Innovative Behavior of Minorities, Women, and Immigrants

The relationship between the innovative behavior and the minority status, gender, and immigration status of, for example, owners, directors, principal investigators, and project managers has only begun to be explored, especially within and among entrepreneurial organizations. Data limitations are certainly one culprit for the paucity of research in this area, but also the economics literature has been slow to move from a technical capital (i.e., investments in R&D) to an innovative behavior focus to an alternative focus that examines the relationship between dimensions of human capital of those who are involved with R&D investments and resulting innovative behavior. The chapters in this edited volume advance this body of thought. These chapters represent foundational research for a nature versus nurture discussion as it relates to innovative behavior, especially a discussion that considers the innovative behavior within and among entrepreneurial organizations.

The chapters in this book were originally published as a special issue of *Economics of Innovation and New Technology.*

Albert N. Link is Virginia Batte Phillips Distinguished Professor at the University of North Carolina at Greensboro, USA. He is Editor-in-Chief of the *Journal of Technology Transfer*, Co-editor of *Foundations and Trends in Entrepreneurship*, and founding Editor of *Annals of Science and Technology Policy.*

Cristiano Antonelli is Chair of Political Economy at the University of Turin and Fellow of the Collegio Carlo Alberto, Italy. He is Managing Editor of *Economics of Innovation and New Technology* and a member of many editorial boards across journals in information economics, communications, and policy.

Innovative Behavior of Minorities, Women, and Immigrants

Edited by
Albert N. Link and Cristiano Antonelli

Routledge
Taylor & Francis Group
LONDON AND NEW YORK

First published 2023
by Routledge
4 Park Square, Milton Park, Abingdon, Oxon, OX14 4RN

and by Routledge
605 Third Avenue, New York, NY 10158

Routledge is an imprint of the Taylor & Francis Group, an informa business

British Library Cataloguing-in-Publication Data
A catalogue record for this book is available from the British Library

ISBN13: 978-1-032-36958-7 (hbk)
ISBN13: 978-1-032-36959-4 (pbk)
ISBN13: 978-1-003-33467-5 (ebk)

DOI: 10.4324/9781003334675

Typeset in Myriad Pro
by codeMantra

Publisher's Note
The publisher accepts responsibility for any inconsistencies that may have arisen during the conversion of this book from journal articles to book chapters, namely the inclusion of journal terminology.

Disclaimer
Every effort has been made to contact copyright holders for their permission to reprint material in this book. The publishers would be grateful to hear from any copyright holder who is not here acknowledged and will undertake to rectify any errors or omissions in future editions of this book.

Contents

Citation Information

The chapters in this book were originally published in the journal *Economics of Innovation and New Technology*, volume 31, issue 1–2 (2022). When citing this material, please use the original page numbering for each article, as follows:

Introduction

Innovative behavior of minorities, women, and Immigrants
Albert N. Link
Economics of Innovation and New Technology, volume 31, issue 1–2 (2022) pp. 1–2

Chapter 1

The role of gender in linking external sources of knowledge and R&D intensity
S. Amoroso and D. B. Audretsch
Economics of Innovation and New Technology, volume 31, issue 1–2 (2022) pp. 3–19

Chapter 2

Entrepreneurial universities and innovative behavior: the impact of gender diversity
Matthias Menter
Economics of Innovation and New Technology, volume 31, issue 1–2 (2022) pp. 20–34

Chapter 3

Does workforce diversity matter on corporate venturing?
Maribel Guerrero
Economics of Innovation and New Technology, volume 31, issue 1–2 (2022) pp. 35–53

Chapter 4

A gender study of principal investigator lead public R&D centres and funding
James A. Cunningham, Alejandro Escribá-Esteve, María José Foncubierta-Rodríguez, Fernando Martín-Alcázar and José Luis Perea-Vicente
Economics of Innovation and New Technology, volume 31, issue 1–2 (2022) pp. 54–69

Chapter 5

Does blockchain technology democratize entrepreneurial finance? An empirical comparison of ICOs, venture capital, and REITs
Christian Fisch, Michele Meoli and Silvio Vismara
Economics of Innovation and New Technology, volume 31, issue 1–2 (2022). pp. 70–89

Chapter 6

Innovation in women-led firms: an empirical analysis
David B. Audretsch, Maksim Belitski and Candida Brush
Economics of Innovation and New Technology, volume 31, issue 1–2 (2022) pp. 90–110

Chapter 7

The use of intellectual property protection mechanisms by publicly supported firms
Albert N. Link and Martijn van Hasselt
Economics of Innovation and New Technology, volume 31, issue 1–2 (2022) pp. 111–121

Notes on Contributors

Sara Amoroso, European Commission, Joint Research Centre, Seville, Spain.

David B. Audretsch, School of Public and Environmental Affairs, Indiana University Bloomington, USA.

Maksim Belitski, Henley Business School, University of Reading, UK.

Candida Brush, Franklin W. Olin Chair-Entrepreneurship Division, Babson College, Arthur M. Blank Center for Entrepreneurship, Babson Park, USA.

James A. Cunningham, Department of Entrepreneurship, Innovation and Strategy, Newcastle Business School, Northumbria University, Newcastle upon Tyne, UK.

Alejandro Escribá-Esteve, University of Valencia, Spain.

Christian Fisch, Faculty of Management, Trier University, Germany.

María José Foncubierta-Rodríguez, Department of Management, Faculty of Economics and Business Sciences, University of Cádiz, Spain.

Maribel Guerrero, Facultad de Economía y Negocios, Universidad del Desarrollo, Santiago de Chile, Chile.

Martijn van Hasselt, Department of Economics, University of North Carolina at Greensboro, USA.

Albert N. Link, Department of Economics, University of North Carolina at Greensboro, USA.

Fernando Martín-Alcázar, Departamento de Organización de Empresas, Universidad de Cádiz, Spain.

Matthias Menter, Faculty of Economics and Business Administration, Friedrich Schiller University Jena, Germany.

Michele Meoli, Department of Management, Information and Production Engineering, University of Bergamo, Dalmine, Italy.

José Luis Perea-Vicente, Departamento de Organización de Empresas, Universidad de Cádiz, Spain.

Silvio Vismara, Department of Management, University of Bergamo, Italy.

INTRODUCTION

Innovative behavior of minorities, women, and immigrants

Albert N. Link

The relationship between innovative behavior and the minority status, gender, and immigration status of, for example, owners, directors, principal investigators, and project managers has only begun to be explored, especially within and among entrepreneurial organizations. Data limitations are certainly one culprit for the paucity of research in this area, but also the economics literature has been slow to move from an R&D (i.e. technical capital) → innovative behavior focus to one that examines the relationship between dimensions of human capital of those who are involved with R&D investments and resulting innovative behavior. The papers in this Special Issues advance this body of thought.

'The Role of Gender in Linking External Sources of Knowledge and R&D Intensity' by Sara Amoroso and David B. Audretsch examines how female-founded firms differ from male ones in translating the knowledge from external sources into R&D efforts. Findings from their empirical analysis suggest that female-founded firms have an advantage compared to male-founded firms in reaping the benefits of knowledge acquired from research institutes and value-chain partners.

'Entrepreneurial Universities and Innovative Behavior: The Impact of Gender Diversity,' by Matthias Menter, investigates the impact of gender diversity on university innovation outcomes across three university missions: teaching, research, and the commercialization of knowledge. The findings presented in this study reveal that gender diversity matters, yet gender diversity follows an inverted U-shaped relationship. This empirical finding further indicates the existence of a threshold effect in that a minimum level of gender diversity is necessary to drive augmented innovative behavior within universities.

'Does Workforce Diversity Matter on Corp[orate Venturing?' by Maribel Guerrero, examines workforce diversity in corporate venturing activities. By adopting a mixed theoretical approach (corporate entrepreneurship, employee ambidexterity, and intellectual capital), the study tests empirically a set of hypotheses using a sample of 17217 employees across 20 countries. The study shows insights into women's and migrants' engagement in corporate venturing by identifying opportunities (using their exploration abilities) and taking advantage of intellectual capital (using their human capital and social capital).

'A Gender Study of Principal Investigator (PI) Lead Public R&D Centres and Funding,' by James A. Cunningham, Alejandro Escribá-Esteve, María José Foncubierta-Rodríguez, Fernando Martín-Alcázar, and José Luis Perea-Vicente, builds on the literature that highlights the growing and intense competition between R&D centers to secure competitive based public funds in order to survive and thrive. Set in Spain, this study firstly examines if a consistent set of priorities defined by R&D center lead PIs secures more competitive funding. Secondly it examines whether the PI's gender moderates the effect of his/her priorities on the amount of competitive public funds that the R&D team of the PI obtains.

'Does Blockchain Technology Democratize Entrepreneurial Finance? An Empirical Comparison of ICOs, Venture Capital, and REITs,' by Christian Fisch, Michele Meoli, and Silvio Vismara, investigates whether gender, ethnicity, and geography affect the choice of initial coin offerings (ICOs) vs.

traditional financing alternatives to finance startups. The paper documents the inclusive potential of digital finance with regard to the participation and likelihood of success of ethnic minorities. In contrast, digital finance does not alleviate the access barriers faced by female entrepreneurs.

'Innovation in Women-led Firms: An Empirical Analysis,' by David B. Audretsch, Maksim Belitski, and Candida Brush,' emphasizes that the availability of resources for innovation is paramount for innovation in women-led firms. The analyses in this paper examine how nature – a pervasive and arbitrary type of institutional environment as well as access to resources – is associated with different propensities to innovate between women and men-led firms.

'The Use of Intellectual Property Protection Mechanisms by Publicly Supported Firms,' by Albert N. Link and Martijn van Hasselt, investigates empirically the use intellectual property protection mechanisms (IPPMs) by technology-based firms to appropriate the returns to their research investments. The authors identify empirically a number of significant nature and nurture covariates with the use of a portfolio of formal IPPMs consisting of patents, copyrights, and trademarks. However, their multivariate empirical analyses show that caution is needed in generalizing about such covariates when discussing any one particular formal IPPM.

This collection of papers represents foundational research for a nature/nurture discussion as it relates to innovative behavior, especially as it relates to innovative behavior in entrepreneurial organizations.

Disclosure statement

No potential conflict of interest was reported by the author(s).

ᴑ OPEN ACCESS

The role of gender in linking external sources of knowledge and R&D intensity

S. Amoroso and D. B. Audretsch

ABSTRACT

Scholars examining the effect of knowledge spillovers on R&D and innovation all agree on one thing – there is a strong relationship between the firm's R&D effort and knowledge spillover. The sign of this relationship depends, however, on many things, such as the type of spillovers (horizontal, vertical, or from other sources), the level of appropriability, the type of firm (e.g. age and sector), and the measurement of the spillover itself. A missing piece of evidence to this literature is the role of gender in the founding team of the firm. Our contribution is to fill this gap by explicitly analysing the role played by gender in the founding team. Given that the relationship between a firm's R&D intensity and external knowledge spillovers is ultimately context-specific, we analyse the differences between male-owned and female-owned young entrepreneurial firms with respect to the influence that knowledge spillovers have on their R&D intensity.

1. Introduction

Despite the rising number of successful female entrepreneurs (Fackelmann and De Concini 2020),[1] women still face many constraints limiting their ability to grow their businesses. Female-owned entrepreneurial firms are not only smaller, less experienced, younger, less profitable, and more risk averse than male ones (Link and Strong 2016), but research suggests that they are also less growth and profit oriented (Liao, Welsch, and Stoica 2003; Carter 2007).

As R&D plays a central role in long-term productivity, both at the firm- (Coad and Rao 2010) and aggregate-levels (Stokey 1995), scholars have started to look at the role of R&D and innovation as one of the factors contributing to the gender gap in the performance of start-ups (Gottschalk and Niefert 2013; Marvel, Lee, and Wolfe 2015; Link and van Hasselt 2020; Quiroz-Rojas and Teruel 2020). Female-owned firms invest less in R&D and innovate less than male-owned firms. This is in part due to the fact that female firms are concentrated in less innovative sectors (Fontana, Malerba, and Marinoni 2016), but also because women have a lower propensity to patent relative to men (Cook and Kongcharoen 2010). However, recent evidence shows that when comparing the patenting rates of both male and female firms in the same high-tech sectors, firms owned by males seem to lag behind (Demiralp, Morrison, and Zayed 2018).

The role of R&D spillovers and external sources of knowledge has long been studied since mid-1980s (Levin and Reiss 1984; Spence 1984; Cohen and Levinthal 1989; Cohen and Levin 1989), as they can create both positive and negative incentives to invest in R&D.[2] External sources of knowledge are especially important for the survival of young entrepreneurial companies (Caloghirou, Protogerou, and Tsakanikas 2014; Protogerou, Caloghirou, and Vonortas 2017; Amoroso, Audretsch, and Link 2018). However, it is unclear how firms adjust their internal R&D activities when dealing with external knowledge, in particular when different types of sources or partners are involved. Indeed, absorbing and integrating information from a university, which primarily focuses on basic research, may require a larger investment in R&D to be able to level up and put that information to use, compared to the information coming from a competitor or a value-chain partner, who may have similar and/or complementary knowledge and capabilities.

Only a few recent studies have looked at the interplay between internal R&D and external knowledge sources (Chen, Vanhaverbeke, and Du 2016; Doloreux, Shearmur, and Rodriguez 2018; Basit and Medase 2019; Audretsch and Link 2019); however, none of them have specifically taken into account the role of gender. Theoretically, female-led firms could have an advantage in accessing the external source of knowledge. In fact, some studies suggest that women seem to have certain advantages in managerial functions related to people. These advantages are due to the fact that women invest more time in networking and conducting market research (for an overview of the economics of women's entrepreneurship Galindo and Ribeiro 2011, see). Social networks constitute key channels for information and resources exchange that can enhance the success of a new venture (Coleman 1988).

So far, the analysis of the role of gender in the relationship between external sources of knowledge and R&D investment has been largely neglected. This paper constitutes the first attempt at analysing the theoretical and empirical differences between male-owned and female-owned entrepreneurial firms with respect to their ability to exploit external knowledge spillovers, thereby increasing or reducing their R&D intensity.

In the next section, we review the literature on the relationship between R&D investment and knowledge spillovers, focusing on studies that concern female entrepreneurship. Section 3 describes the data and the empirical methodology, while Section 4 presents the results. We discuss and draw our conclusions in Section 5.

2. Knowledge spillovers and firm-level R&D investment

The essence of knowledge spillovers traces back to Nelson (1959) and Arrow (1962), who were among the first scholars to recognise the peculiar economic characteristics of information as a commodity that can be reproduced infinitely at virtually no cost. Access to free information may reduce the incentive to invest in R&D, as the involuntary spillovers from the R&D of one firm may allow other firms to achieve results with less research effort (Jaffe 1986). Spence (1984) suggested that research collaborations are a way of internalising the knowledge spillovers. Following Spence's work, many studies focused on the effects of R&D cooperation on R&D incentives and welfare and found that internalising the knowledge spillovers by cooperating leads to higher R&D and welfare only when the R&D spillovers rates are high (Katz 1986; D'Aspremont and Jacquemin 1988; Kamien, Muller, and Zang 1992). Cohen and Levinthal (1989) stressed the importance of investing in R&D to increase the possibility to absorb others' knowledge and to ultimately increase the return to incoming spillovers.

The importance of external knowledge has been further emphasised in the seminal work of Chesbrough (2003), introducing the open innovation paradigm, where internal R&D is seen again as a tool to identify, understand, absorb, complement, and integrate external knowledge (see West and Bogers 2014, for a thorough review on open innovation studies). Moilanen, Østbye, and Woll (2014) study the relationship between external knowledge, absorptive capacity and innovative performance for SMEs and find that absorptive capacity is an important mediator for transforming external knowledge inflows into higher innovative performance, especially for R&D intensive SMEs.Gesing et al. (2015) find that firms' ability to capture value from collaboration and internal R&D depends on the governance mechanisms. In particular, internal R&D increases the return from collaborations only if the relationship between collaboration partners is informal and not contract-based. A recent study from Audretsch and Belitski (2020) investigates the relationship between investments in R&D, knowledge spillovers, innovation, and their impact on productivity, and finds that the availability of knowledge spillovers increases the intensity of investing in internal R&D.

The industrial organisation (IO) literature looked at the relationship between incoming and outgoing spillovers[3] and how firms usually attempt to manage spillovers by minimising outgoing spillovers while at the same time maximising incoming ones (Amir 2000; Cassiman, Pérez-Castrillo, and Veugelers 2002; Martin 2002; Amir, Jin, and Troege 2008; Hagedoorn and Wang 2012). While classical IO research on R&D spillovers has typically considered only horizontal spillovers (i.e. spillovers from firms competing in the same industry), empirical IO and innovation management studies looked at different sources of knowledge as reported in firms' surveys (Belderbos et al. 2004; Cantù et al. 2015; Audretsch and Link 2019). Some studies focused on the importance of various sources of knowledge for innovation, R&D cooperation, and firm performance (Nieto and Santamaria 2007; Cappelli, Czarnitzki, and Kraft 2014; Basit and Medase 2019), while others analysed the relationship between sources of knowledge and the characteristics of young entrepreneurial firms' founders (Caloghirou, Protogerou, and Tsakanikas 2014; Fontana, Malerba, and Marinoni 2016; Amoroso, Audretsch, and Link 2018; Hodges and Link 2018).

The empirical findings of these studies suggest heterogeneity in the role of spillovers, with some studies reporting negative or no effect of knowledge sources from the customers on innovation output (Lööf and Heshmati 2002; Monjon and Waelbroeck 2003), while others find evidence of positive effect of sourcing from value-chain partners and horizontal connections, but we do not find support for complementarity between firm's R&D effort and collaborations with universities and research labs (Chen, Vanhaverbeke, and Du 2016). More recently, Basit and Medase (2019) using firm-level data from the German Community Innovation Survey (CIS) examine and finds the positive effects of horizontal and vertical spillovers on firm innovation.

2.1. The role of appropriability regimes

Many scholars have argued that sectoral appropriability conditions of sectors are an important environmental factor that influences a firm's resource-seeking behaviours such as searching for similar or complementary external sources of knowledge (Cohen and Walsh 2001; Cassiman and Veugelers 2002; Zobel, Lokshin, and Hagedoorn 2017; Seo, Chung, and Yoon 2017).

Therefore, in this study we explore the effect of knowledge spillovers on firm R&D efforts depending on the level of appropriability conditions, i.e. the degree to which different appropriability mechanisms or strategies increase the R&D rents.

2.2. Female entrepreneurship and R&D investment

Because female entrepreneurship is steadily growing all over the world, the number of studies analysing female-owned enterprises grows accordingly. Despite the academic findings related to gender and the economic performance of entrepreneurial firms being mixed, the general picture suggests that female entrepreneurial firms are generally smaller, younger, more risk averse, and less profitable than male ones (see Link and Strong 2016, for a thorough review).

Another empirical regularity is that female-owned firms invest less in R&D and innovate less. One reason for this is that female entrepreneurs are typically concentrated in less innovative sectors such as service and low-tech manufacturing (Amoroso and Link 2018, 2019). By contrast, male-owned firms are more R&D intensive and tend to be more innovative than female-owned ones. Due to the high risk associated with R&D investment and the reported high-risk aversion of women, research has started to look at the relationship between gender and firm innovation. Cook and Kongcharoen (2010) show that in the US women are less likely to patent than men, while Demiralp,

Morrison, and Zayed (2018) go further with US data to show that men-owned businesses in STEM fields are less likely to generate IP (including patents, trademarks, and copyrights) than female-owned firms.

In this paper, we investigate the relationship between R&D investment and the gender of firms' founders.

2.3. Female entrepreneurship and sources of knowledge

Innovation management scholars have posited that women are restricted in their access to networks and are not able to use their networks for resource acquisition or growth (Carter 2007; Nissan, Carrasco, and Castaño 2012; Achtenhagen et al. 2013; Ozkazanc-Pan and Muntean 2018). Atherton (2003) and Fuentes-Fuentes, Bojica, and Ruiz-Arroyo (2015) suggest that, especially for start-ups and small businesses, the relationship with customers, suppliers, competitors, support organisms and services should be considered when investigating knowledge acquisition through business and entrepreneurial networks. In particular, Fuentes-Fuentes, Bojica, and Ruiz-Arroyo (2015) using a survey on Spanish women entrepreneurs show that information gathered from customers and other business-related contacts, relative to market trends and technical and market know-how, has a positive influence on entrepreneurial orientation, which in turn has a positive effect on firm performance. Given that the key components of entrepreneurial orientation[4] deal with firm engagement in R&D and risky activities, it follows that female entrepreneurs with a high entrepreneurial orientation are more involved in R&D. Even though the authors do not use R&D investment or intensity to proxy the entrepreneurial orientation, we think that one interpretation of their study is that the acquisition of the external source of knowledge for female entrepreneurs is positively associated with their engagement in R&D activities. Unfortunately, the study considers only knowledge acquisition from business ties, such as customers and collaborators (suppliers, financial institutions, business associations and government entities) and it does differentiate among different sources of knowledge used.

Nonetheless, in this paper, we advance and test the hypothesis that the acquisition of external source of knowledge for female entrepreneurs is positively associated with their R&D investment. In addition, we empirically explore the heterogeneity among the different sources of external knowledge.

3. Data and methodology

To analyse the relationship between R&D intensity, gender, and various sources of knowledge used by young entrepreneurial firms, we use data from the AEGIS (Advancing Knowledge-Intensive Entrepreneurship and Innovation for Economic Growth and Social Well-being in Europe) project, funded by the European Commission's 7th Framework Programme (FP7), under Theme 8 'Socio-Economic Sciences and Humanities'. The focus of the AEGIS project was on small knowledge-intensive entrepreneurial firms. As part of the AEGIS project, a broad-based survey of 4004 firms established between 2001 and 2007 across 10 European countries was conducted from late 2010 to 2011. The countries included in the survey were (alphabetically): Croatia, Czech Republic, Denmark, France, Germany, Greece, Italy, Portugal, Sweden, and the United Kingdom. Both high-tech and low-tech manufacturing sectors, and knowledge-intensive business services sector are represented in the database.

Similar to the Eurostat's Community Innovation Surveys, the AEGIS survey collected companies' assessment of the importance of certain information sources. The survey question is:

Please evaluate the importance of the following sources of knowledge for exploring new business opportunities on a 5-point scale, where 1 is not important and 5 is extremely important.

(1) Clients or customers

(2) Suppliers
(3) Competitors
(4) Public research institutes
(5) Universities
(6) External commercial labs/R&D firms/technical institutes
(7) In-house (know-how, R&D laboratories in your firm)
(8) Trade fairs, conferences and exhibitions
(9) Scientific journals and other trade or technical publications
(10) Participation in nationally funded research programmes
(11) Participation in EU funded research programmes (Framework Programmes)

Given that we relate external sources of knowledge to firm R&D intensity, we exclude the category n. 7 'In-house (know-how, R&D laboratories in your firm)'. Additionally, the literature on knowledge spillovers considers a narrower categorisation of sources of knowledge, as the average importance of knowledge sources is similar among homogeneous sources (Amoroso, Audretsch, and Link 2018; Hodges and Link 2018). Thus, following this literature, and the clustering of homogenous sources, we created 5 categories from the above 10: Vertical sources, Horizontal sources, Research Institutes, Research Programmes, and Publications & Conferences (see Table 1). Moreover, we transformed these responses into dichotomous variable where 1 is important (a survey response of 4 or 5) and 0 is not important (a survey response of 1, 2, or 3).[5]

To relate the R&D intensity to different sources of knowledge, we estimate the following Tobit model:

$$RDint_i^* = f_i(Spill^k, Female\ leader, X) + \epsilon_i$$
$$RDint_i = RDint_i^* \quad \text{if} \quad RDint_i > 0$$

where the R&D intensity of firm *i* is regressed on *k* types of external knowledge sources, *Spill*, namely horizontal, vertical, research institutes, research programmes, and publications&conferences (*k*=*Ver, Hor,Rinst,Rprog,PubConf*), a gender variable indicating if the first-listed founder is a woman, *Female leader* (we also use the share of female founders in the founding team, % *Women*), and a set of control variables *X*. As control variables, we include the firm size (log of employees), the average experience of founders, the average age and education categories, product or process innovation, the perceived market concentration, country and sector (*FE*, pseudo 2-digit NACE rev.1.1) dummies, $X = (log(empl), exp, age, edu, inno, compet, FE)$. Table 2 reports summary statistics and a description of the variables; Table 3 displays the pairwise correlation coefficients between variables.

Table 4 reports 2-sample *t*-tests of differences in the importance of external knowledge spillovers by gender of the first-listed founder. Vertical knowledge spillovers (i.e. knowledge acquired from clients and suppliers) and spillovers from publications and conferences are the most important sources of external knowledge for both female- and male-founded firms (roughly 90% and 50% of firms classified these two sources of knowledge as important for entrepreneurial activities).

Table 1. Categorisation of external sources of knowledge.

AEGIS 10 original categories	5 new categories
Clients or customers	Vertical
Suppliers	Vertical
Competitors	Horizontal
Public research institutes	Research Institutes
Universities	Research Institutes
External commercial labs/R&D firms/technical institutes	Research Institutes
Trade fairs, conferences, and exhibitions	Publications & Conferences
Scientific journal and other trade or technical publications	Publications&Conferences
Participation in nationally funded research programmes	Research Programmes
Participation in EU funded research programmes	Research Programmes

Table 2. Summary statistics.

Variable	Mean	SD	Min	Max
RDint (% of sales)	12.46	19.35	0	100
Vertical	0.90	0.30	0	1
Horizontal	0.43	0.50	0	1
Research Institutes	0.25	0.43	0	1
Research Programmes	0.18	0.38	0	1
Publications&Conferences	0.49	0.50	0	1
Female leader	0.15	0.36	0	1
% Women	18.34	30.92	0	100
log(empl)	1.69	1.17	−0.69	7.3
Exp	12.23	9.23	0	55
Age	2.99	0.79	1	4
Edu	2.76	1.10	0	5
Inno	0.64	0.48	0	1
Compet	1.48	0.62	1	3

Notes: The importance of external sources of knowledge has been re-codified. Originally, they range from 1 (not important) to 5 (extremely important). The values 1–3 have been codified as 0 and the values 4–5 as 1.

A *female-owned* firm is a firm where the first-listed founder is a woman. % Wmn founders is the share of founders. The maximum number of founders is 4 and the average number of founders is 2.

Experience, *Age* and *Edu* are the average experience (in years), age groups (1–4) and education level (1–5) of all founders of a firm.

Compet takes value 1 when the firm's market is not very concentrated (many competitors) and 3 when is very concentrated (oligopolistic).

Knowledge from competitors (horizontal) and research institutes is also important for 43% and 25% of firms; however, these sources of knowledge are statistically significantly more important for female-founded firms than for male-founded ones. Finally, the knowledge acquired via the participation to public research programmes is important for only less than 20% of the firms.

To analyse the relationship between R&D intensity and knowledge spillovers from a gender perspective, we include interaction effects between spillovers and the gender variable. Moreover, following Cohen and Walsh (2001), we explore the relationship between knowledge spillovers and firm R&D efforts under different levels of appropriability conditions. To measure the appropriability conditions, similar to Seo, Chung, and Yoon (2017), we use an industry-level measure of the use of intellectual property mechanisms (IPPMs). In the AEGIS survey, firms are asked to report whether they used any IPPMs in the last three years (2007–2009) such as patents, trademarks, copyrights, confidentiality agreements, secrecy, lead-time advantages, and design complexity. We take the average number of IPPMs used by firms in each sector and split the sample in two groups – sectors with an average number of IPPMs above the median (16 sectors and 1950 firms) and sectors below the median (10 sectors and 2054 firms). Table 5 reports the number of firms per sector, categorised as either 'low' appropriability conditions, or 'high' appropriability. The share of firms with a female first-listed founder is similar between the two samples (7.7% and 7.5% in the low and high appropriability samples, respectively; see Table 6).

In the next section, we present and discuss the results from the Tobit regression model for the whole sample and for the two samples of firms in sectors with low or high appropriability conditions.

4. Results and discussion

Table 7 reports the marginal effects of the five sources of external knowledge on the R&D intensity of small entrepreneurial firms in Europe. The first column (1) displays the results of the simplest specification where R&D intensity depends only on spillovers, the gender dummy, and country-sector dummies. Column (2) includes all other control variables. Between the two specifications the regression coefficients do not vary much. In general, vertical and horizontal sources of knowledge are not related to the R&D intensity, while research institutes, participation to research programmes, and access to publications and conference increase the R&D spending of 7.3, 3.8, and 3.2 percentage points (ppt), respectively (column (2)).

Table 3. Pairwise correlation coefficients.

Variables	(1)	(2)	(3)	(4)	(5)	(6)	(7)	(8)	(9)	(10)	(11)	(12)
(1) RDint	1											
(2) Vertical	0	1										
(3) Horizontal	0.04*	0.13*	1									
(4) Research Institutes	0.18*	0.05*	0.17*	1								
(5) Research Programmes	0.18*	0.06*	0.13*	0.40*	1							
(6) Publications&Conferences	0.14*	0.10*	0.14*	0.25*	0.24*	1						
(7) Female leader	−0.05*	0.01	0.02	0.02	0.01	0.02	1					
(8) log(empl)	0.03	0.03	0.07*	0.03	0.11*	0.01	−0.11*	1				
(9) Exp	0	0.01	−0.03	0.04*	0	0	−0.11*	−0.01	1			
(10) Age	−0.04*	0	−0.03	0.03	0.01	0	−0.06*	0	0.47*	1		
(11) Edu	0.15*	−0.03*	−0.04*	0.02	0.04*	0.06*	0	−0.06*	−0.04*	0.01	1	
(12) Inno	0.21*	0.03	0.05*	0.11*	0.12*	0.12*	−0.02	0.16*	−0.04*	−0.04*	0.05*	1
(13) Compet	0.17*	0	−0.06*	0.03	0.08*	0.02	−0.04*	0.01	0	0.06*	0.03*	0.08*

* shows significance at the .05 level.

Table 4. The importance of sources of external knowledge by gender.

	Vertical	Horizontal	Research Institutes	Research Programmes	Publications Conferences	N. firms
Male leader	0.90	0.43	0.25	0.18	0.49	3,395
Female leader	0.91	0.46	0.27	0.19	0.52	609
2-sample *t*-test	−0.94	−1.34*	−1.48*	−0.52	−1.24	

Note: The table reports the average importance (0 = not important, 1 = important) of the five sources of external knowledge. Significance code ****p*<0.001, ***p*<0.01, **p*<0.1.

Table 5. Number of firms, by sector and by appropriability conditions.

NACE code	Description	Appropriability Low	Appropriability High
15	Manufacture of food products and beverages	297	
17	Manufacture of textiles	91	
18	Manufacture of wearing apparel; dressing & dyeing of fur		84
19	Leather, manufacture of leather products		34
20	Manufacture of wood&wood products, except furniture	122	
21	Manufacture of pulp, paper and paper products		46
22	Publishing, printing and reproduction of recorded media		572
24	Manufacture of coke, refined petroleum products & nuclear fuel		51
27	Manufacture of basic metals	31	
28	Manufacture of fabricated metal products, except machinery & equipment	214	
29	Manufacture of machinery and equipment n.e.c.		201
30	Manufacture of office machinery and computers		20
31	Manufacture of electrical machinery and apparatus n.e.c.		45
32	Manufacture of radio, television and communication equipment and apparatus		35
33	Manufacture of medical, precision and optical instruments, watches and clocks		67
35.3	Manufacture of aircraft and spacecraft		1
36.1	Manufacture of furniture	111	
64.2	Telecommunications		24
72	Computer and related activities		518
73	Research and development		71
74.1	Legal, accounting, book-keeping and auditing activities; tax consultancy; market research and public opinion polling; business and management consultancy; holdings	767	
74.2	Architectural and engineering activities and related technical consultancy	317	
74.3	Technical testing and analysis	60	
74.4	Advertising		116
74.5	Labour recruitment and provision of personnel	44	
74.8	Miscellaneous business activities n.e.c.		65
Total		2054	1950

Table 6. Distribution of firms by gender of the first-listed founder and appropriability conditions, absolute numbers and (percentages).

	Appropriability Low	Appropriability High	Row total
Male leader	1745	1650	3395
	(43.6)	(41.2)	(84.8)
Female leader	309	300	609
	(7.7)	(7.5)	(15.2)
Column total	2054	1950	4004
	(51.3)	(48.7)	(100)

The dummy for female-founded firms is negatively related to the R&D intensity, confirming that women-led firms have a lower R&D intensity, probably due to their risk aversion to the uncertain nature of R&D investment. In particular, the average R&D intensity is 2.8 percentage points lower in female-founded firms than in male-founded ones. When looking at the share of women in the founding team (column (4)), we obtain a similar result – an increase of 10 percentage points

Table 7. Estimation results from Tobit regression model.

Dep. var: $RDint \mid RDint > 0$	(1)	(2)	(3)	(4)	(5)
Vertical	0.307	0.087	−0.769	0.108	0.411
	(1.390)	(1.405)	(1.502)	(1.405)	(1.417)
Horizontal	0.588	0.608	0.514	0.624	0.635
	(0.857)	(0.847)	(0.916)	(0.847)	(0.847)
Research Institutes	7.882***	7.310***	6.552***	7.296***	7.290***
	(1.035)	(1.023)	(1.106)	(1.023)	(1.022)
Research Programmes	6.266***	3.768***	3.947***	3.779***	3.774***
	(1.157)	(1.152)	(1.248)	(1.152)	(1.151)
Publications&Conferences	4.397***	3.157***	3.119***	3.151***	3.129***
	(0.868)	(0.860)	(0.924)	(0.860)	(0.861)
Female leader	−3.884***	−2.853**	−10.591**		
	(1.186)	(1.192)	(4.292)		
% Women				−0.036**	−0.138***
				(0.014)	(0.049)
Ver×Female [% Wmn]			6.673		[0.114]**
			(4.289)		(0.049)
Hor×Female [% Wmn]			0.686		[0.001]
			(2.371)		(0.028)
RInst×Female [% Wmn]			4.764*		[0.057]*
			(2.861)		(0.034)
RProg×Female [% Wmn]			−1.263		[−0.010]
			(3.176)		(0.038)
PubConf×Female [% Wmn]			0.217		[−0.030]
			(2.464)		(0.029)
ln(empl)		0.741*	0.756**	0.756**	0.761**
		(0.384)	(0.384)	(0.384)	(0.384)
exp		0.107**	0.108**	0.108**	0.109**
		(0.051)	(0.051)	(0.051)	(0.051)
age		−2.078***	−2.097***	−2.097***	−2.095***
		(0.601)	(0.601)	(0.601)	(0.600)
edu		2.240***	2.244***	2.244***	2.223***
		(0.402)	(0.403)	(0.403)	(0.403)
inno		10.776***	10.774***	10.774***	10.752***
		(0.898)	(0.899)	(0.899)	(0.898)
compet		5.627***	5.666***	5.666***	5.602***
		(0.667)	(0.667)	(0.667)	(0.667)
var(e.RDint)	581.012***	517.487***	516.907***	516.907***	514.844***
	(16.791)	(15.445)	(15.427)	(15.427)	(15.364)
N	3947	3602	3602	3602	3602

Notes: The table reports the marginal effects of the five sources of external knowledge on R&D intensity. The coefficients can be interpreted as the average R&D intensity being β percentage points higher for knowledge sources that are considered important (equal to 1).
Country and 2-digit sector dummies included but not reported.
Significance code ***p<0.001, **p<0.01, *p<0.1.

(e.g. going from 0% to 10%) in the share of female founders corresponds to a lower R&D intensity (0.36 percentage points lower).

The regression coefficients of the control variables are in line with what other studies find. The larger and more innovative firms invest more in R&D; younger, more educated, and more experienced founding teams are also more R&D intensive (Protogerou, Caloghirou, and Vonortas 2017; Amoroso and Link 2018). Finally, firms have a higher R&D intensity when the market concentration is high (few competitors).

The main variables of interest are the interactions between knowledge sources and the gender dummy. Columns (3) and (5) report the results for an econometric specification that takes into account such interactions. In column (3), there is some evidence that female-founded firms have an advantage compared to male-founded ones in reaping the benefits of knowledge acquired from research institutes. Similarly, knowledge spillovers from research institutes correspond to higher R&D intensity for a larger share of women in the founding team.[6] Figure 1 reports the

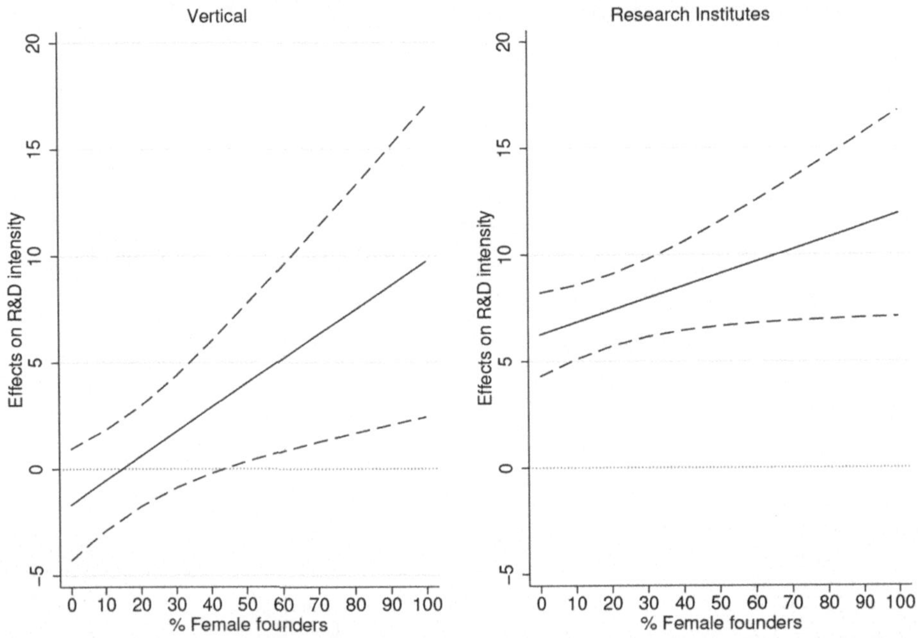

Figure 1. Average marginal effects of vertical (value chain) and research institutes sources of knowledge by share of female founders (90% CIs).

average marginal effects of knowledge from value chain business ties (vertical) and research institutes, by share of female founders. The effect of the increase in the number of women among the founders is more accentuated for vertical spillovers. It seems that once the team has more than 40% of female founders, vertical spillovers become more associated with R&D investment. The effect of research institutes spillovers is not as strong. In fact, once reached a minimum of 30–40% of women, the effect flattens out.

Our results are in line with Fuentes-Fuentes, Bojica, and Ruiz-Arroyo (2015) who find that the acquisition of external knowledge has a positive effect on the engagement in R&D and risky activities of women entrepreneurs. Moreover, we add a deeper layer of understanding to their findings, in that we are able to distinguish between sources of knowledge. Not only do we confirm that firms' clients are a critical source of knowledge that leads to innovative activities (Argote 2013), but we also show that other sources of knowledge are important for the R&D activities of female-founded firms, such as research institutes. Overall, our findings suggest that, compared to men, female collaborative orientation (Sorenson, Folker, and Brigham 2008) pays off in terms of complementing internal R&D capabilities with the acquisition of valuable external knowledge resources.

Table 8 reports the results for specifications including the role of appropriability. Columns (1) and (2) include the dummy *appropriability* which is equal to one if the firm in one of the sectors characterised by high appropriability (see Table 5) and the interaction between such dummy and the spillovers variables. The results do not differ from those of Table 7 and no direct statistically significant effect is found for the appropriability variable nor for the interaction terms. However, separate estimations for the two samples of sectors (columns (High) and (Low)) offer two very different pictures. The participation in public research programmes is only associated with higher R&D efforts in sectors with a low appropriability level. Knowledge from research institutes corresponds to higher R&D intensity for firms in high appropriability sectors (the average R&D intensity is 3.4 ppt higher then in the low appropriability ones). Finally, there is a gender difference in the R&D intensity only in the high appropriability, more innovative sectors, where female-led firms report a lower average R&D intensity.

Table 8. Estimation results from Tobit regression model (by appropriability conditions).

Dep. var: *RDint*|*RDint* > 0	(1)	(2)	(High)	(Low)
Vertical	−0.769	0.273	−1.732	0.657
	(1.502)	(2.071)	(2.239)	(1.983)
Horizontal	0.514	0.014	2.034	−1.150
	(0.916)	(1.244)	(1.372)	(1.200)
Research Institutes	6.552***	6.059***	8.356***	5.019***
	(1.106)	(1.465)	(1.702)	(1.413)
Research Programmes	3.947***	5.099***	1.752	6.019***
	(1.248)	(1.693)	(1.862)	(1.643)
Publications&Conferences	3.119***	2.655**	3.444**	2.791**
	(0.924)	(1.263)	(1.375)	(1.219)
Female leader	−10.591**	−10.643**	−12.916**	−8.290
	(4.292)	(4.299)	(6.342)	(5.732)
Ver×Female	6.673	6.594	10.832*	2.689
	(4.289)	(4.296)	(6.377)	(5.689)
Hor×Female	0.686	0.785	−5.818	7.033**
	(2.371)	(2.372)	(3.654)	(3.063)
Rinst×Female	4.764*	4.817*	−0.878	9.719***
	(2.861)	(2.860)	(4.470)	(3.620)
Rprog×Female	−1.263	−1.377	4.460	−5.826
	(3.176)	(3.176)	(4.910)	(4.054)
PubConf×Female	0.217	0.318	0.276	−0.381
	(2.464)	(2.464)	(3.784)	(3.191)
appropriability	2.457	3.525		
	(3.592)	(4.507)		
Ver×appro		−1.935		
		(2.812)		
Hor×appro		0.973		
		(1.686)		
Rinst×appro		1.045		
		(2.035)		
Rprog×appro		−2.312		
		(2.270)		
PubConf×appro		0.901		
		(1.705)		
log(empl)	0.756**	0.757**	1.009*	0.554
	(0.384)	(0.384)	(0.592)	(0.490)
exp	0.108**	0.108**	0.096	0.107*
	(0.051)	(0.051)	(0.082)	(0.064)
age	−2.097***	−2.091***	−2.329**	−1.844**
	(0.601)	(0.601)	(0.913)	(0.780)
edu	2.244***	2.248***	3.108***	1.407***
	(0.403)	(0.403)	(0.598)	(0.534)
inno	10.774***	10.790***	12.221***	9.746***
	(0.899)	(0.900)	(1.408)	(1.133)
compet	5.666***	5.649***	6.721***	4.466***
	(0.667)	(0.667)	(1.006)	(0.870)
var(e.RDint)	516.907***	516.441***	574.052***	442.836***
	(15.427)	(15.414)	(23.895)	(18.971)
N	3602	3602	1729	1873

Notes: The table reports the marginal effects of the five sources of external knowledge on R&D intensity. The coefficients can be interpreted as the average R&D intensity being β percentage points higher for knowledge sources that are considered important (equal to 1).

Country and 2-digit sector dummies included but not reported.

Significance code ***p<0.001, **p<0.01, *p<0.1.

The interaction effects reveal a more nuanced story for the role of gender entrepreneurship in the relationship between external knowledge and R&D investment. In sectors with high levels of appropriability, information from customers and suppliers still remains more valuable for female founded firms than for male-founded ones. These sources of information may be more relevant to obtain access to external knowledge resources in sectors with high appropriability, because suppliers and customers are not direct competitors. Indeed, in low appropriability sectors, the R&D intensity of firms with female first-listed founders is positively associated with spillovers from competitors (horizontal) and research institutes.

Overall, our findings indicate that both female- and male-founded firms complement their internal R&D strategies with the acquisition of external source of knowledge such as research institutes, publications and conferences, and the participation to research programmes (in sectors with low appropriability conditions). However, only female-led firms are able to also benefit from what are thought to be most important sources of knowledge, i.e. competitors and customers (Liao, Welsch, and Stoica 2003)

These results could be due not only to the fact that women have more collaborative and cooperative approaches to leading and organising (Sorenson, Folker, and Brigham 2008), but also because women tend to value stakeholders more highly than men do (Posner and Munson 1981). Moreover, as firms develop and grow, the professional relationships become increasingly significant to the entrepreneur's networks. This has been shown to be particularly relevant for women entrepreneurs in two Scandinavian countries Achtenhagen et al. (2013). Also, the stronger relationship of spillovers from research institutes and R&D intensity of female-founded firms could stem from the fact that public research institutes and universities may follow more inclusive social norms that emphasise gender equality (Fang, Shams, and Xu 2019).

5. Conclusions

There is no consensus regarding the relationship between internal R&D activities and other sources of knowledge, primarily because this relationship varies with the type of knowledge source, and with appropriability conditions (Laursen and Salter 2014). Following the footsteps of Cohen and Levinthal (1989), many studies have analysed the impact of R&D collaboration with different partners, externally sourced R&D, and R&D spillovers on innovation and productivity. However, very few studies have attempted to directly link the two faces of R&D à la Cohen and Levinthal (1989), namely the innovation-generating R&D and the assimilate-and-exploit-existing-information R&D, distinguishing by sources of information. Most importantly, there is no empirical evidence on the role gender of firms' founders and the difference in their ability to exploit external sources of information. By exploiting the unique features of a data sample of knowledge-intensive entrepreneurial firms, we are able to analyse the relationship between different sources of knowledge and firms' R&D intensity, accounting for the gender of first-listed founders.

Differently from previous studies which claimed and found that the most important areas of knowledge emanate from competitors and customers (Liao, Welsch, and Stoica 2003; Fuentes-Fuentes, Bojica, and Ruiz-Arroyo 2015; Chen, Vanhaverbeke, and Du 2016), our estimates show that value-chain (i.e. vertical) or horizontal knowledge spillovers have no effect on R&D intensity of the average firm. The knowledge sources that are mostly associated with internal R&D capabilities are research institutes, public research programmes, and publications and conferences. These results indicate that when the sources of knowledge are less directly related to firms' core business activities, firms' own R&D could be a critical resource:

> When outside knowledge is less targeted to the firm's particular needs and concerns, a firm's own R&D becomes more important in permitting it to recognise, assimilate and exploit valuable knowledge. Sources that produce less targeted knowledge include, for example, university laboratories involved in basic research, while more targeted knowledge may be generated by contract research laboratories or input supplier. (Cohen and Levinthal 1989, 572)

Another important finding is related to the appropriability conditions. According to Teece (1993), high-tech and innovation intensive industries are characterised by high appropriability conditions. By estimating separate regressions for two groups of firms – firms in high and a low appropriability sectors – we observe that the effect on R&D spending of sources of knowledge differs between the two groups. In sectors with high appropriability conditions, knowledge spillovers from research institutes and publications and conferences lead to higher R&D intensity than in low appropriability sectors. The knowledge acquired via the participation in public research programmes has no effect on R&D spending of firms in high appropriability sectors. A potential explanation is that while a firm can extract useful information and knowledge by participating in research programmes, it may also involuntarily spill over some of its tacit know-how (Amoroso and Vannuccini 2019). The possibility of giving away useful knowledge to other firms (competitors, value-chain partners, or firms in a research consortium) does not create the incentive to invest more in R&D. This type of knowledge is, however, the most valuable in sectors with low appropriability conditions.

The main contribution of this paper is, however, the analysis of the role of female founders. While most studies focus on the economic or innovative performance of women entrepreneurs, we look instead at the knowledge absorptive capability from a gender perspective. More specifically, we examine how female first-listed founded firms differ from male ones in translating the knowledge from external sources into R&D efforts. Our findings suggest that female-led firms have an advantage compared to male-led ones in reaping the benefits of knowledge acquired from research institutes and value-chain partners. Moreover, in sectors with low appropriability conditions, female-founded firms are able to complement their internal R&D with information from competitors as well. These results align with the theoretical underpinnings of management and organisational studies which suggest that women have a preference and tendency to organise and manage their activities as collaborative networks, where they use their relational skills to create and develop connections with both professional and personal contacts (Sorenson, Folker, and Brigham 2008; Achtenhagen et al. 2013). This feminine approach to managing and organising in collaborative networks is associated with higher R&D intensity, which is seen as a key component of the entrepreneurial orientation (Wiklund and Shepherd 2003).

From a policy perspective, these results are especially relevant. Indeed, our results suggest that encouraging the natural tendency of women entrepreneurs to rely on formal and informal collaborative networks and supporting social structures may offset and even reverse their aversion to risky investment such as R&D.

In spite of its contributions, the present study has its limitations. Methodologically, the choice of censored regression (Tobit model) takes into account the truncation of the error term due to the fact that we observe the R&D intensity only for a part of the sample. However, this approach may introduce a specification error as we restrict the way in which the explanatory variables simultaneously determine the probability of performing R&D and the intensity of R&D spending. Indeed, the knowledge spillover variables may not affect the probability of engaging in R&D, but only affect R&D performance. A second estimation problem stems from the endogeneity of market concentration and innovation which are endogenous variables and must be seen as simultaneously determined within a system. Moreover, our analysis is based on a cross-sectional survey and cannot be used to understand the evolution and the dynamic relationship between internal R&D and different sources of external knowledge. Lastly, we do not take into account cooperations as an additional way in which firms may access pools of knowledge. For example, consulting with a research institute or a university to solve a technical problem, or collaborating with universities to develop a new technology, may correspond to different levels of internal R&D.

Notes

1. US Chamber of Commerce Foundation.
2. Bloom, Schankerman, and Van Reenen (2013) explains that 'R&D generates at least two distinct types of 'spillover' effects. The first is technology (or knowledge) spillovers, which may increase the productivity of other firms that operate in similar technology areas. The second type of spillover is the product market rivalry effect of R&D. Whereas technology spillovers are beneficial to other firms, R&D by product market rivals has a negative effect on a firm's value due to business stealing.' (1347).
3. The incoming spillovers are measures of the importance of external information flows for the firm's innovation process. The outgoing spillovers derive from knowledge leaking out of the company or organisation.

4. The entrepreneurial orientation is defined as a set of strategic actions taken by managers and entrepreneurs which are driven by perceptions of opportunity, and oriented towards the exploitation of these opportunities (Wiklund and Shepherd 2003). According to Lumpkin and Dess (1996), the three main components of entrepreneurial orientation are innovativeness, risk-taking propensity, and proactiveness. Innovativeness is the firm's engagement in experimentation and R&D activities that may result in new products or technological processes. Proactiveness refers to the firm's forward-looking perspective to anticipate future needs by seeking new opportunities. It may play a significant role for the R&D investment. Risk-taking propensity involves the willingness to commit significant resources to exploit opportunities or engage in business strategies with a highly uncertain outcome.
5. We categorise 3 as not important since firms scoring 3 on a Likert 1-5 scale are not actually rating the source of knowledge as important.
6. In the interaction terms between spillovers and the share of women, we normalised the share of women founders to have a zero population mean, so that we can interpret the average effect of spillovers as β_k. For example, the average increase in R&D due to knowledge spillovers from research programmes is 3.774 ppt.

Acknowledgements

The authors wish to thank Mercedes Teruel, Michele Pezzoni, Enrico Santarelli, the guest editor Al Link, and the anonymous referee for their valuable comments on a previous version of this paper. Any remaining errors are ours alone. The views expressed are purely those of the authors and may not in any circumstances be regarded as stating an official position of the European Commission.

Disclosure statement

No potential conflict of interest was reported by the author(s).

References

Achtenhagen, Leona, Malin Tillmar, Maria Bogren, Yvonne von Friedrichs, Oystein Rennemo, and Oystein Widding. 2013. "Networking Women Entrepreneurs: Fruitful for Business Growth?" *International Journal of Gender and Entrepreneurship* 5 (1): 60–77.

Amir, Rabah. 2000. "Modelling Imperfectly Appropriable R&D Via Spillovers." *International Journal of Industrial Organization* 18 (7): 1013–1032. Accessed March 18, 2020. https://linkinghub.elsevier.com/retrieve/pii/S0167718700000710.

Amir, Rabah, Jim Y. Jin, and Michael Troege. 2008. "On Additive Spillovers and Returns to Scale in R&D." *International Journal of Industrial Organization* 26 (3): 695–703. Accessed March 18, 2020. https://linkinghub.elsevier.com/retrieve/pii/S016771870700063X.

Amoroso, Sara, David B. Audretsch, and Albert N. Link. 2018. "Sources of Knowledge Used by Entrepreneurial Firms in the European High-tech Sector." *Eurasian Business Review* 8 (1): 55–70. Accessed March 18, 2020. https://doi.org/10.1007/s40821-017-0078-4.

Amoroso, Sara, and Albert N. Link. 2018. "Under the AEGIS of Knowledge-intensive Entrepreneurship: Employment Growth and Gender of Founders Among European Firms." *Small Business Economics* 50 (4): 899–915. Accessed March 18, 2020. http://link.springer.com/10.1007/s11187-017-9920-4.

Amoroso, Sara, and Albert N. Link. 2019. "Intellectual Property Protection Mechanisms and the Characteristics of Founding Teams." JRC Working Papers on Corporate R&D and Innovation 01/2019. Seville: European Commission, Joint Research Centre (JRC). http://hdl.handle.net/10419/202182.

Amoroso, Sara, and Simone Vannuccini. 2019. *Teaming up with Large R&D Investors: Good or Bad for Knowledge Production and Diffusion?* Technical Report 2019/05. European Commission, Joint Research Centre (JRC).

Argote, Linda. 2013. *Organizational Learning: Creating, Retaining and Transferring Knowledge*. 2nd ed. New York: Springer. OCLC: 830340473.

Arrow, Kenneth. 1962. "Economic Welfare and the Allocation of Resources for Invention." In *The Rate and Direction of Inventive Activity: Economic and Social Factors*, edited by Universities-National Bureau Committee for Economic Research, Committee on Economic Growth of the Social Science Research Council Volume, 609–626. Princeton, NJ: Princeton University Press. Accessed March 17, 2020. https://www.nber.org/chapters/c2144.

Atherton, Andrew. 2003. "The Uncertainty of Knowing: An Analysis of the Nature of Knowledge in a Small Business Context." *Human Relations* 56 (11): 1379–1398. Accessed March 22, 2020. http://journals.sagepub.com/doi/10.1177/00187267035611005.

Audretsch, David B., and Maksim Belitski. 2020. "The Role of R&D and Knowledge Spillovers in Innovation and Productivity." *European Economic Review* 123: 103391. http://www.sciencedirect.com/science/article/pii/S0014292120300234.

Audretsch, David B., and Albert N. Link. 2019. *Sources of Knowledge and Entrepreneurial Behavior*. Toronto: University of Toronto Press.

Basit, Shoaib Abdul, and Kehinde Medase. 2019. "The Diversity of Knowledge Sources and Its Impact on Firm-level Innovation." *European Journal of Innovation Management* 22 (4): 681–714.

Belderbos, René, Martin Carree, Bert Diederen, Boris Lokshin, and Reinhilde Veugelers. 2004. "Heterogeneity in R&D Cooperation Strategies." *International Journal of Industrial Organization* 22 (8–9): 1237–1263.

Bloom, Nicholas, Mark Schankerman, and John Van Reenen. 2013. "Identifying Technology Spillovers and Product Market Rivalry." *Econometrica* 81 (4): 1347–1393.

Caloghirou, Yannis D., Aimilia Protogerou, and Aggelos Tsakanikas. 2014. "Exploring Knowledge-Intensive Entrepreneurship in High-Tech and Low-Tech Manufacturing Sectors: Differences and Similarities." In *Knowledge-Intensive Entrepreneurship in Low-Tech Industries*, edited by Hartmut Hirsch-Kreinsen and Isabel Schwinge, 17–41. Cheltenham: Edward Elgar Publishing. Accessed March 18, 2020. http://www.elgaronline.com/view/9781783472031.00009.xml.

Cantù, Chiara, Daniela Corsaro, Annalisa Tunisini, Graciela Corral de Zubielqui, Janice Jones, Pi-Shen Seet, and Noel Lindsay. 2015. "Knowledge Transfer Between Actors in the Innovation System: A Study of Higher Education Institutions (HEIS) and SMES." *Journal of Business & Industrial Marketing* 30 (3/4): 436–458.

Cappelli, Riccardo, Dirk Czarnitzki, and Kornelius Kraft. 2014. "Sources of Spillovers for Imitation and Innovation." *Research Policy* 43 (1): 115–120. Accessed March 18, 2020. https://linkinghub.elsevier.com/retrieve/pii/S0048733313001327.

Carter, Nancy M., ed. 2007. *Female Entrepreneurship: Implications for Education, Training and Policy*. Routledge Advances in Management and Business Studies. Vol. 30. London: Routledge. OCLC: 255159491.

Cassiman, Bruno, David Pérez-Castrillo, and Reinhilde Veugelers. 2002. "Endogenizing Know-how Flows Through the Nature of R&D Investments." *International Journal of Industrial Organization* 20 (6): 775–799. Accessed March 18, 2020. https://linkinghub.elsevier.com/retrieve/pii/S0167718701000844.

Cassiman, Bruno, and Reinhilde Veugelers. 2002. "R&D Cooperation and Spillovers: Some Empirical Evidence From Belgium." *American Economic Review* 92 (4): 1169–1184.

Chen, Yufen, Wim Vanhaverbeke, and Jingshu Du. 2016. "The Interaction Between Internal R&D and Different Types of External Knowledge Sourcing: An Empirical Study of Chinese Innovative Firms: Interaction Between Internal R&D and Different Types of External Knowledge Sourcing." *R&D Management* 46 (S3): 1006–1023. Accessed March 17, 2020. http://doi.wiley.com/10.1111/radm.12162.

Chesbrough, Henry William. 2003. *Open Innovation: The New Imperative for Creating and Profiting From Technology*. Boston, MA: Harvard Business School Press.

Coad, Alex, and Rekha Rao. 2010. "Firm Growth and R&D Expenditure." *Economics of Innovation and New Technology* 19 (2): 127–145. https://doi.org/10.1080/10438590802472531.

Cohen, Wesley M., and Richard C. Levin. 1989. "Empirical Studies of Innovation and Market Structure." Chap. 18 in *Handbook of Industrial Organization*. Vol. 2, edited by Richard Schmalensee and Robert Willig, 1059–1107. Amsterdam: Elsevier. http://www.sciencedirect.com/science/article/pii/S1573448X89020066.

Cohen, Wesley M., and Daniel A. Levinthal. 1989. "Innovation and Learning: The Two Faces of R & D." *The Economic Journal* 99 (397): 569–596. Accessed March 6, 2020. www.jstor.org/stable/2233763.

Cohen, Wesley M., and John P. Walsh. 2001. "R&D Spillovers, Appropriability and R&D Intensity: A Survey Based Approach." In *Papers and Proceedings of the Advanced Technology Program's International Conference on the Economic Evaluation of Technological Change*, edited by Richard N. Spivack, 22–29. Washington, DC: U.S. Government Printing Office.

Coleman, James S. 1988. "Social Capital in the Creation of Human Capital." *American Journal of Sociology* 94: S95–S120.

Cook, Lisa D., and Chaleampong Kongcharoen. 2010. "The Idea Gap in Pink and Black." SSRN Scholarly Paper ID 1673676. Rochester, NY: Social Science Research Network. Accessed March 19, 2020. https://papers.ssrn.com/abstract=1673676.

D'Aspremont, Claude, and Alexis Jacquemin. 1988. "Cooperative and Noncooperative R & D in Duopoly with Spillovers." *The American Economic Review* 78 (5): 1133–1137. Accessed March 17, 2020. https://www.jstor.org/stable/1807173.

Demiralp, Berna, Laura T. R. Morrison, and Stephanie Zayed. 2018. "On the Commercialization Path: Entrepreneurship and Intellectual Property Outputs Among Women in STEM." *Technology & Innovation* 19 (4): 707–726. Accessed March 19, 2020. http://www.ingentaconnect.com/content/10.21300/19.4.2018.707.

Doloreux, David, Richard Shearmur, and Mercedes Rodriguez. 2018. "Internal R&D and External Information in Knowledge-intensive Business Service Innovation: Complements, Substitutes Or Independent?" *Technological and Economic Development of Economy* 24 (6): 2255–2276.

Fackelmann, Surya, and Alessandro De Concini. 2020. "Funding Women Entrepreneurs: How to Empower Growth." https://www.eib.org/attachments/thematic/why_are_women_entrepreneurs_missing_out_on_funding_en.pdf.

Fang, Sheng, Heba Shams, and Lixin Colin Xu. 2019. "Foreign Direct Investment and Female Entrepreneurship." World Bank Policy Research Working Paper (9083).

Fontana, Roberto, Franco Malerba, and Astrid Marinoni. 2016. "Knowledge Intensive Entrepreneurship in Different Sectoral Systems. A Taxonomy." In *Dynamics of Knowledge Intensive Entrepreneurship: Business Strategy and Public Policy*, edited by Franco Malerba, Yannis Caloghirou, Maureen McKelvey, Slavo Radoševic, 191–213. London: Routledge, Taylor & Francis Group. Accessed March 18, 2020. https://iris.unibocconi.it/handle/11565/3989858.

Fuentes-Fuentes, María del Mar, Ana M. Bojica, and Matilde Ruiz-Arroyo. 2015. "Entrepreneurial Orientation and Knowledge Acquisition: Effects on Performance in the Specific Context of Women-owned Firms." *International Entrepreneurship and Management Journal* 11 (3): 695–717. Accessed March 20, 2020. http://link.springer.com/10.1007/s11365-014-0336-1.

Galindo, Miguel-Angel, and Domingo Ribeiro. 2011. *Women's Entrepreneurship and Economics: New Perspectives, Practices, and Policies*. Vol. 1000. New York: Springer-Verlag.

Gesing, Judith, David Antons, Erk P. Piening, Mario Rese, and Torsten Oliver Salge. 2015. "Joining Forces Or Going It Alone? On the Interplay Among External Collaboration Partner Types, Interfirm Governance Modes, and Internal R&D: Joining Forces Or Going It Alone." *Journal of Product Innovation Management* 32 (3): 424–440. Accessed October 11, 2020. http://doi.wiley.com/10.1111/jpim.12227.

Gottschalk, Sandra, and Michaela Niefert. 2013. "Gender Differences in Business Success of German Start-up Firms." *International Journal of Entrepreneurship and Small Business* 18 (1): 15–46.

Hagedoorn, John, and Ning Wang. 2012. "Is there Complementarity Or Substitutability Between Internal and External R&D Strategies?" *Research Policy* 41 (6): 1072–1083. Accessed March 18, 2020. https://linkinghub.elsevier.com/retrieve/pii/S0048733312000558.

Hodges, Nancy J., and Albert N. Link. 2018. "Sources of Knowledge Used by KIE Textile and Apparel Firms." In *Knowledge-Intensive Entrepreneurship: An Analysis of the European Textile and Apparel Industries*, edited by Nancy J. Hodges and Albert N. Link, International Studies in Entrepreneurship, 81–103. Cham: Springer International Publishing. Accessed March 18, 2020. https://doi.org/10.1007/978-3-319-68777-3_6.

Jaffe, Adam B. 1986. "Technological Opportunity and Spillovers of R & D: Evidence From Firms' Patents, Profits, and Market Value." *The American Economic Review* 76 (5): 984–1001. Accessed March 17, 2020. https://www.jstor.org/stable/1816464.

Kamien, Morton I., Eitan Muller, and Israel Zang. 1992. "Research Joint Ventures and R&D Cartels." *The American Economic Review* 82 (5): 1293–1306. Accessed March 17, 2020. https://www.jstor.org/stable/2117479.

Katz, Michael L. 1986. "An Analysis of Cooperative Research and Development." *The RAND Journal of Economics* 17 (4): 527–543. Accessed March 17, 2020. https://www.jstor.org/stable/2555479.

Laursen, Keld, and Ammon J. Salter. 2014. "The Paradox of Openness: Appropriability, External Search and Collaboration." *Research Policy* 43 (5): 867–878. http://www.sciencedirect.com/science/article/pii/S0048733313001832.

Levin, Richard, and Peter C. Reiss. 1984. "Tests of a Schumpeterian Model of R&D and Market Structure." In *R&D, Patents, and Productivity*, edited by Zvi Griliches, 175–208. Chicago, IL: University of Chicago Press. https://EconPapers.repec.org/RePEc:nbr:nberch:10049.

Liao, Jianwen, Harold Welsch, and Michael Stoica. 2003. "Organizational Absorptive Capacity and Responsiveness: An Empirical Investigation of Growth-Oriented SMEs." *Entrepreneurship Theory and Practice* 28 (1): 63–86. Accessed March 27, 2020. http://journals.sagepub.com/doi/10.1111/1540-8520.00032.

Link, Albert N., and Derek R. Strong. 2016. "Gender and Entrepreneurship: An Annotated Bibliography." *Foundations and Trends® in Entrepreneurship* 12 (4–5): 287–441. Accessed March 18, 2020. http://www.nowpublishers.com/article/Details/ENT-068.

Link, Albert N., and Martijn van Hasselt. 2020. "Exploring the Impact of R&D on Patenting Activity in Small Women-owned and Minority-owned Entrepreneurial Firms." *Small Business Economics* 54 (4): 1061–1066.

Lööf, Hans, and Almas Heshmati. 2002. "Knowledge Capital and Performance Heterogeneity." *International Journal of Production Economics* 76 (1): 61–85. Accessed March 18, 2020. https://linkinghub.elsevier.com/retrieve/pii/S0925527301001475.

Lumpkin, G. T., and Gregory G. Dess. 1996. "Clarifying the Entrepreneurial Orientation Construct and Linking It To Performance." *Academy of Management Review* 21 (1): 135–172. Accessed March 21, 2020. http://journals.aom.org/doi/10.5465/amr.1996.9602161568.

Martin, Stephen. 2002. "Spillovers, Appropriability, and R&D." *Journal of Economics* 75 (1): 1–32. Accessed March 18, 2020. https://www.jstor.org/stable/41794929.

Marvel, Matthew R., In Hyeock Lee, and Marcus T. Wolfe. 2015. "Entrepreneur Gender and Firm Innovation Activity: a Multilevel Perspective." *IEEE Transactions on Engineering Management* 62 (4): 558–567.

Moilanen, Mikko, Stein Østbye, and Kristin Woll. 2014. "Non-R&D SMEs: External Knowledge, Absorptive Capacity and Product Innovation." *Small Business Economics* 43 (2): 447–462.

Monjon, Stéphanie, and Patrick Waelbroeck. 2003. "Assessing Spillovers From Universities to Firms: Evidence From French Firm-level Data." *International Journal of Industrial Organization* 21 (9): 1255–1270. Accessed March 18, 2020. https://linkinghub.elsevier.com/retrieve/pii/S0167718703000821.

Nelson, Richard R. 1959. "The Simple Economics of Basic Scientific Research." *Journal of Political Economy* 67 (3): 297–306. Accessed March 17, 2020. https://www.journals.uchicago.edu/doi/10.1086/258177.

Nieto, María Jesús, and Lluis Santamaría. 2007. "The Importance of Diverse Collaborative Networks for the Novelty of Product Innovation." *Technovation* 27 (6-7): 367–377. Accessed March 18, 2020. https://linkinghub.elsevier.com/retrieve/pii/S0166497206001064.

Nissan, Edward, Inmaculada Carrasco, and María-Soledad Castaño. 2012. "Women Entrepreneurship, Innovation, and Internationalization." In *Women's Entrepreneurship and Economics: New Perspectives, Practices, and Policies*, edited by Miguel-Angel Galindo and Domingo Ribeiro, 125–142. New York, NY: Springer. https://doi.org/10.1007/978-1-4614-1293-9_9.

Ozkazanc-Pan, Banu, and Susan Clark Muntean. 2018. "Networking Towards (in)equality: Women Entrepreneurs in Technology." *Gender, Work & Organization* 25 (4): 379–400. Accessed March 22, 2020. https://onlinelibrary.wiley.com/doi/abs/10.1111/gwao.12225.

Posner, Barry Z., and J. Michael Munson. 1981. "Gender Differences in Managerial Values." *Psychological Reports* 49 (3): 867–881. Accessed March 24, 2020. http://journals.sagepub.com/doi/10.2466/pr0.1981.49.3.867.

Protogerou, Aimilia, Yannis Caloghirou, and Nicholas S. Vonortas. 2017. "Determinants of Young Firms' Innovative Performance: Empirical Evidence From Europe." *Research Policy* 46 (7): 1312–1326. http://www.sciencedirect.com/science/article/pii/S004873331730094X.

Quiroz-Rojas, Paula, and Mercedes Teruel. 2020. "Does Gender Matter for Innovative and Non-innovative Firms' Growth? An Empirical Analysis of Chilean Managers." *Innovation and Development* 18: 1–19.

Seo, Hangyeol, Yanghon Chung, and Hyungseok (David) Yoon. 2017. "R&D Cooperation and Unintended Innovation Performance: Role of Appropriability Regimes and Sectoral Characteristics." *Technovation*66–67: 28–42. http://www.sciencedirect.com/science/article/pii/S0166497217301906.

Sorenson, Ritch L., Cathleen A. Folker, and Keith H. Brigham. 2008. "The Collaborative Network Orientation: Achieving Business Success Through Collaborative Relationships." *Entrepreneurship Theory and Practice* 32 (4): 615–634.

Spence, A. 1984. "Cost Reduction, Competition, and Industry Performance." *Econometrica* 52 (1): 101–21. https://EconPapers.repec.org/RePEc:ecm:emetrp:v:52:y:1984:i:1:p:101-21.

Stokey, Nancy L. 1995. "R&D and Economic Growth." *The Review of Economic Studies* 62 (3): 469–489.

Teece, David J. 1993. "Profiting From Technological Innovation: Implications for Integration, Collaboration, Licensing and Public Policy." *Research Policy* 22 (2): 112–113.

West, Joel, and Marcel Bogers. 2014. "Leveraging External Sources of Innovation: a Review of Research on Open Innovation." *Journal of Product Innovation Management* 31 (4): 814–831.

Wiklund, Johan, and Dean Shepherd. 2003. "Knowledge-based Resources, Entrepreneurial Orientation, and the Performance of Small and Medium-sized Businesses." *Strategic Management Journal* 24 (13): 1307–1314. Accessed March 21, 2020. http://doi.wiley.com/10.1002/smj.360.

Zobel, Ann-Kristin, Boris Lokshin, and John Hagedoorn. 2017. "Formal and Informal Appropriation Mechanisms: The Role of Openness and Innovativeness." *Technovation* 59: 44–54.

Entrepreneurial universities and innovative behavior: the impact of gender diversity

Matthias Menter

ABSTRACT

Whereas the impact of entrepreneurial universities is rather well understood, the underlying mechanisms that foster and accelerate university innovation outcomes are much less clear. Besides institutional factors, especially individual characteristics of scientists may decisively influence the quality of university outcomes. The purpose of this paper is to investigate the impact of gender diversity on university innovation outcomes across all three university missions, i.e. teaching, research and the commercialization of knowledge. The results of this study suggest that gender diversity positively affects university innovation outcomes in the context of universities' mission implementation, yet follows an inverted U-shape. Whereas a higher share of female scientists seems to be particularly conducive for innovative behavior with regard to teaching and research activities, male scientists seem to be better able to produce radical innovations, i.e. transfer new knowledge from academia towards the market. The findings further suggest that there seems to be a certain threshold in that a minimum level of gender diversity is necessary to drive augmented innovative behavior within universities. Based on these findings, recommendations for university managers and policy makers are derived as well as future avenues of research are outlined.

1. Introduction

The impact of (entrepreneurial) universities on economic growth and prosperity has been proven in numerous studies (Hayter and Link 2015; Lehmann and Menter 2016; Link 2000; Urbano and Guerrero 2013; Valero and Van Reenen 2019). Universities serve as the drivers of new ideas, products, and innovations through their multiple missions of teaching, research and the commercialization of knowledge, thus constitute an important pillar of regional development strategies:

> The entrepreneurial university serves as a conduit of spillovers contributing to economic and social development through its multiple missions of teaching, research, and entrepreneurial activities. In particular, the outcomes of its missions are associated with the determinants of production functions (e.g. human capital, knowledge capital, social capital, and entrepreneurship capital). (Guerrero, Cunningham, and Urbano 2015, 748)

Entrepreneurial universities hence succeed in creating environments that are conducive for innovative entrepreneurship and incentivize scholars to constantly challenge the status-quo. This innovative behavior is thereby reflected and applied across all three university missions and ultimately results in augmented levels of entrepreneurship capital (Audretsch, Keilbach, and Lehmann 2006).

Whereas the influence of entrepreneurial universities is rather well understood, the underlying mechanisms that foster and accelerate university innovation outcomes are much less clear. In this context, research has mainly been devoted to the organizational architecture of universities and the critical role of selected organizational units such as technology transfer offices, liaison offices, incubators, or science parks, i.e. institutional factors (Chapple et al. 2005; Hülsbeck, Lehmann, and Starnecker 2013; Link and Scott 2005; Siegel, Waldman, and Link 2003). However, also individual factors, i.e. the inherent characteristics of individual scientists, might have an essential impact on the quality of university outcomes (see Wu, Welch, and Huang 2015).

Especially the role and impact of gender diversity, that is the equitable ratio of men and women across occupations[1], has attracted increasing research attention among scholars to explain differences in performance and innovation outcomes. This strand of literature is yet mostly concerned about the private sector, looking at firm-relevant aspects such as board composition (Campbell and Mínguez-Vera 2008; Joecks, Pull, and Vetter 2013; Owen and Temesvary 2018), team composition in R&D departments (Díaz-García, González-Moreno, and Jose Sáez-Martínez 2013; Sastre 2014), or financial performance (Dwyer, Richard, and Chadwick 2003; Fernando, Jain, and Tripathy 2020), almost neglecting public sector organizations such as universities. However, especially universities are an interesting object of investigation, since studies confirm the existence of a gender gap within academia (Kuschel et al. 2020; Weisshaar 2017), particularly in the context of academic entrepreneurship (Abreu and Grinevich 2017; Rosa and Dawson 2006).

The purpose of this paper is to address this research gap and investigate the impact of gender diversity on university innovation outcomes across all three university missions, i.e. teaching, research and the commercialization of knowledge. Literature suggests that gender diversity and the associated gender composition of teams matter; e.g. Hoogendoorn, Oosterbeek, and Van Praag (2013) find that teams with an equal gender mix outperform male-dominated teams. Applying these benefits to the academic sector implies that gender diversity may play a significant role in fulfilling universities' missions: A gender-balanced workforce may offer more multifaceted approaches towards innovative teaching (e.g. through the utilization of digital tools and technologies), may augment the overall research performance (e.g. through the investigation of new and relevant phenomena) and may be better able to address market needs through the commercialization of knowledge (e.g. through the addressing of current and future market needs).

Set in the German context, this study examines the impact of gender diversity on the German higher education landscape, i.e. how a diverse workforce of female and male scientists affects the mission implementation of German universities. Universities' innovative outcomes across all three missions are thereby at the focus of this study – teaching, research and the commercialization of knowledge. The results of this study suggest that gender diversity positively affects university innovation outcomes in the context of universities' mission implementation, yet follows an inverted U-shape. Whereas a higher share of female scientists seems to be particularly conducive for innovative behavior with regard to teaching and research activities, male scientists seem to be better able to produce radical innovations, i.e. transfer new knowledge from academia towards the market. The findings further suggest that there seems to be a certain threshold in that a minimum level of gender diversity is necessary to drive augmented innovative behavior within universities. Based on these findings, recommendations for university managers and policy makers are derived how to (1) establish a more gender-balanced workforce within the academic context, (2) leverage the potentials of a more gender-balanced workforce and (3) ensure a continuous variety and inclusiveness within universities.

This study contributes to the literature on entrepreneurial universities and innovative behavior by unveiling the role and impact of gender diversity, highlighting the potential downsides of a male-dominated academic environment. It further sheds light on the antecendents of the existing gender gap in academia and proposes several mechanisms how to overcome existing obstacles for women. Both female and male scientists inhere the potential of pushing technological boundaries. This study opens up trajectories how university managers may better leverage the potentials of a more gender-balanced workforce and ensure a continuous variety and inclusiveness within universities.

The remainder of this study is structured as follows. The next section provides a literature review of entrepreneurial universities as well as the role and impact of gender diversity. The third section describes the methodological approach and explains the data. Section four presents the results of this study, whereas section five discusses the findings. A final section concludes and outlines recommendations for university managers and policy makers.

2. Literature review

2.1. Entrepreneurial universities and innovative behavior

Knowledge serves as a key factor of production and has been perceived – at least since Romer (1986) – as a key driver of economic prosperity. Endogenous growth theory suggests that investments in new technological knowledge are associated with knowledge spillovers which may be translated into innovative activities and ultimately result in economic growth (Romer 1990). Considering the assumptions of the endogenous growth theory, the knowledge spillover theory of entrepreneurship complements that entrepreneurial action is needed to exploit knowledge spillovers and transform knowledge into innovation (Acs et al. 2009, 2013). The growing awareness that knowledge and knowledge spillovers are a necessary, yet not a sufficient prerequisite for economic growth finally induced – among others – a paradigm shift within universities and the entire academic sector, which had previously only been perceived as knowledge creating institutions: 'The universities needed to become more entrepreneurial in that they pro-actively engaged in entrepreneurial activity to facilitate knowledge spillovers for commercialization out of the universities' (Audretsch 2014, 317). Etzkowitz (2014, 223) describes this transformative change as the 'entrepreneurial university wave' and concludes that 'traditional academic roles are revised to include entrepreneurial elements, both to attract external resources and to see that knowledge is put to use'.

The emergence of entrepreneurial universities was thereby accompanied by a mission reorientation of universities (Romero, Ferreira, and Fernandes 2020). Whereas the core tasks of universities traditionally revolved around teaching and research, the shift towards an entrepreneurial paradigm resulted in a so-called 'third mission' of universities, that is the commercialization of scientific knowledge through entrepreneurship and business-related activities (Gulbrandsen and Slipersaeter 2007). In broader terms, the 'third mission' of universities may be associated with outreach activities meant to give something back to society, hence disseminate knowledge to contribute to innovation-driven social change.

Policy makers worldwide tried to accelerate this transformative change within the higher education landscape and implemented policy instruments meant to facilitate the shift towards an entrepreneurial paradigm, with the most prominent legislative change being the so-called Bayh-Dole Act of 1980 in the United States (see Aldridge and Audretsch 2011). These legislative changes resulted in an enormous increase of innovative activities such as patenting among universities, the creation of organizational units specifically devoted to facilitating the commercialization of research (e.g. technology transfer offices) as well as additional support of universities to engage in the 'third mission': 'Since the passage of the Bayh-Dole Act in 1980, there has been widespread and growing public sector support for the commercialization of university-based research' (Leyden and Link 2015, 83). In their study of US science parks, Link and Scott (2003) show that an entrepreneurial orientation may ultimately also affect the perception of the academic missions of universities.

Hence, the transformation from traditional towards entrepreneurial universities has resulted in increased levels of innovative behavior in the context of the commercialization of knowledge, yet also beyond, that is in the context of teaching and research. The utilization of new technologies and the adaption to the digital economy with its new opportunities and challenges are hence reactions of universities in the context of this changing paradigm. The introduction of digital campuses, e-learning and massive open online courses (MOOCs) can thereby be seen as visible examples of universities' reponses towards the fast-moving digital economy. Guerrero, Heaton, and Urbano (2020) describe the introcution of MOOCs as a strategy tool in the digital transformation of entrepreneurial universities, enabling universities to attract large audiences worldwide in a rather short time period.

In order to cope with these institutional changes, university managers need to rely on the innovative behaviors of universities' scientists to adopt and apply these new technologies and exploit resulting (entrepreneurial) opportunities. Only a creative pool of scientists might ultimately enable the transformation towards an entrepreneurial university. However, despite the general agreement on the impact of the transition of universities towards an entrepreneurial paradigm, i.e. increased innovative behavior and outcomes within and beyond academic spheres, the underlying mechanisms that may stimulate innovative outcomes within universities, thus enable the transformation of universities, largely remain vague.

2.2. The role and impact of gender diversity

Among the various influencing factors enhancing innovative behavior and outcomes of universities on an individual basis, especially the role and impact of gender diversity has attracted increasing research attention (see Neves and Brito 2020; Riegraf et al. 2010). In this context, especially the existence of a gender gap in academia has been investigated intensively (Kuschel et al. 2020; Xie and Shauman 2003), ultimately affecting the scientific productivity of women: among others, female academics seem to be less likely to patent, license, or create their own spin-off, hence engage in academic entrepreneurship. The so-called 'leaky pipeline' model suggests that those differences may be associated with higher shares of women dropping out of research at various stages of the scientific career paths in comparison to their male counterparts (Pell 1996; Wickware 1997). This drop out occurs at various points, starting in school (choice of subjects), continues when transitioning to higher education and my even apply to (tenured) faculty positions.

As a consequence, women are underrepresented especially in senior faculty positions and face less opportunities, e.g. for commercializing their research or engaging in university-industry collaborations. In their study of UK-based academics, Abreu and Grinevich (2017, 784) find that female academics are confronted with significant obstacles to commercialization that affects their scientific performance negatively: 'Female academics are severely constrained in their opportunities for commercialization by their less senior status, and lack of entrepreneurial experience'. Efforts to close this gender gap are omnipresent. Besides the imperative to ensure gender equality and offer both male and female academics the same basic requirements to progress and perform, closing the gender gap might also be associated with an increase in the overall scientific performance of a university.

Ruiz-Jiménez, del Mar Fuentes-Fuentes, and Ruiz-Arroyo (2016) show that the knowledge combination capabilities and innovation performance are positively moderated by gender diversity. This positive moderation effect is also confirmed by Lauring and Villesèche (2019). Pitts and Wise (2010) further suggest that gender diversity positively affects organizational success and also Herring (2009) finds a positive relationship between gender diversity and performance. An explanation for the expected positive externalities of gender diversity is provided by Van Knippenberg and Schippers (2007, 517) by taking an information/ decision-making perspective: 'Diversity may introduce differences in knowledge, expertise, and perspectives that may help work groups reach higher quality and more creative and innovative outcomes'. Hence, the heterogeneity of male and female perspectives and skills may ultimately result in augmented scientific performance. Similarly, Wegge et al. (2008) argue that gender-diverse teams outperform. The first hypothesis thus posits a positive linear relationship between gender diversity and universities' innovative outcomes (across all three missions, i.e. teaching, research and the commercialization of knowledge).

H1: Gender diversity positively affects universities' innovative outcomes (across all three university missions)

Besides this rather positive notion of gender diversity, other studies have taken a more critical look at the role and impact of gender diversity. In their comprehensive literature reviews, Jackson, Joshi, and Erhardt (2003), Terjesen, Sealy, and Singh (2009) and Sciarelli et al. (2020) find inconsistent results with regard to the effect of gender diversity on performance. Van Knippenberg, De Dreu, and Homan (2004, 1008) claim that differences between group members (such as gender) may lead to disruptions that may ultimately affect team performance negatively, subsumed under the so-called 'social categorization perspective', and suggest that 'all dimensions of diversity may have positive as well as negative effects'. Shore et al. (2009) therefore argues that an inverted U-shaped relationship between gender diversity and performance may exist. In support of this curvilinear effect, Richard et al. (2004) and Dahlin, Weingart, and Hinds (2005) provide evidence that moderate levels of diversity may be associated with more positive outcomes than higher or lower levels of diversity. The second hypothesis thus posits that the relationship between gender diversity and universities' innovative outcomes (across all three missions, i.e. teaching, research and the commercialization of knowledge) follows an inverted U-shaped curvilinear relationship.

H2: The relationship between gender diversity and universities' innovative outcomes (across all three university missions) follows an inverted U-shaped curvilinear relationship

3. Data and methodology

3.1. Dataset

This paper examines the impact of gender diversity on universities' innovative outcomes across all three missions – teaching, research and the commercialization of knowledge. Set in the German context, 102 universities are investigated, using a timeframe ranging from 2000 to 2017. Following the broad literature on board and team composition, gender diversity within universities is measured as the number of female research fellows in relation to all research fellows of a university (e.g. Campbell and Mínguez-Vera 2008). Hence, the percentage of female research fellows in universities is calculated. Based on this operationalization, a gender diversity of 0.5 (or 50%) would imply an equal distribution of male and female scientists, i.e. a gender-balanced workforce.

In order to operationalize innovative behavior of universities in the context of teaching, the offering of MOOCs is employed, retrieved from university homepages as well as email correspondence with all investigated universities. According to Teece (2018, 98), MOOCs 'prove to be the most significant advance in the pedagogic part of higher education in a millennium'. MOOCs offer the opportunity to convey knowledge online to an almost unrestricted amount of participants for free: 'The shimmery hope is that free courses can bring the best education in the world to the most remote corners of the planet, help people in their careers, and expand intellectual and personal networks' (Pappano 2012). Initially adopted by reputed universities such as Harvard University, Massachusetts Institute of Technology (MIT), Stanford University or University California at Berkeley (UCB), entrepreneurial universities around the world have followed these examples and have included such online courses in their teaching portfolio as a new and innovative offer in the context of distance learning (North, Richardson, and North 2014).

With regard to research, published research papers in natural sciences classified as 'highly cited in the field', according to Web of Science, are utilized, i.e. key papers in their fields, reflected by rapid and significant numbers of citations. Innovative behavior in academic writing is associated with opening up new research trajectories, hence creating new research fields that push existing technological boundaries and can therefore be referred to as innovative outcomes of scientific research (Ranga, Debackere, and Tunzelmann 2003). The engagement in new and promising research fields is one form of being entrepreneurial, as is the challenging of status-quo thinking.

Concerning innovative behavior in the context of the commercialization of knowledge, radical innovations (as classified by the OECD[2]) of universities are taken as a proxy, retrieved from the European database PATSTAT. Radical innovations may lead to a radical technological change, hence a paradigm shift (see Verhoeven, Bakker, and Veugelers 2016), whereby the underlying concept itself can be dated back to Schumpeter (1939). Collaborations with industry might thereby augment the probability for the emergence of radical innovations (Arant et al. 2019). The concept of radicalness of a patent thereby refers to the number of IPC technology classes the focal patent is based on (backward citations), but in which the patent itself is not classified (Squicciarini, Dernis, and Criscuolo 2013). Hence, radicalness is the expression of the creative recombination of existing knowledge, i.e. the entrepreneurial exploitation of an existing knowledge stock.

Control variables for established university specifics such as scientific orientation (measured by a dummy variable that takes the value 1 if a university is a technical university and 0 otherwise), openness towards university-industry collaborations (measured by the total amount of third-party funds received from industry), and size (measured by the total amount of students) as well as established regional specifics such as regional density (measured by the number of citizens per square kilometer), regional innovativeness (measured by the number of patents per workforce, in 10,000) and regional entrepreneurship (measured by the number of start-ups per workforce, in 10,000) are further included. As utilized by the German Statistics Office, regions in terms of spatial planning regions (*Raumordnungsregionen*, RORs) are considered, where the respective university is located in.

3.2. Descriptive statistics

The transformation from a traditional towards an entrepreneurial university is a long-term process that involves both institutional as well as individual factors (Cunningham and Menter 2020). Hence, whereas some universities might have already fully adopted an entrepreneurial paradigm, other universities might just be undergoing transformative change. The resulting heterogeneity within the higher education landscape is also reflected in the data of this study as indicated by the large spread of the independent variables, i.e. innovative outcomes across all three missions – teaching, research and the commercialization of knowledge (see Table 1). However, the heterogeneity within the German higher education landscape is not only reflected in the entrepreneurial orientation of universities but also in terms of their size (as indicated by the variable university size) and industry focus (as indicated by the variable university-industry collaborations). Interestingly,

Table 1. Descriptive statistics.

Variable	Obs	Mean	SD	Min	Max	Description/Source
Innovative teaching outcomes	1,854	0.18	1.15	0	17	Number of offered massive open online courses (MOOCs); Source: University websites, Email correspondence with analyzed universities
Innovative research outcomes	1,854	10.65	25.53	0	206	Number of published research papers in natural sciences classified as 'highly cited in the field'; Source: Web of Science
Innovative commercialization outcomes	1,854	1.20	2.53	0	23.4	Number of radical innovations (as classified by the OECD) of universities, Source: PATSTAT
Gender diversity	1,741	0.35	0.10	0.02	0.92	Number of female research fellows in relation to all research fellows of a university; Source: German Statistics Office
Scientific orientation	1,854	0.18	0.39	0	1	Indication of technical university (dummy variable); Source: German Statistics Office
University-industry collaborations	1,637	10,707	14,287	0	117,320	Amount of university third-party funding by industry (in 1,000 €); Source: German Statistics Office
University size	1,766	15,127	13,376	10	80,464	Number of university students: Source: German Statistics Office
Regional innovativeness	1,734	4.74	3.12	0.17	14.63	Patents per workforce (in 10,000); Source: OECD REGPAT Database, German Statistics Office
Regional entrepreneurship	1,751	41.42	16.23	6.67	122.61	Start-ups per workforce (in 10,000); Source: Start-up Compendium, German Statistics Office
Regional density	1,734	815.80	1,103	58.71	3,981	Citizens per square kilometer; Source: German Statistics Office

Note: This table shows descriptive data on 102 German universities observed from 2000 to 2017.

universities also differ significantly with regard to aspects of gender diversity (as indicated by the variable gender diversity). Overall, the average number of female scientists has increased significantly within the observation period of this study (2000: 27.7% vs. 2017: 40.8%). Large differences are yet not only present in academic but also in regional spheres. Whereas some universities are located in highly entrepreneurial (as indicated by the variable regional entrepreneurship) and innovative (as indicated by the variable regional innovativeness) regions, other universities may not benefit from such fertile environments.

An analysis of the bivariate correlations reveals further insights (see Table 2). Strong university-industry linkages highly correlate with innovative research ($r = 0.49$) and commercialization ($r = 0.48$) outcomes. Innovative research outcomes are further highly correlated with innovative commercialization outcomes ($r = 0.42$). University size thereby seems to be positively associated with university-industry collaborations ($r = 0.61$), innovative research outcomes ($r = 0.50$) and innovative commercialization outcomes ($r = 0.40$).

3.3. Methodology

Due to the structure of the data, count panel regression models seem to be most appropriate for all three dependent variables (innovative outcomes across all three missions – teaching, research and the commercialization of knowledge). Throughout all three model specifications, random-effects negative binomial models are utilized (see Model I to III). The following estimation model is thereby taken as the basis:

where Y_{rt} refers to the three innovative outcomes across all three missions of university *r* at time *t*, respectively. Based on the derived hypothesis, a linear as well as a polynomial term of the variable gender diversity are included. The vector *University context* contains the scientific orientation of a university, the university size as well as the openness towards university-industry collaborations. The vector *Regional context* includes regional innovativeness, regional entrepreneurship and regional density. As usual, ε_{rt} represents the error term. In order to test the robustness of the results, population-averaged negative binomial models with robust standard errors are utilized (see Model IV to VI).

4. Results

The results of this study are reported in Table 3. Gender diversity seems to positively affect innovative outcomes across all three missions – teaching ($\beta = 51.26; p < 0.05$), research ($\beta = 33.09; p < 0.01$) and the commercialization of knowledge ($\beta = 28.73; p < 0.01$). Hence, these findings confirm H1 in that an increase in the number of female scientists leads to augmented innovative behavior within universities which ultimately results in an increase of innovative outcomes. The included squared terms of gender diversity enter all three regressions negative and statistically significant,

Table 2. Correlation matrix.

		1	2	3	4	5	6	7	8	9
1	Innovative teaching outcomes	1								
2	Innovative research outcomes	0.39	1							
3	Innovative commercialization outcomes	0.10	0.42	1						
4	Gender diversity	0.10	0.23	0.00	1					
5	University-industry collaborations	0.08	0.49	0.48	−0.04	1				
6	University size	0.18	0.50	0.40	0.14	0.61	1			
7	Regional innovativeness	−0.09	−0.01	0.07	−0.21	0.24	0.04	1		
8	Regional entrepreneurship	−0.10	−0.20	−0.18	−0.18	−0.10	−0.07	−0.16	1	
9	Regional density	0.00	−0.02	0.04	−0.05	−0.05	−0.01	−0.11	0.49	1

Note: This table reports the correlation coefficients among the dependent and independent variables employed in our regressions.

Table 3. Estimation results.

	Model I (Innovative teaching outcomes)	*Model II (Innovative research outcomes)*	*Model III (Innovative commercialization outcomes)*
GENDER			
Gender diversity	**51.26****	**33.09*****	**28.73*****
	(23.55)	**(6.35)**	**(4.62)**
Gender diversity (sqr)	**−61.37****	**−31.74*****	**−36.30*****
	(29.54)	**(8.15)**	**(6.20)**
UNIVERSITY			
Scientific orientation	**1.32***	**1.25*****	0.12
	(0.73)	**(0.24)**	(0.35)
University-industry collaborations	−0.00	−0.00	**0.00*****
	(0.00)	(0.00)	**(0.00)**
University size	**0.00****	−0.00	−0.00
	(0.00)	(0.00)	(0.00)
REGION			
Regional innovativeness	0.13	**0.16*****	**0.06*****
	(0.11)	**(0.02)**	**(0.02)**
Regional entrepreneurship	−0.00	−0.01	−0.01
	(0.03)	(0.01)	(0.02)
Regional density	0.00	0.00	0.00
	(0.00)	(0.00)	(0.00)
Year dummies	Yes	Yes	Yes
N	1,598	1,598	1,598
n	102	102	102

Note: This table reports the results of the random-effects negative binomial panel regressions. The estimation is based on a sample of 102 German universities ranging from 2000 to 2017. The dependent variables are innovative teaching outcomes measured by the number of offered massive open online courses (MOOCs), innovative research outcomes measured by the number of published research papers in natural sciences classified as 'highly cited in the field' and innovative commercialization outcomes measured by the number of radical innovations (as classified by the OECD) of universities, respectively. Standard errors are reported in parentheses.
*$p < .10$; ** $p < .05$; ***$p < .01$.

suggesting an inverted U-shaped relationship between gender diversity and universities' innovative outcomes across all three university missions. An increase in the number of female scientists leads to augmented innovative behavior within universities, yet only up to a certain point. H2 can thus also be confirmed.

Beyond aspects of gender, the scientific orientation of a university seems to decisively affect innovative behavior within universities. Whereas it is rather obvious that a specialization in engineering, technology, applied science, and natural sciences is conducive for innovative research in the field of natural sciences ($\beta = 1.25; p < 0.01$), the same holds true for innovative outcomes in the context of teaching ($\beta = 1.32; p < 0.1$). In addition, strong linkages with industry seem to particularly stimulate the generation of radical patents ($\beta = 0.00; p < 0.01$). From a regional perspective, especially innovative activities seem to positively affect innovative outcomes – at least in the context of research and the commercialization of knowledge. The alternative regression approach shows similar results and thus confirms the robustness of the findings (see Table 4).

Further insights can be derived by plotting the relationship between gender diversity and universities' innovative outcomes (see Figure 1). Especially innovative behavior in the context of teaching and research activities seems to be further stimulated by an increase in the number of female scientists, reaching a maximum at a share of approx. 60% of female scientists. Vice versa, innovative behavior in the context of the commercialization of knowledge seems to reach its maximum at a share of approx. 40% of female scientists. The visualizations further suggest that a certain threshold with regard to the level of female scientists needs to be exceeded in order to realize augmented innovation outcomes. Whereas this threshold is rather high for innovative outcomes in the context of teaching and research (approx. 20% of female scientists), commercialization activities

Table 4. Robustness tests.

	Model IV (Innovative teaching outcomes)	***Model V (Innovative research outcomes)***	***Model VI (Innovative commercialization outcomes)***
GENDER			
Gender diversity	**50.91***** **(17.86)**	**60.07***** **(7.25)**	**23.78***** **(8.11)**
Gender diversity (sqr)	**−64.58***** **(24.97)**	**−69.25***** **(8.85)**	**−31.55***** **(10.58)**
UNIVERSITY			
Scientific orientation	0.25 (0.70)	**1.15***** **(0.29)**	**0.78**** **(0.34)**
University-industry collaborations	−0.00 (0.00)	**0.00***** **(0.00)**	**0.00***** **(0.00)**
University size	**0.00***** **(0.00)**	**0.00***** **(0.00)**	**0.00***** **(0.00)**
REGION			
Regional innovativeness	0.06 (0.08)	**0.17***** **(0.03)**	**0.11***** **(0.02)**
Regional entrepreneurship	0.02 (0.03)	−0.02 (0.02)	−0.01 (0.01)
Regional density	−0.00 (0.00)	0.00 (0.00)	0.00 (0.00)
Year dummies	Yes	Yes	Yes
N	1,598	1,598	1,598
n	102	102	102

Note: This table reports the results of the population-averaged negative binomial panel regressions. The estimation is based on a sample of 102 German universities ranging from 2000 to 2017. The dependent variables are innovative teaching outcomes measured by the number of offered massive open online courses (MOOCs), innovative research outcomes measured by the number of published research papers in natural sciences classified as 'highly cited in the field' and innovative commercialization outcomes measured by the number of radical innovations (as classified by the OECD) of universities, respectively. Robust standard errors are reported in parentheses.
$^*p < .10$; $^{**}p < .05$; $^{***}p < .01$.

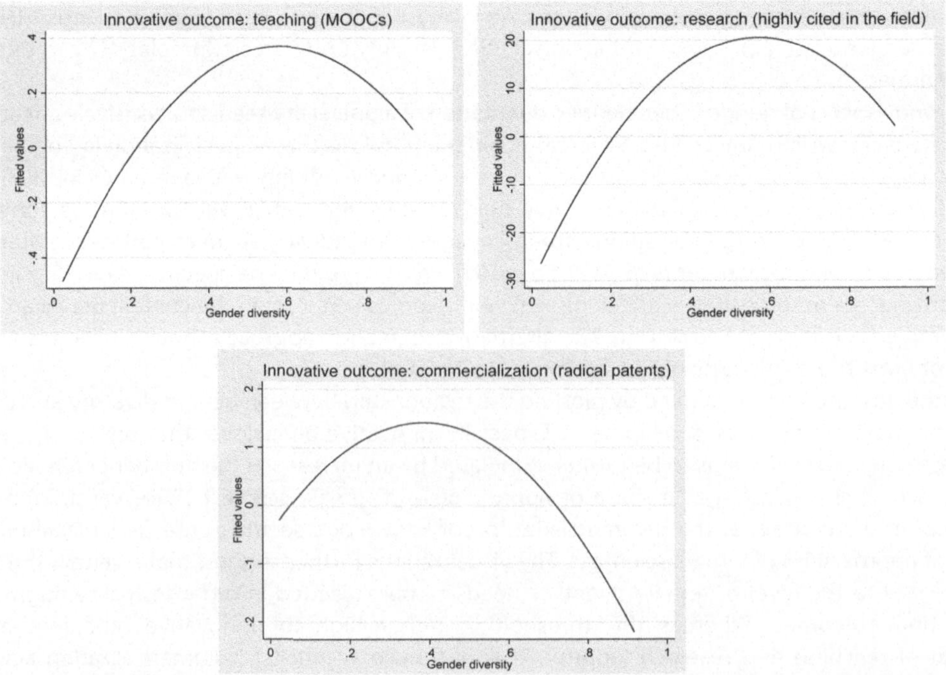

Figure 1. Visualization of estimation results.

do not seem to require lots of engagement of female scientists to stimulate innovative behavior (approx. 5% of female scientists).

5. Discussion

The results of this study reveal that huge differences with regard to gender diversity and innovative outcomes across the German higher education landscape exist. Leading entrepreneurial universities in Germany seem to proactively foster gender diversity, which is among others reflected by the innovative behavior of respective institutions in the context of their mission implementation. However, the findings of this study suggest that innovative outcomes across all three university missions seem to be affected differently by gender diversity. Whereas the innovative behavior in the context of teaching and research activities seem to benefit from a surplus of female scientists, innovative behavior in the context of the commercialization of knowledge seems to be rather driven by male scientists.

An explanation for this paradox is provided by Cunningham et al. (2017, 245) who also find differences between male and female scientists with regard to innovative behavior in the context of the commercialization of knowledge: 'Our findings provide some evidence that male PIs have more commercial experience, are more externally orientated and are involved in more academic entrepreneurship activities than female PIs'. In her study of Italian scientists, Baldini (2011) notes that industry engagement and experience is positively correlated with patenting activities. Hence, the lack of commercial experience might be one explanation for different patterns in the context of the commercialization of knowledge. Male scientists may thus be able to translate higher levels of commercial experience into higher levels of patenting activities. Also other studies confirm that female scientists are less likely to patent their research outcomes in comparison to their male counterparts (Ding, Murray, and Stuart 2006; Leahey and Blume 2017; Thursby and Thursby 2005).

This quantitative deficit of patents filed by female scientists of course does not imply that also the quality of filed patents is lower. On the contrary, Long (1992), Whittington and Smith-Doerr (2005) as well as Colyvas et al. (2012) show that patents from female scientists might be of the same quality and impact in comparison to patents from their male peers or even of higher quality and impact. Parker et al. (2017, 134) mention further reasons that might result in lower commercial engagement of female scientists such as fewer network contacts as well as different network structures that ultimately limit the amount of opportunities for commercial science, and conclude that female scientists are 'less likely to engage in commercially oriented activities due to their focus on traditional academic responsibilities, including teaching and service'. This finding might also explain why a surplus of female scientists leads to augmented innovation performance in the context of teaching and research.

The existence of a threshold effect in the context of gender diversity is another major outcome of this study. Based on the described results, low levels of gender diversity seem to negatively affect innovative outcomes, hence restrain innovative behavior. However, as shown in the data, context matters: whereas low levels of female scientists seem to affect innovative teaching and research outcomes negatively, high levels of female scientists seem to affect innovative commercialization outcomes negatively, too. Hence, a balance between male and female scientists seems to be most conducive, whereby deviations from the golden mean, i.e. gender balance, seem to be reasonable, given that prerequisites for certain activities seem to be gender biased, e.g. commercial experience affecting patenting activities positively. University managers need to take these patterns into consideration and simultenously try to eliminate obstacles that prevent female scientists from exploiting their full potential.

This study further shows that besides individual factors, also institutional factors influence innovative behavior and thus innovative outcomes within academia and thereby confirms previous studies (Perkmann et al. 2013). The scientific orientation as well as openness towards university-industry collaborations constitute key determinants that may positively affect innovative outcomes in the context of research and the commercialization of knowledge, respectively. Perkmann and Walsh (2009) provide evidence that especially applied university-industry collaborations may enable exploratory learning and may result in new (radical) ideas and innovations. The findings further suggest that also the external environment may stimulate innovative behavior and thus entrepreneurial innovation outcomes (Autio et al. 2014). Highly innovative regions seem to have a positive impact on universities' innovative outcomes, hence stimulate innovative behavior.

As with all empirical papers, this study is subject to a number of limitations. Whereas this study focuses on the quantity of innovation outcomes, also the quality of innovation outcomes needs to be taken into consideration. In addition, the empirical setting only accounts for female scientists in (post) entry-level positions within the university context (e.g. early-stage and postdoctoral researchers), yet neglects female scientists in senior positions (e.g. professors), where women are even more underrepresented (Winchester and Browning 2015). Also the operationalization of innovative outcomes does not capture the entire spectrum, as e.g. innovative commercialization activities might also include the creation of spin-offs, industry engagement through consulting activities, etc. Moreover, further control variables might be included to better capture the influences on innovative behavior on a university level (STEM distribution per university) as well as a regional level (gender diversity). Finally, the generalizability of the derived results may be limited due to the country-specific higher education legislations that may decisively affect innovative behavior and outcomes (Cunningham et al. 2019).

6. Conclusion

The objective of this study is to disentangle the underlying mechanisms that enable entrepreneurial universities to create impact within and beyond academic spheres. By focusing on individual factors in general and the role of gender diversity in specific, the findings of this study reveal that gender diversity may have opposing effects in the context of universities' mission implementation, i.e. generating innovative outcomes in teaching, research and the commercialization of knowledge. Whereas larger shares of female scientists may create more innovative outcomes in teaching and research, male scientists seem to be better able to produce commercial outcomes such as (radical) patents. However, the results also suggest that various other factors beyond gender aspects, e.g. institutional and regional factors, may also affect innovative outcomes of universities and thus give impetus to more nuanced approaches of university managers and policy makers aimed at augmenting the innovative behavior of scientists and ultimately the innovative outcomes of universities.

University managers and policy makers have already tried to establish a more diverse workforce within the academic context by introducing e.g. gender quotas to overcome existing barriers for women, promote gender equality, and benefit from a more diverse workforce that should ultimately lead to an increased academic performance (Sagaria 2007). However, the findings of this study show that it is not only about encouraging women to stay in academia (although well represented among PhD graduates (48%), women only account for 22% of leading positions in higher-education institutes (EC 2019a)), but also about addressing issues that deter female scientists from producing the same scientific outputs as their male counterparts. As stated earlier, women seem to have less opportunities for commercial science that may result in fewer opportunities to boost their scientific performance, resulting in less (financial) support for their research activities. The European Commission describes this as a vicious circle in which women researchers are caught in (EC 2019b).

Hence, the task of university managers and policy makers should go far beyond retaining women in academia but address challenges women face within the academic system and their day-to-day work. Once, the problems women currently face are solved or at least reduced, positive outcomes of recruiting and retaining female scientists will arise naturally. Both male and female scientists bear the potential of pushing technological boundaries and create new ideas and knowledge. From a university manager perspective, it is ultimately about leveraging gender diversity to improve universities' performance across all three missions – teaching, research and the commercialization of knowledge – to create a culture that encourages and strives for innovative outcomes through innovative behavior. University managers should on the one hand incorporate aspects of gender diversity in their leadership role and encourage female scientists to play a more active role in academia across all different levels (from entry-level positions to senior positions). On the other hand, university managers need to remove structural factors that impede women from achieving the same outcomes as their male counterparts. Shepherd (2017, 86) therefore argues that

> efforts to 'fix' the women, for example female-only development programmes like Aurora and Leadership Matters, are unlikely to be sufficient to achieve gender equality. Rather, a mix of change interventions may be required that also seek to 'fix' the organization, i.e. in terms of systemic and procedural changes.

Future studies should examine processes and mechanisms within universities that – intentionally or not – allow for gender discrimination and thus induce unequal scientific outcomes between male and female scientists. More research also needs to be devoted to the evaluation of policy tools and instruments meant to reduce those obstacles for female scientists. Ideally, university managers and policy makers should create an environment which truly supports innovative behavior within and beyond academic spheres for both genders. Hence, evidence-based guidance is needed to eliminate unequal treatment – not only in the context of gender diversity, but diversity in general (culture, race, religion, age, gender, etc.). In addition, scholars should investigate further factors stimulating and encouraging innovative behavior within entrepreneurial universities, taking into consideration the multitude of influencing factors ranging from individual and institutional to regional factors. Finally, more research attention should be devoted to the nature/nurture discussion affecting innovative behavior in the context of entrepreneurial organizations in general and entrepreneurial universities in specific.

Notes

1. Gender diversity may also include people of non-binary genders, which is yet out of scope of this study.
2. See Squicciarini, Dernis, and Criscuolo (2013) for a detailed description of the indicator construction.

Disclosure statement

No potential conflict of interest was reported by the author(s).

ORCID

Matthias Menter http://orcid.org/0000-0001-6981-6778

References

Abreu, M., and V. Grinevich. 2017. "Gender Patterns in Academic Entrepreneurship." *The Journal of Technology Transfer* 42 (4): 763–794.

Acs, Z. J., D. B. Audretsch, and E. E. Lehmann. 2013. "The Knowledge Spillover Theory of Entrepreneurship." *Small Business Economics* 41 (4): 757–774.

Acs, Z. J., P. Braunerhjelm, D. B. Audretsch, and B. Carlsson. 2009. "The Knowledge Spillover Theory of Entrepreneurship." *Small Business Economics* 32 (1): 15–30.

Aldridge, T. T., and D. B. Audretsch. 2011. "The Bayh-Dole Act and Scientist Entrepreneurship." *Research Policy* 40 (8): 1058–1067.

Arant, W., D. Fornahl, N. Grashof, K. Hesse, and C. Söllner. 2019. "University-industry Collaborations: The key to Radical Innovations?" *Review of Regional Research* 39 (2): 119–141.

Audretsch, D. B. 2014. "From the Entrepreneurial University to the University for the Entrepreneurial Society." *The Journal of Technology Transfer* 39 (3): 313–321.

Audretsch, D. B., M. Keilbach, and E. E. Lehmann. 2006. *Entrepreneurship and Economic Growth*. Oxford: Oxford University Press.

Autio, E., M. Kenney, P. Mustar, D. Siegel, and M. Wright. 2014. "Entrepreneurial Innovation: The Importance of Context." *Research Policy* 43 (7): 1097–1108.

Baldini, N. 2011. "University Patenting: Patterns of Faculty Motivations." *Technology Analysis & Strategic Management* 23 (2): 103–121.

Campbell, K., and A. Mínguez-Vera. 2008. "Gender Diversity in the Boardroom and Firm Financial Performance." *Journal of Business Ethics* 83 (3): 435–451.

Chapple, W., A. Lockett, D. Siegel, and M. Wright. 2005. "Assessing the Relative Performance of UK University Technology Transfer Offices: Parametric and Non-Parametric Evidence." *Research Policy* 34 (3): 369–384.

Colyvas, J. A., K. Snellman, J. Bercovitz, and M. Feldman. 2012. "Disentangling Effort and Performance: A Renewed Look at Gender Differences in Commercializing Medical School Research." *The Journal of Technology Transfer* 37 (4): 478–489.

Cunningham, J. A., E. E. Lehmann, M. Menter, and N. Seitz. 2019. "The Impact of University Focused Technology Transfer Policies on Regional Innovation and Entrepreneurship." *The Journal of Technology Transfer* 44 (5): 1451–1475.

Cunningham, J. A., and M. Menter. 2020. "Transformative Change in Higher Education: Entrepreneurial Universities and High-Technology Entrepreneurship." *Industry and Innovation* forthcoming: 1–22. doi:10.1080/13662716.2020.1763263.

Cunningham, J. A., P. O'Reilly, B. Dolan, C. O'Kane, and V. Mangematin. 2017. "Gender Differences and Academic Entrepreneurship: A Study of Scientists in the Principal Investigator Role." In *Gender and Entrepreneurial Activity*, edited by A. N. Link, 221–251. Cheltenham: Edward Elgar Publishing.

Dahlin, K. B., L. R. Weingart, and P. J. Hinds. 2005. "Team Diversity and Information use." *Academy of Management Journal* 48 (6): 1107–1123.

Díaz-García, C., A. González-Moreno, and F. Jose Sáez-Martínez. 2013. "Gender Diversity Within R&D Teams: Its Impact on Radicalness of Innovation." *Innovation* 15 (2): 149–160.

Ding, W. W., F. Murray, and T. E. Stuart. 2006. "Gender Differences in Patenting in the Academic Life Sciences." *Science* 313 (5787): 665–667.

Dwyer, S., O. C. Richard, and K. Chadwick. 2003. "Gender Diversity in Management and Firm Performance: The Influence of Growth Orientation and Organizational Culture." *Journal of Business Research* 56 (12): 1009–1019.

EC. 2019a. *Closing Gender Gaps in Research and Innovation*. Brussels: European Commission: Horizon 2020.

EC. 2019b. *She Figures 2018*. Brussels: European Commission: Horizon 2020.

Etzkowitz, H. 2014. "The Entrepreneurial University Wave: From Ivory Tower to Global Economic Engine." *Industry and Higher Education* 28 (4): 223–232.

Fernando, G. D., S. S. Jain, and A. Tripathy. 2020. "This Cloud has a Silver Lining: Gender Diversity, Managerial Ability, and Firm Performance." *Journal of Business Research* 117: 484–496.

Guerrero, M., J. A. Cunningham, and D. Urbano. 2015. "Economic Impact of Entrepreneurial Universities' Activities: An Exploratory Study of the United Kingdom." *Research Policy* 44 (3): 748–764.

Guerrero, M., S. Heaton, and D. Urbano. 2020. "Building Universities' Intrapreneurial Capabilities in the Digital Era: The Role and Impacts of Massive Open Online Courses (MOOCs)." *Technovation* 102139. doi:10.1016/j.technovation.2020.102139.

Gulbrandsen, M., and S. Slipersaeter. 2007. "The Third Mission and the Entrepreneurial University Model." In *Universities and Strategic Knowledge Creation*, edited by A. Bonaccorsi, and C. Daraio, 112–143. Cheltenham: Edward Elgar Publishing.

Hayter, C. S., and A. N. Link. 2015. "On the Economic Impact of University Proof of Concept Centers." *The Journal of Technology Transfer* 40 (1): 178–183.

Herring, C. 2009. "Does Diversity pay?: Race, Gender, and the Business Case for Diversity." *American Sociological Review* 74 (2): 208–224.

Hoogendoorn, S., H. Oosterbeek, and M. Van Praag. 2013. "The Impact of Gender Diversity on the Performance of Business Teams: Evidence from a Field Experiment." *Management Science* 59 (7): 1514–1528.

Hülsbeck, M., E. E. Lehmann, and A. Starnecker. 2013. "Performance of Technology Transfer Offices in Germany." *The Journal of Technology Transfer* 38 (3): 199–215.

Jackson, S. E., A. Joshi, and N. L. Erhardt. 2003. "Recent Research on Team and Organizational Diversity: SWOT Analysis and Implications." *Journal of Management* 29 (6): 801–830.

Joecks, J., K. Pull, and K. Vetter. 2013. "Gender Diversity in the Boardroom and Firm Performance: What Exactly Constitutes a "Critical Mass?"." *Journal of Business Ethics* 118 (1): 61–72.

Kuschel, K., K. Ettl, C. Díaz-García, and G. A. Alsos. 2020. "Stemming the Gender Gap in STEM Entrepreneurship–Insights into Women's Entrepreneurship in Science, Technology, Engineering, and Mathematics." *International Entrepreneurship and Management Journal*, 1–15. doi:10.1007/s11365-020-00642-5.

Lauring, J., and F. Villesèche. 2019. "The Performance of Gender Diverse Teams: What is the Relation Between Diversity Attitudes and Degree of Diversity?" *European Management Review* 16 (2): 243–254.

Leahey, E., and A. Blume. 2017. "Elucidating the Process: Why Women Patent Less Than Men." In *Gender and Entrepreneurial Activity*, edited by A. N. Link, 151–167. Cheltenham: Edward Elgar Publishing.

Lehmann, E. E., and M. Menter. 2016. "University–Industry Collaboration and Regional Wealth." *The Journal of Technology Transfer* 41 (6): 1284–1307.

Leyden, D. P., and A. N. Link. 2015. *Public Sector Entrepreneurship: US Technology and Innovation Policy*. New York: Oxford University Press.

Link, A. N. 2000. "Assessing the Economic Impacts of University R&D and Identifying Roles for Technology Transfer Officers." *Industry and Higher Education* 14 (1): 24–32.

Link, A. N., and J. T. Scott. 2003. "US Science Parks: the Diffusion of an Innovation and its Effects on the Academic Missions of Universities." *International Journal of Industrial Organization* 21 (9): 1323–1356.

Link, A., and J. Scott. 2005. "Opening the Ivory Tower's Door: An Analysis of the Determinants of the Formation of US University Spin-off Companies." *Research Policy* 34 (7): 1106–1112.

Long, J. S. 1992. "Measures of Sex Differences in Scientific Productivity." *Social Forces* 71 (1): 159–178.

Neves, S., and C. Brito. 2020. "Academic Entrepreneurship Intentions: A Systematic Literature Review." *Journal of Management Development* forthcoming. doi:10.1108/JMD-11-2019-0451.

North, S. M., R. Richardson, and M. M. North. 2014. "To Adapt MOOCs, or Not? That Is No Longer the Question." *Universal Journal of Educational Research* 2 (1): 69–72.

Owen, A. L., and J. Temesvary. 2018. "The Performance Effects of Gender Diversity on Bank Boards." *Journal of Banking & Finance* 90: 50–63.

Pappano, L. 2012. "The Year of the MOOC." *The New York Times*, November 2, 2012. http://www.nytimes.com/2012/11/04/education/edlife/massive-open-online-courses-are-multiplying-at-a-rapid-pace.html?pagewanted=all&_r=0.

Parker, M., C. S. Hayter, L. Lynch, and R. Mohammed. 2017. "Barriers to Academic Entrepreneurship among Women: A Review of the Constituent Literatures." In *Gender and Entrepreneurial Activity*, edited by A. N. Link, 117–150. Cheltenham: Edward Elgar Publishing.

Pell, A. N. 1996. "Fixing the Leaky Pipeline: Women Scientists in Academia." *Journal of Animal Science* 74 (11): 2843–2848.

Perkmann, M., V. Tartari, M. McKelvey, E. Autio, A. Broström, P. D'Este, S. Krabel, et al. 2013. "Academic Engagement and Commercialisation: A Review of the Literature on University–Industry Relations." *Research Policy* 42 (2): 423–442.

Perkmann, M., and K. Walsh. 2009. "The Two Faces of Collaboration: Impacts of University-Industry Relations on Public Research." *Industrial and Corporate Change* 18 (6): 1033–1065.

Pitts, D. W., and L. R. Wise. 2010. "Workforce Diversity in the New Millennium: Prospects for Research." *Review of Public Personnel Administration* 30 (1): 44–69.

Ranga, L., K. Debackere, and N. Tunzelmann. 2003. "Entrepreneurial Universities and the Dynamics of Academic Knowledge Production: A Case Study of Basic vs. Applied Research in Belgium." *Scientometrics* 58 (2): 301–320.

Richard, O. C., T. Barnett, S. Dwyer, and K. Chadwick. 2004. "Cultural Diversity in Management, Firm Performance, and the Moderating Role of Entrepreneurial Orientation Dimensions." *Academy of Management Journal* 47 (2): 255–266.

Riegraf, B., B. Aulenbacher, E. Kirsch-Auwärter, and U. Müller. 2010. *Gender Change in Academia: Re-Mapping the Fields of Work, Knowledge, and Politics from a Gender Perspective*. Berlin: Springer Science & Business Media.

Romer, P. M. 1986. "Increasing Returns and Long-run Growth." *Journal of Political Economy* 94 (5): 1002–1037.

Romer, P. M. 1990. "Endogenous Technological Change." *Journal of Political Economy* 98 (5, Part 2): 71–102.

Romero, E. C., J. J. Ferreira, and C. I. Fernandes. 2020. "The Multiple Faces of the Entrepreneurial University: A Review of the Prevailing Theoretical Approaches." *The Journal of Technology Transfer*, 1–23. doi:10.1007/s10961-020-09815-4.

Rosa, P., and A. Dawson. 2006. "Gender and the Commercialization of University Science: Academic Founders of Spinout Companies." *Entrepreneurship and Regional Development* 18 (4): 341–366.

Ruiz-Jiménez, J. M., M. del Mar Fuentes-Fuentes, and M. Ruiz-Arroyo. 2016. "Knowledge Combination Capability and Innovation: The Effects of Gender Diversity on top Management Teams in Technology-Based Firms." *Journal of Business Ethics* 135 (3): 503–515.

Sagaria, M. 2007. *Women, Universities, and Change: Gender Equality in the European Union and the United States*. New York: Palgrave Macmillan.

Sastre, J. F. 2014. "The Impact of R&D Teams' Gender Diversity on Innovation Outputs." *International Journal of Entrepreneurship and Small Business* 24 (1): 142–162.

Schumpeter, J. A. 1939. *Business Cycles*. New York: McGraw-Hill.

Sciarelli, M., G. C. Landi, L. Turriziani, and M. Tani. 2020. "Academic Entrepreneurship: Founding and Governance Determinants in University Spin-off Ventures." *The Journal of Technology Transfer*, 1–25. doi:10.1007/s10961-020-09798-2.

Shepherd, S. 2017. "Why are there so Few Female Leaders in Higher Education: A Case of Structure or Agency?" *Management in Education* 31 (2): 82–87.

Shore, L. M., B. G. Chung-Herrera, M. A. Dean, K. H. Ehrhart, D. I. Jung, A. E. Randel, and G. Singh. 2009. "Diversity in Organizations: Where are We Now and Where are We Going?" *Human Resource Management Review* 19 (2): 117–133.

Siegel, D. S., D. Waldman, and A. N. Link. 2003. "Assessing the Impact of Organizational Practices on the Relative Productivity of University Technology Transfer Offices: An Exploratory Study." *Research Policy* 32 (1): 27–48.

Squicciarini, M., H. Dernis, and C. Criscuolo. 2013. *Measuring Patent Quality: Indicators of Technological and Economic Value*. Paris: Organisation for Economic Cooperation and Development (OECD).

Teece, D. J. 2018. "Managing the University: Why "Organized Anarchy" is Unacceptable in the Age of Massive Open Online Courses." *Strategic Organization* 16 (1): 92–102.

Terjesen, S., R. Sealy, and V. Singh. 2009. "Women Directors on Corporate Boards: A Review and Research Agenda." *Corporate Governance: An International Review* 17 (3): 320–337.

Thursby, J. G., and M. C. Thursby. 2005. "Gender Patterns of Research and Licensing Activity of Science and Engineering Faculty." *The Journal of Technology Transfer* 30 (4): 343–353.

Urbano, D., and M. Guerrero. 2013. "Entrepreneurial Universities: Socioeconomic Impacts of Academic Entrepreneurship in a European Region." *Economic Development Quarterly* 27 (1): 40–55.

Valero, A., and J. Van Reenen. 2019. "The Economic Impact of Universities: Evidence from Across the Globe." *Economics of Education Review* 68: 53–67.

Van Knippenberg, D., C. K. De Dreu, and A. C. Homan. 2004. "Work Group Diversity and Group Performance: An Integrative Model and Research Agenda." *Journal of Applied Psychology* 89 (6): 1008.

Van Knippenberg, D., and M. C. Schippers. 2007. "Work Group Diversity." *Annual Review of Psychology* 58: 515–541.

Verhoeven, D., J. Bakker, and R. Veugelers. 2016. "Measuring Technological Novelty with Patent-Based Indicators." *Research Policy* 45 (3): 707–723.

Wegge, J., C. Roth, B. Neubach, K. H. Schmidt, and R. Kanfer. 2008. "Age and Gender Diversity as Determinants of Performance and Health in a Public Organization: The Role of Task Complexity and Group Size." *Journal of Applied Psychology* 93 (6): 1301–1313.

Weisshaar, K. 2017. "Publish and Perish? An Assessment of Gender Gaps in Promotion to Tenure in Academia." *Social Forces* 96 (2): 529–560.

Whittington, K. B., and L. Smith-Doerr. 2005. "Gender and Commercial Science: Women's Patenting in the Life Sciences." *The Journal of Technology Transfer* 30 (4): 355–370.

Wickware, P. 1997. "Along the Leaky Pipeline." *Nature* 390 (6656): 202–203.

Winchester, H. P., and L. Browning. 2015. "Gender Equality in Academia: a Critical Reflection." *Journal of Higher Education Policy and Management* 37 (3): 269–281.

Wu, Y., E. W. Welch, and W. L. Huang. 2015. "Commercialization of University Inventions: Individual and Institutional Factors Affecting Licensing of University Patents." *Technovation* 36: 12–25.

Xie, Y., and K. A. Shauman. 2003. *Women in Science: Career Processes and Outcomes*. Cambridge, MA: Harvard University Press.

Does workforce diversity matter on corporate venturing?

Maribel Guerrero

ABSTRACT

Ongoing academic debates demand a better understanding of the effect of workforce diversity (not only top managers) on unexplored outcomes (not only financial performance). We proposed/tested a conceptual model that theorizes the moderate role of workforce demographics corporate venturing drivers by adopting different theoretical approaches. Using a sample of 17217 employees across 20 countries, our findings highlight that women and migrant workers contribute to corporate venturing by identifying business opportunities (exploration experiences) and taking advantage of intellectual capital (human capital and social capital). Several implications for leaders who manage a diversified workforce emerge from this study.

Introduction

Workforce diversity refers to the composition of work units in terms of the cultural or demographic characteristics salient and symbolically meaningful in the relationships among group members (DiTomaso, Post, and Parks-Yancy 2007, 474). Prior studies have classified workforce diversity into two dimensions. The first dimension is related to demographic characteristics (i.e. age, income, gender, and nationality) that exhibit differences between various individuals (Friedman and DiTomaso 1996; Jasso 2001; Peroni, Riillo, and Sarracino 2016). The second dimension is related to cultural characteristics (i.e. values, beliefs, cognitions) that are not noticeable to individuals within an organization (Yadav and Lenka 2020). This study understood a diversified workforce as organizations integrated by employees with different demographic backgrounds regarding generational cohorts, gender, personal income, and immigration status.

Over the past decades, workforce diversity was analyzed with diverse lenses in management and entrepreneurship fields. *Firstly, in the management literature,* diversity management research emerged as a new organizational paradigm (Gilbert, Stead, and Ivancevich 1999) focused on effectively managing workforce by valuing its diversity (Sessa 1992). Diversity management research has analyzed human resources practices to manage diversity, inequalities, work-life balance (D'Netto and Sohal 1999; DiTomaso, Post, and Parks-Yancy 2007; Yee, Miquel-Romero, and Cruz-Ros 2020), as well as the positive effects of diversity on performance (Sung and Choi 2019; Lee and Kim 2020; Kim et al. 2020). A recent literature review on workforce diversity has highlighted the repeatedly investigated effect of diversified top managers' teams on organizational performance (Yadav and Lenka 2020, 13). However, workforce diversity research needs to be conducted across countries for exploring the effect of employees' diversity (not only managers) on unexplored outcomes (Yadav and Lenka

2020, 12). Secondly, *in the entrepreneurship literature*, corporate entrepreneurship represents the firms' ability to be innovative, risk-taking, competitive, proactive, and adaptable through the development of renewal/innovation strategies (strategic entrepreneurship) and the creation of ventures (corporate venturing) (Guth and Ginsberg 1990; Sharma and Chrisman 1999). Diversity research in corporate entrepreneurship has limited the analysis to the top or middle managers that pursue corporate entrepreneurship within innovative (multinational) firms (Hayton 2005; Heavey and Simsek 2013; Boone et al. 2019; Garrett et al. 2020). The achievement of corporate venturing strategies requires leadership and the workforce's full involvement. Consequently, workforce diversity may play a relevant role in the employees' propensity to become self-employed, intrapreneurs, or continue to be employed within entrepreneurial organizations (Marino, Parrotta, and Pozzoli 2012; Yeganegi et al. 2019). However, little is known about the contribution of workforce diversity in corporate entrepreneurship outcomes as the creation of innovative ventures under the umbrella of their employers (Junni et al. 2015; Guerrero, Amorós, and Urbano 2019; Mom et al. 2019; Yeganegi et al. 2019).

Inspired by the literature's stated gaps, this study examines the effect of a diversified workforce on corporate venturing activities. By adopting different theoretical approaches (corporate entrepreneurship, employee ambidexterity, and intellectual capital), we propose a conceptual model that theorizes how workforce demographics moderate corporate venturing drivers. The assumption that workforce diversity matters in venturing corporate activities is tested by using a sample of 17217 employees across 20 countries.

Our results contribute to the workforce diversity literature (Yadav and Lenka 2020) and the corporate venturing literature (Guerrero, Amorós, and Urbano 2019; Yeganegi et al. 2019) with insights into how the workforce's engagement in corporate venturing by identifying business opportunities (exploration experiences) and taking advantage of intellectual capital (human capital and social capital) depends on its demographics (gender, age, nationality, income). The study also encourages future research into how nature/nurture conditions within innovative/entrepreneurial organizations to generate value for shareholders are influenced by diversified workforce' behaviors (Narayanan, Yang, and Zahra 2009; Guerrero, Amorós, and Urbano 2019; Yadav and Lenka 2020). Regarding practical implications, changing the workforce's demographic dynamics should lead many organizations to rethink or re-design organizational strategies, innovative/entrepreneurial behaviors, and cultures (Sung and Choi 2019).

The remainder of this paper is organized as follows: Section 2 develops the conceptual framework. Section 3 presents the methodology used in the study. Section 4 discusses the main findings. Finally, Section 5 presents the main conclusions, implications for decision-makers, and future lines of research.

Conceptual framework

Corporate venturing and employees' diversity

According to Guerrero, Amorós, and Urbano (2019), there is a consensus about three critical components behind any corporate venturing: the workplace (organization) that provides favorable conditions for achieving the corporate venturing activities; the (ambidexterity) process that includes the exploration and exploitation of new opportunities that be transformed into innovative and entrepreneurial initiatives; and the workforce (employees) who lead and execute the innovative and entrepreneurial processes.

Given the complexity of studying the labor force's diversity, we identify three theoretical approaches to examine the contribution of the labor force's demographics to create ventures for employers (corporate venturing). First, *paying attention to the workplace*, the corporate entrepreneurship literature explains how organizational support may encourage the flourishment of creativity, innovation, and entrepreneurship (Narayanan, Yang, and Zahra 2009; Alpkan et al. 2010). According to Colombo, Rossi-Lamastra, and Matassini (2015), entrepreneurial organizations' climate is characterized by autonomy, a meaningful job, and adequate rewards systems. Extant studies have explained that perceptions, values, motivations, and other attributes are configured according to the individuals' generational cohorts (Parry and Urwin 2011), nationality (Boone et al. 2019), and gender (Petrie and Roman 2004). The workforce's perceptions of organizational supports will vary depending on their demographic characteristics. Second, *paying attention to the exploration/exploitation process*, the organizational ambidexterity literature explains how employees' abilities shifted depending on their involvement in exploration or exploitation activities (Mom, Van Den Bosch, and Volberda 2009; Good and Michel 2013; Li, Lin, and Tien 2016). Management research has validated an individual-behavioral orientation toward ambidexterity capabilities associated with accomplishing the tensions/problems related to exploration and exploitation processes (Mom, Van Den Bosch, and Volberda 2009). Innovation literature has also recognized how diversified teams contribute to achieving ambidexterity processes and the highest performance (Mom, Fourné, and Jansen 2015). Third, *paying attention to the employees,* the intellectual capital literature explains how the effects of intellectual capital facets (i.e. human, social, investor, and entrepreneurial capital) on organizational ambidexterity (Kostopoulos, Bozionelos, and Syrigos 2015; Turner, Maylor, and Swart 2015) and corporate venturing (Guerrero and Peña-Legazkue 2013, 2019). Intellectual capital is a determinant in the propensity to pursues corporate venturing opportunities (Ireland, Covin, and Kuratko 2009; Parker 2011; Guerrero, Amorós, and Urbano 2019). Although the relationship between diversified workforce and innovation/entrepreneurship outcomes is scared, many entrepreneurial organizations are integrated by a heterogeneous labor force, including women workers, migrant workers, elderly workers, and low-income workers (Guerrero, Amorós, and Urbano 2019). This workforce diversity may influence on any organizational activity and outcome.

Hypotheses

Workforce diversity and perceptions of the organizational environment

An organizational climate is the primary driver of innovative and entrepreneurial initiatives (Ireland, Covin, and Kuratko 2009; Narayanan, Yang, and Zahra 2009; Alpkan et al. 2010; Antoncic and Antoncic 2011; Lee, Woo, and Joshi 2017). A good combination of organizational climate' components (autonomy, rewards, and meaningful) is strongly related to the (un)success of innovative and entrepreneurial initiatives (Colombo, Rossi-Lamastra, and Matassini 2015). *Workplace autonomy* is an organizational climate that encourages creativity, innovation, and entrepreneurship (Kuratko, Hornsby, and Hayton 2015). A few studies have studied diversity in workplace autonomy (Petrie and Roman 2004). Job autonomy represents the opportunity of balancing work and family lives for all labor groups (Green and Cohen 1995), especially for entrepreneurial women (Úbeda-García et al. 2017; Ruiz, Amoros, and Guerrero 2019). Job flexibility also represents a non-monetary return derived from participating in innovative and entrepreneurial initiatives that motivate low-income and immigrant workers (Kim, Aldrich, and Keister 2006; Stone and Stubbs 2007). Likewise, *rewards systems* are part of an organizational climate that enhances employees' motivations (Gibson, Greenwood, and Murphy 2009; Patel, Messersmith, and Lepak 2013) and, combined with job autonomy, reinforces entrepreneurial/innovative employees' intentions (Guerrero, Amorós, and Urbano 2019). The incentive system represents an encouragement for corporate employee-entrepreneurs involvement in corporate venturing because it represents a trade-off based on ambitions, values, and motivations (Monsen, Patzelt, and Saxton 2010; Guerrero, Amorós, and Urbano 2019) that differ among gender, ethnicity, generational cohort, and educational level. A *meaningful job* is also related to organizational value systems and personal goals that may vary per generational cohort, ethnicity, and educational level (Fairlie 2011). The workforce experienced a meaningful job when values, demands, and motivations are aligned at personal and organizational levels (Scroggins 2008). Employees' perceptions of having meaningful work facilitate personal growth and contribute to greater motivation and satisfaction. These employees' perceptions vary according to personal backgrounds in terms of generational cohorts (Guerrero, Amorós, and Urbano 2019), gender, ethnicity, or migration status (Culpan and Wright 2002; Brandes et al. 2010). It explains why groups with similar backgrounds help develop entrepreneurial initiatives due to the high intra-group solidarity, shared values, norms, and attitudes that facilitate economic activities (Peroni, Riillo, and Sarracino 2016). Assuming that the workforce's perceptions about organizational support strengthen their engagement in corporate venturing, we suggest the following hypotheses:

Hypothesis 1a: Favorable organizational supports increase the employees' engagement in corporate venturing

Hypothesis 1b: Diversity in the labor force positively moderate the effect of favorable organizational supports on corporate venturing activities.

Workforce diversity and ambidexterity experience

Employee ambidexterity is the ability related to employees' behavioral orientation towards combining exploitation and exploration processes simultaneously within a specified period (Mom, Fourné, and Jansen 2015, 135). Employee ambidexterity represents the good combination of exploration abilities (e.g. the identification or generation of innovative and entrepreneurial opportunities) and exploitation abilities (e.g. the exploit of identified opportunities via strategies, resources, and capabilities) that are responsible for the successful employees' innovative performance (Rosing and Zacher 2017, 697). Exploration and exploitation learning processes increase performance and variability (March 1991, 83). If innovations/technologies are novel, the advantages will be superior for the workforce familiar with the required knowledge and capabilities to explore/exploit them. The accumulation of knowledge about the link between ambidexterity and workforce demographics is limited and inconclusive (Yadav and Lenka 2020). According to Ang et al. (2007), the difference in race, gender, age, ethnicity, and nationality may positively affect firms' engagement in corporate entrepreneurship. A few studies have found that gender diversity in teams is beneficial for introducing untypical ways of exploring and exploiting innovation opportunities (Zacher and Rosing 2015; Zacher, Robinson, and Rosing 2016; Jahanshahi, Nawaser, and Brem 2018). Boone et al. (2019) also found a positive effect of nationality diversity on innovation and entrepreneurship processes, but this effect depends on social relationships at the team-level and country-level. Some insights showed how entrepreneurial attitudes and employees' ambidexterity abilities vary across generational cohorts (Guerrero, Amorós, and Urbano 2019). Younger generations are more ambidexterity-oriented than the older generations. Therefore, balanced and diversified teams (gender, nationality, age) provide different perceptions and capabilities during exploration/exploitation of innovation and entrepreneurship opportunities (Díaz-García, González-Moreno, and Saez-Martinez 2013; Cropley and Cropley 2017). Assuming that the ambidexterity workforce's experiences strengthen their engagement in corporate venturing, we suggest the following hypotheses:

Hypothesis 2a: Ambidexterity experience increase the employees' engagement in corporate venturing

Hypothesis 2b: Diversity in the labor force positively moderate ambidexterity experience on corporate venturing activities.

Workforce diversity and intellectual capital

Intellectual capital is represented by human capital, social capital, investor capital, and entrepreneurial capital (Kostopoulos, Bozionelos, and Syrigos 2015). Previous studies have shown the positive effect of diversified intellectual capital on entrepreneurship and innovation (Bosma 2013; Guerrero, Amorós, and Urbano 2019). Entrepreneurship literature has recognized different knowledge sources that contribute to corporate venturing (Parker 2011). Prior studies also identify different intellectual capitals during exploration/exploitation processes: *human capital* increases the entrepreneurial intention of employees depending on their educational level and experiences (Millan et al. 2014), *entrepreneurial capital* reduces the barriers as the knowledge filters during innovation and entrepreneurship processes depending on employees' demographic backgrounds (Guerrero and Urbano

2014), *investors' capital* represents a valuable workforce's learning experience that provides useful information and specific facilities for creating ventures (Ucbasaran, Westhead, and Wright 2009), and *social capital* represents a window of workforce's contacts that represents a source of multiple resources/capabilities required for developing corporate ventures (Heavey, Simsek, and Fox 2015). The demographic backgrounds (age, gender, income, and nationality) explain differences in the workforce's intellectual capital (Parker 2011; Guerrero, Amorós, and Urbano 2019) and the workforce's feasibility of participating in corporate venture activities (Van Auken, Fry, and Stephens 2006). Assuming that the workforce's intellectual capitals strengthen their engagement in corporate venturing, we suggest the following hypotheses:

Hypothesis 3a: Intellectual capital increase the employees' engagement in corporate venturing

Hypothesis 3b: Diversity in the labor force positively moderate the effect of intellectual capital on corporate venturing activities.

Proposed model

Figure 1 shows the proposed conceptual model. Based on our literature review, we assume that a diversified workforce positively moderates the effect of individual-level drivers of corporate venturing. We first assume that the probability of workforce's engagement in corporate venturing increases when: employees have favorable perceptions about the organizational climate in terms of autonomy, a meaningful job, and reward systems (H1a); employees have an ambidexterity experience (H2a); employees have different intellectual capitals (H3). We then assume a positive moderation effect (H1b, H2b, H3b) produced by the workforce' diversity in terms of demographics characteristics (gender, age, nationality, and income).

Methodology

Data collection

We used individual-level data from the Adult Population Survey (APS) of the Global Entrepreneurship Monitor (Reynolds et al. 2005). The 2012 and 2013 waves included a set of questions that

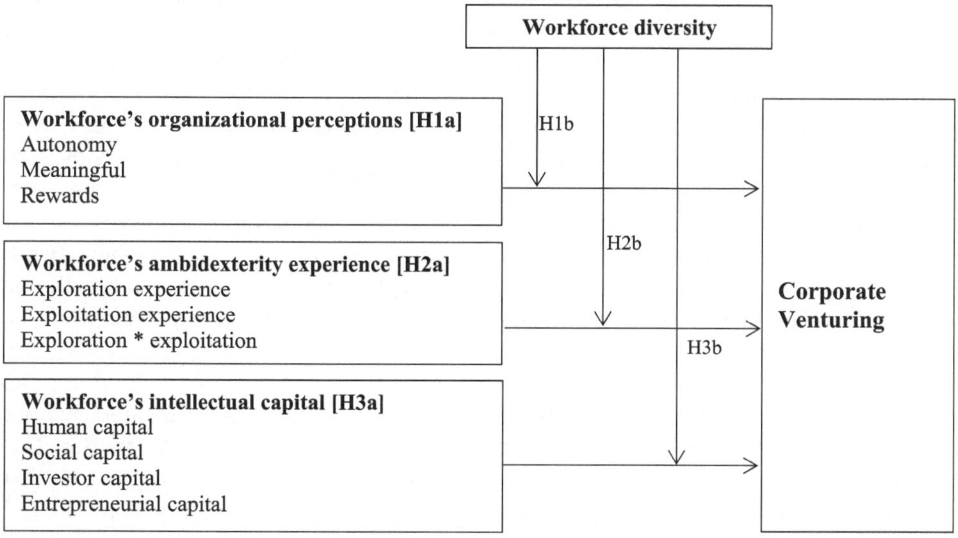

Figure 1. Proposed Conceptual Model. Source: Authors.

captured information about (1) entrepreneurial employee activities (e.g. venture creation), (2) workplace characteristics (e.g. employees' perceptions about a meaningful job, autonomy, and income satisfaction), (3) migration (e.g. place of born, first or second generation of immigrants) and (4) innovation (e.g. employees' innovation goals, organizational' innovation goals). Our sample consists of 17,217 employees across 20 countries.[1] The country-level data came from the World Bank Open Data.

Description of variables

Corporate venturing captures when an employee has (not) undertaken entrepreneurial actions in the last three years to create a new venture for his/her employer (Bosma et al. 2013; Guerrero and Peña-Legazkue 2019). Specifically, this variable takes value one if when the employee answered 'yes' to the three previous criteria and zero otherwise (Guerrero, Amorós, and Urbano 2019): (a) employees' involvement in developing intrapreneurial activities for their primary employer in the last three years; (b) employees that are currently trying to create a new venture for their employer; and (c) employees are operating a new venture for fewer than 42 months.

The first explanatory variable captures the employees' perceptions of workplace characteristics measured with a Likert scale (1 = lower to 5 = higher). This explanatory variable included three proxies: *a meaningful job* measured the perceptions that the employee has a meaningful job (Alrumaithi, Guerrero, and Peña 2015; Guerrero, Amorós, and Urbano 2019); *job autonomy* measured the perceptions that the employee can decide how to do his or her work (Hornsby, Kuratko, and Zahra 2002; Kuratko, Hornsby, and Hayton 2015); and *rewards* measured the perceptions that employees are satisfied with their current income (Monsen, Patzelt, and Saxton 2010).

The second explanatory variable captures the employees' ambidexterity experience through three proxies (Yeganegi et al. 2019; Guerrero, Amorós, and Urbano 2019). *Exploration experience* is measured by a dichotomous variable that takes the value 1 when the employee has been involved in the idea development but not implementing the idea for their employer in the previous three years. *Exploitation experience* is measured by a dichotomous variable that takes the value 1 when the employee has been involved in implementing the idea but not in idea development for their employer in the previous three years. *Ambidexterity experience* is measured by a dichotomous variable that takes the value 1 when the employee has been involved in both idea development and idea implementation for their employer in the previous three years.

The third explanatory variable captures five employees' intellectual capital (Kostopoulos, Bozionelos, and Syrigos 2015; Turner, Maylor, and Swart 2015). *Human capital* is measured by a dichotomous variable that takes the value 1 when the employee has a college degree (Alpkan et al. 2010; Parker 2011). *Social capital* is measured by a dichotomous variable that takes the value 1 when the employee mentioned that know someone who has started a business in the past two years (Bosma 2013; Guerrero, Amorós, and Urbano 2019). *Investor capital* is measured by a dichotomous variable that takes the value 1 when the employee had investor experience in the past three years (Bosma 2013). *Entrepreneurial capital* is measured by a dichotomous variable that takes the value 1 when the employee had entrepreneurial experience in the previous year (Millan et al. 2014). *Opportunity perceptions* are measured by a dichotomous variable that takes the value 1 when the employee perceives entrepreneurial opportunities in the next six months (Guerrero and Peña-Legazkue, 2013).

The four explanatory variable captures the moderation effect of a diversified workforce captured through four proxies demographics characteristics: the *women workers* are measured by a dichotomous variable that takes the value 1 when the employee reported a female gender (Guerrero, Amorós, and Urbano 2019); the *migrant workers* are measured by a binary variable that takes the value 1 when the employee born in a different country (Peroni, Riillo, and Sarracino 2016; Boone et al. 2019); the *elderly workers* are measured by a dichotomous variable that takes the value 1 when the employee born from 1946 to 1964 (Guerrero, Amorós, and Urbano 2019); and the *low-*

income workers are measured by a binary variable that takes the value 1 when the employee reported personal income lower than 33,000 dollars/year (Bosma 2013).

The control variables added to our model based on previous studies (Parker 2011; Bosma et al. 2013; Guerrero, Amorós, and Urbano 2019) were: the size of employers' organizations in terms of the number of employees that were included in our analysis as a natural logarithm (*lnSize*); the organization type is measured by a dichotomous variable that takes value 1 when the organization was private, otherwise, if it was public (*Organization type*); the natural logarithm of total unemployment per country (*Labor market conditions*); the natural logarithm of the industry value added per country (*Competitive intensity*); the natural logarithm of high-technology manufactured exports per country (*Technological intensity*); and the natural logarithm of R&D expenditure per country (*Innovation intensity*).

Statistical Model

Given the dichotomous nature of our dependent variable, we used a logistic analysis. We show our results via odds ratios because it is a single summary score of the effect, and the probabilities are more intuitive than simple coefficients (see Mickiewicz et al. 2019; Guerrero, Amorós, and Urbano 2019). The odds demonstrate the probability that an outcome (corporate venturing) will occur in the presence of an explanatory variable (e.g. workforce's organizational perceptions, workforce's ambidexterity experience, workforce's intellectual capitals). An odds ratio value lower than 1 indicates a negative coefficient, and an odds ratio value greater than or equal to 1 indicates a positive coefficient (Langer 2017). Based on these arguments, we decided to show our results using odd ratios.

To test our hypotheses, we first ran three models per exploratory variable: workforce's perceptions of organizational climate (Models 1), workforce's ambidexterity experience (Models 2), and workforce's intellectual capitals (Model 3). We then created interactions between each exploratory variable and each workforce's demographic characteristics (our workforce diversity measure) to test its moderation effects. Table 1 shows the correlation matrix and descriptive. The correlation matrix reveals that most of the explanatory variables are not highly correlated. According to descriptive statistics, the prevalence of workers that have created a corporate venture for their employers in the last three years is approximately 9% (Appendix 1). On average, of the total sample, the workforce demographics are represented by women workers (44%), migrant workers (5%), elderly workers (22%), and low-income workers (22%). Workers also have positive perceptions about a favorable climate towards corporate entrepreneurship (three on a five-point Likert scale).

Findings and discussion

Workforce's demographic characteristics

All models show a significant effect on corporate venturing (see Model 1a, Model 2a, and Model 3a). However, migrant workers represented the unique demographic characteristic that positively influences innovative and entrepreneurial activities. Therefore, nationality diversity increases the probability that workers be engaged in corporate entrepreneurship. A plausible explanation is that migrants knew information about home/host markets that may prevent potential entry problems or be sources of innovative opportunities. Previous studies found that diversified workers' nationalities strengthen a team's ability to scan and interpret the available international information associated with corporate venturing and innovation (Peroni, Riillo, and Sarracino 2016; Boone et al. 2019). Concerning the direct effect of gender and age, we observe that a worker's probability of creating corporate ventures decreases when they are women and elderly workers. An explanation could be that women/elderly workers are segregated into less rewarded job tasks than men/youngest workers that take advantage of power/negotiation skills into more challenging working conditions (Petrie

Table 1. Correlation matrix

	Variables	Mean	Std. Dev.	Min	Max	1	2	3	4	5	6	7	8	9
1	Corporate venturing	0.094	0.292	0	1	1								
2	Type_private	0.640	0.480	0	1	0.0628*	1							
3	lnsize	4.119	2.114	1.609	13.816	0.0069	−0.0115*	1						
4	lnUnemployment	2.242	0.699	1.131	4.190	0.0145*	−0.0391*	0.0061	1					
5	lnTech	2.162	1.324	−2.303	4.190	−0.0504*	0.0778*	0.0026	−0.1146*	1				
6	lnR&D	0.050	1.315	−2.303	4.190	−0.0972*	−0.0184*	0.0111*	0.3215*	0.5905*	1			
7	lnIndustry	33.573	11.881	11.920	95.490	0.0392*	0.0372*	−0.0034	0.2982*	−0.1032*	0.3516*	1		
8	Women workers	0.439	0.496	0	1	−0.0621*	−0.1388*	0.0016	0.0147*	0.0631*	0.0580*	−0.0419*	1	
9	Migrant workers	0.045	0.206	0	1	0.0025	0.0108*	0.0021	0.0807*	0.0658*	0.1255*	0.0051	0.0141*	1
10	Elderly workers	0.223	0.416	0	1	−0.0586*	−0.1183*	0.0410*	0.0049	0.0404*	0.0574*	−0.0775*	0.0260*	0.0222*
11	Low-income workers	0.223	0.416	0	1	−0.0185*	0.0449*	−0.0024	−0.0146*	−0.0321*	−0.0036	0.0642*	0.0247*	0.0128*
12	Autonomy	3.250	1.416	1	5	0.0797*	0.0435*	−0.0116*	−0.0904*	−0.0679*	−0.1861*	0.1800*	−0.0279*	−0.0064
13	Meaningful	3.273	1.554	1	5	0.0788*	0.0294*	−0.0194*	−0.0811*	−0.1435*	−0.2410*	0.2474*	−0.0277*	−0.0389*
14	Rewards	3.198	1.354	1	5	0.0549*	0.0042	−0.0084	−0.0602*	−0.1010*	−0.1966*	0.2068*	−0.0138*	−0.0401*
15	Exploration experience	0.108	0.310	0	1	0.0031	−0.0071	0.0007	0.0048	0.003	0.0045	−0.0019	−0.0046	0.0077
16	Exploitation experience	0.069	0.253	0	1	−0.0055	−0.0077	0.0023	0.0031	−0.0008	−0.0004	−0.0051	−0.0003	−0.0013
17	Ambidexterity experience	0.036	0.187	0	1	0.0021	−0.0049	0.0039	0.0026	0.0002	0.0011	0.0002	−0.0025	0.0081
18	Human capital	0.307	0.461	0	1	0.0228*	−0.1816*	0.0097*	0.0841*	0.0610*	0.1566*	0.0483*	0.0771*	0.0566*
19	Social capital	0.396	0.489	0	1	0.1694*	0.0379*	−0.0011	−0.0412*	−0.0823*	−0.0962*	0.0387*	−0.0643*	−0.0318*
20	Investor capital	0.060	0.238	0	1	0.1013*	0.005	0.0019	0.0032	−0.0910*	−0.0859*	0.0212*	−0.0447*	−0.0098*
21	Entrepreneurship capital	0.028	0.166	0	1	0.0819*	0.0163*	0.0028	0.0175*	−0.0877*	−0.0830*	0.0199*	−0.0186*	−0.0097*
22	Opportunity	0.381	0.486	0	1	0.1683*	0.0356*	−0.006	−0.0205*	−0.1389*	−0.1335*	0.0213*	−0.0596*	−0.0179*

	Variables	10	11	12	13	14	15	16	17	18	19	20	21	22
10	Elderly workers	1												
11	Low-income workers	0.0130*	1											
12	Autonomy	−0.0201*	0.0245*	1										
13	Meaningful	−0.0158*	0.0220*	0.5309*	1									
14	Rewards	0.0164*	−0.0103	0.4697*	0.7163*	1								
15	Exploration experience	−0.0043	0.0011	0.0002	−0.0013	0.0007	1							
16	Exploitation experience	0.0206*	0.0008	−0.0057	−0.0034	0.0044	0.3670*	1						
17	Ambidexterity experience	0.0017	−0.0012	0.0000	0.0002	0.0067	0.5580*	0.7131*	1					
18	Human capital	−0.0293*	−0.1854*	−0.0041	−0.0097	−0.0036	0.0024	0.0018	0.0014	1				
19	Social capital	−0.0963*	−0.0598*	0.0614*	0.0698*	0.0471*	−0.0009	−0.0027	0.0009	0.0583*	1			
20	Investor capital	−0.0082*	−0.0381*	0.0335*	0.0382*	0.0377*	0.0005	−0.005	−0.0021	0.0341*	0.1327*	1		
21	Entrepreneurship capital	−0.0227*	0.0137*	0.0262*	0.0257*	0.0098	0.0008	0.001	−0.0043	−0.0141*	0.0790*	0.0666*	1	
22	Opportunity	−0.0673*	−0.0221*	0.0783*	0.0885*	0.0602*	0.0026	−0.0059	−0.0004	0.0105*	0.2155*	0.0923*	0.0528*	1

Notes: Significant level at the 1%.

and Roman 2004). However, given the inconclusive nature of workforce diversity literature, it is relevant to explore the moderation effect of the workforce's demographic background for a better understanding of the workforce diversity in corporate venturing.

Workforce's organizational perceptions and corporate venturing

Table 2 shows the increasing or decreasing probability of corporate venturing associated with the workers' perception of organizational supports (Model 1).

Regarding the workforce's perceptions, Model 1a shows that a good workforce's perceptions about workplace autonomy (1.041; $p < 0.100$) and the meaningful job (1.047; $p < 0.100$) increase the workforce's engagement in corporate venturing. Model 1a did not show enough insights regarding the influence of rewards perception on corporate venturing. Results suggest that non-monetary returns expressed in terms of autonomy and consistency with values highly influence the workforce' engagement in corporate venturing (Petrie and Roman 2004; Guerrero, Amorós, and Urbano 2019), supporting H1a.

Concerning the moderation effect, Model 1b shows that workforce diversity reinforces the positive effect of *job autonomy* on corporate venturing through generational cohorts (1.031; $p < 0.100$) and personal income ranges (1.092; $p < 0.100$). Our results show that motivated workers (elderly and low-income) by non-economy incentives (e.g. flexibility to do their work) are likely to participate in creating innovative initiatives with a risk assumed by their employers (Patel, Messersmith, and Lepak 2013; Lee, Woo, and Joshi 2017; Guerrero, Amorós, and Urbano 2019). A few studies found that race/gender segregation was not significantly associated with workplace autonomy (Petrie and Roman 2004). A plausible explanation is that the lack of autonomy in one's workplace is a means of inequality. Model 1c shows that workforce diversity reinforces the positive effect of a *meaningful job* on corporate venturing when workers are women (1.061; $p < 0.100$) and migrant (1.067; $p < 0.100$). Given the workforce's nature, women/migrants are highly motivated by generating significant contributions to the community (Fairlie 2011), consistent with personal values and organizational purposes (Monsen, Patzelt, and Saxton 2010). In this vein, women/migrants will be interested in participating in innovative and entrepreneurial processes aligned with their values, motivations, and expectations (Scroggins 2008). Model 1d shows that the workforce's *income diversity* reinforces rewards' positive effect on corporate venturing (1.132; $p < 0.100$). Low-income workers' primary motivation is increasing their salary or rewards conditions (Gibson, Greenwood, and Murphy 2009). The workforce's income diversity shows that workers' engagement in corporate venturing activities is motivated by the returns or rewards (Monsen, Patzelt, and Saxton 2010). Our results show that diversity in the labor force positively moderates the perception of organizational supports on corporate venturing (supporting H1b).

Workforce's ambidexterity experiences and corporate venturing

Table 3 shows the increasing or decreasing probability of corporate venturing associated with the workforce's ambidexterity experiences (Model 2).

Regarding the workforce's ambidexterity experience, Model 2a show that the prior workforce's experiences in exploration (1.054; $p < 0.100$), exploitation (1.082; $p < 0.010$), and ambidexterity (1.402; $p < 0.100$) increase the workforce's engagement in corporate venturing. Innovation/entrepreneurial projects require teams with abilities to identify potential opportunities (exploration) and abilities to transform these potential opportunities into innovations, new business models, or new ventures (exploitation). Previous studies recognized the relevant contribution of a workforce with a previous leading role experience in the idea development and a previous leading role experience in the idea implementation (Bosma et al. 2013; Guerrero, Amorós, and Urbano 2019). Consequently, a workforce with ambidexterity abilities (simultaneous exploration

Table 2. Logistic Regression (Model 1: Workforce's organizational perceptions).

	Model 1a			Model 1b			Model 1c			Model 1d		
	Odds Ratio	Std. Err.	*P>z*	Odds Ratio	Std. Err.	*P>z*	Odds Ratio	Std. Err.	*P>z*	Odds Ratio	Std. Err.	*P>z*
Country controls												
lnUnemployment	0.592	0.163	**	0.592	0.164	**	0.587	0.164	**	0.587	0.165	**
lnTech	0.715	0.129	*	0.715	0.130	**	0.714	0.131	**	0.714	0.132	**
lnR&D	0.637	0.081	***	0.634	0.081	***	0.633	0.082	***	0.624	0.081	***
lnIndustry	0.981	0.013		0.981	0.013		0.980	0.013		0.982	0.013	
Organizational controls												
Orgatype_private	1.602	0.100	***	1.608	0.100	***	1.613	0.101	***	1.610	0.100	***
lnSize	1.018	0.013	*	1.019	0.013	*	1.020	0.013	*	1.019	0.013	*
Workforce demographics												
Women workers	0.619	0.035	***	0.587	0.082	***	0.513	0.065	***	0.657	0.092	***
Immigrants workers	1.278	0.041	**	1.527	0.440	*	1.077	0.290	*	1.412	0.414	*
Elderly workers	0.614	0.045	***	0.770	0.131	*	0.676	0.105	*	0.662	0.118	**
Low-income workers	0.765	0.054	***	0.570	0.104	***	0.717	0.117	**	0.521	0.093	***
Workforce's organizational perceptions												
Autonomy	1.041	0.023	*	1.039	0.028	*						
Autonomy * women workers				1.016	0.040							
Autonomy * migrant workers				0.942	0.083							
Autonomy * elderly workers				1.031	0.046	*						
Autonomy * low-income workers				1.092	0.053	*						
Meaningful	1.047	0.028	*				1.017	0.028	*			
Meaningful * women workers							1.061	0.037	*			
Meaningful * migrant workers							1.067	0.085	*			
Meaningful * elderly workers							0.968	0.042				
Meaningful * low-income workers							1.021	0.046				
Rewards	0.962	0.027								0.988	0.030	
Rewards * women workers										0.982	0.040	
Rewards * migrant workers										0.972	0.093	
Rewards * elderly workers										0.976	0.051	
Rewards * low-income workers										1.132	0.058	*
N	17217			17217			17217			17217		
Countries	20			20			20			20		
Log likelihood	−5228			−5241			−5248			−5237		
Wald chi2	256.4			259.2			256.9			253.3		
Prob > chi2	***			***			***			***		
LR test vs. logit model	173.3			175.8			181.8			179.4		
Prob >= chibar2	***			***			***			***		

*Significance at the 10% level; **Significance at the 5% level; ***Significance at the 1%.

Table 3. Logistic Regression (Model 2: Workforce' ambidexterity experience).

	Model 2a			Model 2b			Model 2c			Model 2d		
	Odds Ratio	Std. Err.	*P>z*	Odds Ratio	Std. Err.	*P>z*	Odds Ratio	Std. Err.	*P>z*	Odds Ratio	Std. Err.	*P>z*
Country controls												
lnUnemployment	0.590	0.163	**	0.592	0.163	**	0.592	0.163	**	0.592	0.163	**
lnTech	0.713	0.129	**	0.715	0.129	**	0.714	0.129	**	0.715	0.129	*
lnR&D	0.636	0.081	***	0.637	0.081	***	0.636	0.081	***	0.637	0.031	***
lnIndustry	0.981	0.013		0.981	0.013		0.981	0.013		0.981	0.013	
Organizational controls												
Orgatype_private	1.602	0.100	***	1.603	0.100	***	1.602	0.100	***	1.603	0.100	***
lnSize	1.018	0.013		1.018	0.013		1.018	0.013		1.018	0.013	
Workforce demographics												
Women workers	0.590	0.163	**	0.620	0.037	***	0.611	0.036	***	0.615	0.036	***
Immigrants workers	1.713	0.129	**	1.272	0.180	*	1.263	0.174	*	1.312	0.177	**
Elderly workers	0.636	0.081	***	0.606	0.047	***	0.613	0.046	***	0.610	0.045	***
Low-income workers	0.981	0.013		0.756	0.057	***	0.782	0.057	***	0.774	0.056	***
Workforce's organizational perceptions												
Autonomy	1.041	0.023	*	1.041	0.023	*	1.041	0.023	**	1.041	0.023	**
Meaningful	1.047	0.028	*	1.047	0.028	*	1.047	0.028	*	1.046	0.028	*
Rewards	0.962	0.027		0.962	0.027		0.962	0.027		0.962	0.027	
Workforce's ambidexterity experience												
Exploration	1.054	0.108	*	1.004	0.16	*						
Exploration * women workers				1.008	0.181	*						
Exploration * migrant workers				1.047	0.431	**						
Exploration * elderly workers				1.124	0.246							
Exploration * low-income workers				1.103	0.239							
Exploitation	1.082	0.118	**				1.011	0.202	*			
Exploration * women workers							0.823	0.190				
Exploration * migrant workers							1.169	0.646				
Exploration * elderly workers							1.062	0.294				
Exploration * low-income workers							0.68	0.212				
*Exploration * Exploitation*	1.402	0.339	*							1.210	0.314	*
Ambidexterity * women workers										0.841	0.248	
Ambidexterity * migrant workers										0.341	0.355	
Ambidexterity * elderly workers										1.187	0.426	
Ambidexterity * low-income workers										0.712	0.278	
N	17217			17217			17217			17217		
Countries	20			20			20			20		
Log likelihood	−5225			−5227			−5225			−5226		
Wald chi2	261.3			257			260.4			258.7		
Prob > chi2	***			***			***			***		
LR test vs. logit model	173.1			173.1			173.1			173.3		
Prob >= chibar2	***			***			***			***		

*Significance at the 10% level; **Significance at the 5% level; ***Significance at the 1%.

and exploitation abilities) are more likely to participate in corporate entrepreneurship strategies than a workforce without ambidexterity abilities (Zacher, Robinson, and Rosing 2016; Yeganegi et al. 2019). These results support H2a.

Concerning the moderation effect, Model 2b shows that workforce diversity reinforces the positive effect of *previous experience in exploration activities* on corporate venturing through gender (1.008; $p < 0.100$) and nationality (1.047; $p < 0.010$). Literature recognized that teams integrated by gender equality quote (Ahl 2006) and immigrant quotes (Aliaga-Isla and Rialp 2013) are more likely to identify innovations than unbalanced teams. The explanation is that non-native workers are a source of information from their home/host markets that facilitate the generation innovations and reduce entry barriers (Boone et al. 2019). However, we did not find insights about workforce demographics' moderation effect on the relationship between exploitation/ambidexterity and corporate ventures. A plausible explanation is that exploitation roles are limited for top or middle managers teams with direct access to networks, resources, and organizational support. As a result, a reduced number of employees will recognize an ambidexterity experience. It also explains why it is important to analyze the distance to power, workforce diversity, and inequality (DiTomaso, Post, and Parks-Yancy 2007). Our results are partially supporting H2b.

Workforce's intellectual capitals and corporate venturing

Table 4 shows the increasing or decreasing probability of corporate venturing associated with the workforce's intellectual capital (Model 3).

Regarding the workforce's intellectual capital, Model 3a show that human capital (1.296; $p < 0.001$), social capital (2.651; $p < 0.001$), investor capital (1.604; $p < 0.001$), entrepreneurial capital (1.481; $p < 0.001$), and opportunity perceptions (2.222; $p < 0.001$) increase employees' engagement in corporate venturing (supporting H3a). Prior studies have revealed that employees' intellectual capitals are antecedents of corporate entrepreneurship (Ireland, Covin, and Kuratko 2009; Parker 2011; Kostopoulos, Bozionelos, and Syrigos 2015; Turner, Maylor, and Swart 2015; Guerrero, Amorós, and Urbano 2019). However, extant studies have tested separately intellectual capitals' role in entrepreneurial processes without adopting a workforce diversity perspective.

Concerning the moderation effect, Model 3b shows that workforce diversity reinforces the positive effect of *human capital* on corporate venturing through generational cohorts (1.257; $p < 0.100$). Elderly workers' human capital has accumulated knowledge, particular abilities, and unique experiences with/across organizations (Becker 2002; Guerrero, Amorós, and Urbano 2019), representing a core competence for their current entrepreneurial and innovative employer. Although skilled women/migrants' potential role, this study did not find conclusive results about the moderation effect of these workforce groups. Model 3c shows that workforce diversity reinforces the positive effect of *social capital* on corporate venturing through gender (1.274; $p < 0.010$), immigrant status (1.149; $p < 0.100$), and generational cohorts (1.241; $p < 0.010$). This model provides insights into how networks from a diversified workforce benefit the creation of ventures under the parent organization's umbrella (Heavey, Simsek, and Fox 2015). Intuitively, the balanced team configuration will be a good strategy for organizations with an innovative and entrepreneurial orientation. Model 3d shows that workforce diversity reinforces the positive effect of *investor capital* on corporate venturing through elderly workers (1.593; $p < 0.010$) and migrant workers (1.538; $p < 0.100$). Monetary resources and prior experiences in specific markets influence conditioned the configuration of *investor capital.* It explains why having an investor capital is influenced by workers' age older or migratory status. Indeed, women experience small investor experiences with friends and family (Bosma 2013). Our findings are supporting H3b.

Table 4. Logistic Regression (Model 3: Workforces' intellectual capitals)

	Model 3a			Model 3b			Model 3c			Model 3d			Model 3d			Model 3e		
	Odds Ratio	Std. Err.	P>z	Odds Ratio	Std. Err.	P>z	Odds Ratio	Std. Err.	P>z	Odds Ratio	Std. Err.	P>z	Odds Ratio	Std. Err.	P>z	Odds Ratio	Std. Err.	P>z
Country controls																		
lnUnemployment	0.831	0.217		0.610	0.167	*	0.686	0.187		0.633	0.169	*	0.591	0.160	**	0.723	0.194	
lnTech	0.838	0.143		0.728	0.130	*	0.766	0.136		0.749	0.131	*	0.709	0.126	**	0.779	0.137	
lnR&D	0.704	0.085	***	0.621	0.078	***	0.659	0.083	***	0.646	0.080	***	0.646	0.081	***	0.693	0.086	***
lnIndustry	0.995	0.013		0.982	0.013		0.987	0.013		0.984	0.013		0.980	0.013		0.988	0.013	
Organizational controls																		
Orgatype_private	1.640	0.114	***	1.710	0.109	***	1.610	0.103	***	1.624	0.102	***	1.600	0.100	***	1.557	0.104	***
lnSize	1.023	0.014	*	1.017	0.013		1.023	0.013	*	1.018	0.013		1.018	0.013		1.020	0.014	
Workforce demographics																		
Women workers	0.629	0.040	***	0.660	0.047	***	0.553	0.052	***	0.627	0.038	***	0.615	0.036	***	0.523	0.048	***
Immigrants workers	1.375	0.202	**	1.373	0.227	**	1.633	0.304	***	1.264	0.177	*	1.257	0.172	*	1.146	0.246	
Elderly workers	0.686	0.055	***	0.570	0.053	***	0.613	0.070	***	0.650	0.049	***	0.614	0.046	***	0.595	0.066	***
Low-income workers	0.890	0.070		0.820	0.066	**	0.939	0.102		0.786	0.058	***	0.763	0.056	***	0.827	0.090	*
Workforce's organizational perceptions																		
Autonomy	1.040	0.026	*	1.043	0.023	**	1.038	0.024	*	1.039	0.023	*	1.040	0.023	*	1.042	0.025	*
Meaningful	1.023	0.031		1.043	0.028		1.037	0.029		1.049	0.029	*	1.048	0.028	*	1.033	0.030	
Rewards	0.964	0.030		0.960	0.027		0.967	0.028		0.961	0.027	*	0.964	0.027	*	0.964	0.029	
Workforce's ambidexterity experience																		
Exploration	0.995	0.113	*	1.032	0.107	*	1.011	0.107	*	1.051	0.109	*	1.051	0.108	*	1.061	0.116	*
Exploitation	0.62	0.121	**	0.683	0.118	**	0.676	0.119	**	0.677	0.118	**	0.679	0.118	**	0.632	0.122	**
Exploration * Exploitation	1.612	0.438	*	1.443	0.35	*	1.525	0.375	*	1.456	0.354	*	1.372	0.334	*	1.497	0.396	*
Workforce's intellectual capitals																		
Human capital	1.296	0.089	***	1.634	0.135	***												
Human capital * women workers				0.767	0.091	**												
Human capital * migrant workers				0.758	0.207													
Human capital * elderly workers				1.257	0.187	*												
Human capital * low-income workers				1.014	0.183													
Social capital	2.651	0.167	***				3.052	0.244	***									
Social capital * women workers							1.274	0.151	**									
Social capital * migrant workers							1.149	0.17	*									
							1.241	0.184	*									

(*Continued*)

Table 4. Continued.

	Model 3a			Model 3b			Model 3c			Model 3d			Model 3d			Model 3e		
	Odds Ratio	Std. Err.	*P*>z	Odds Ratio	Std. Err.	*P*>z	Odds Ratio	Std. Err.	*P*>z	Odds Ratio	Std. Err.	*P*>z	Odds Ratio	Std. Err.	*P*>z	Odds Ratio	Std. Err.	*P*>z
Social capital * elderly workers																		
Social capital * low-income workers							0.796	0.114	*									
Investor capital	1.604	0.159	***							2.468	0.294	***						
Investor capital * women workers										1.076	0.212							
Investor capital * migrant workers										1.133	0.564							
Investor capital * elderly workers										1.593	0.158	**						
Investor capital * low-income workers										1.001	0.272							
Entrepreneurial capital	1.481	0.201	***										1.643	0.29	***			
Entrepreneurial capital * women workers													1.118	0.294				
Entrepreneurial capital * migrant workers													1.538	1.007	*			
Entrepreneurial capital * elderly workers													1.186	0.416				
Entrepreneurial capital * low-income workers													0.998	0.303				
Opportunity perception	2.222	0.14	***													2.401	0.198	***
Opportunity * women workers																1.374	0.168	***
Opportunity * migrant workers																1.417	0.405	*
Opportunity * elderly workers																1.065	0.166	
Opportunity * low-income workers																0.926	0.138	
N	17217			17217			17217			17217			17217			17217		
Countries	20			20			20			20			20			20		
Log likelihood	−4229			−5179			−4947			−5165			−5199			−4473		
Wald chi2	788.5			316.5			648.9			354.3			282.2			494.8		
Prob > chi2	***			***			***			***			***			***		
LR test vs. logit model: chibar2(01)	119.4			165.5			163.4			155.7			164			141		
Prob >= chibar2	***			***			***			***			***			***		

*Significance at the 10% level; **Significance at the 5% level; ***Significance at the 1%.

Conclusions

Main conclusions

The purpose of this study was to examine how workforce demographics (age, gender, income, and nationality) moderate corporate venturing drivers: the workforce's organizational perceptions (H1a), the workforce's ambidexterity experience (H2a), and the workforce's intellectual capital (H3a). This paper contributes to ongoing academic debates. The *first contribution* relates to the effects of workforce diversity (not only managers) on unexplored organizational outcomes (not only performance) across countries (Yadav and Lenka 2020, 12). Our results proposed/tested a conceptual framework about a diversified workforce's role in corporate entrepreneurship using a sample of 17217 employees across 20 countries. We provide insights into the workforce's contribution of women, multiple generational cohorts, and immigrants to achieve new organizational outcomes through their motivations, abilities, capabilities, and capitals. Our insights open a new window to provide a better theoretical/empirical understanding of the diversified workforce's contributions to their workplaces through multidisciplinary approaches (i.e. management, entrepreneurship, innovation, sociology, economics). The *second contribution* relates to the moderation effects of the workforce's demographic diversity (not limited to the top or middle managers) into the individual-drivers of corporate venturing (Junni et al. 2015; Guerrero, Amorós, and Urbano 2019; Mom et al. 2019; Yeganegi et al. 2019). Our results provided insights into the workforce's engagement in corporate venturing by identifying opportunities (using their exploration abilities) and taking advantage of intellectual capital (using their human capital and social capital), as well as how these drivers are influenced by the demographic background of workers (especially the diversity in terms of gender, age, nationality, and income). Our insights open a new window to provide robust workforce diversity measurements to understand a diversified workforce's critical role in corporate entrepreneurship under uncertain environmental conditions.

Limitations and future research

We acknowledge several limitations and future research opportunities. First, the APS GEM survey provided traditional and unique measures concerning entrepreneurial employee activity, workplace environments, innovation, and migration. Therefore, our measures represented the workers' perceptions without enough details about parent organizations (workplace), the corporate entrepreneurship strategy (process), and the corporate venture organization (outcome). Future research opens an opportunity window for capturing organizational details of the workforce diversity into corporate entrepreneurship processes, the strategic view of the parent organization, and the innovation level of the new corporate venture. Second, like any secondary dataset, the selection of our proxies was supported by previous studies. Our adopted workforce diversity measures demographics characteristics that exhibit differences between employees (Friedman and DiTomaso 1996; Jasso 2001; Peroni, Riillo, and Sarracino 2016). Future studies should consider novel measurements that capture both workforce diversity's dimensions: the demographic and the cultural (Yadav and Lenka 2020). Novel measurements also demand novel quantitative (longitudinal) and qualitative (cases, experiments, action research) methods to capture robust data within organizations. Third, our theory development considers the analysis of diversity management and corporate entrepreneurship literature. Future research should propose theory development by adopting multiple theoretical lenses to understand workforce diversity and corporate entrepreneurship (innovation, entrepreneurship, management, sociology, psychology).

Implications

Several implications emerge from our results. *For the entrepreneurial workforce*, the analysis highlights the workforce propensity into corporate venturing. Our results are relevant for workers with entrepreneurial intentions that could be transformed into entrepreneurial actions by creating ventures under their organizations' umbrella. In this vein, workers should value their demographic backgrounds and promote diversity within their workplaces. *For top/middle managers*, our results provide insights into the benefits of different workforce groups into corporate venturing strategies. Given the current workplace configuration and uncertain external conditions, managers should pay attention to updating human management practices by valuing employees' diversity and cultural/demographic background. It may allow the creation of diversified teams to motivate the identification and implementation of novel marketable ideas. Nowadays, it is also unfortunate that some organizations lack attention to organizational conditions to engage the workforce in innovative and entrepreneurial tasks. *For policymakers*, the United Nations' sustainable development goals are looking for inclusion and diversity. In this vein, policymakers should support these goals by incentivizing diversity/equality within organizations through innovation and entrepreneurship policy frameworks. Directly/indirectly, these actions will generate multiple benefits at an individual level (professional/personal growth), organizational level (sustainable performance), and social level (economic and social outcomes).

Note

1. The list of countries that included in their APS the four set of questions were: Belgium, China, Croatia, Denmark, Estonia, Finland, Greece, Hungary, South Korea, Lithuania, Malaysia, Namibia, Nigeria, Peru, Philippines, Poland, Romania, Slovenia, Slovakia, and United Kingdom.

Disclosure statement

No potential conflict of interest was reported by the author(s).

ORCID

Maribel Guerrero http://orcid.org/0000-0001-7387-1999

References

Ahl, H. 2006. "Why Research on Women Entrepreneurs Needs new Directions." *Entrepreneurship Theory and Practice* 30 (5): 595–621.

Aliaga-Isla, R., and A. Rialp. 2013. "A Systematic Review of Immigrant Entrepreneurship Literature: Previous Findings and Ways Forward." *Entrepreneurship & Regional Development* 25 (9-10): 819–844.

Alpkan, L., C. Bulut, G. Gunday, G. Ulusoy, and K. Kilic. 2010. "Organizational Support for Intrapreneurship and its Interaction with Human Capital to Enhance Innovative Performance." *Management Decision* 48 (5): 732–755.

Alrumaithi, E., M. Guerrero, and I. Peña. 2015. "The Role of Employee's Human Capital and the Work Environment on the Creation of Organizational Spin-Offs: Evidence from Spain." In *Entrepreneurship, Human Capital, and Regional Development*, edited by R. Baptista and J. Leitão, 59–74. UK: Springer International Publishing.

Ang, S., L. Van Dyne, C. Koh, K. Y. Ng, K. J. Templer, C. Tay, and N. A. Chandrasekar. 2007. "Cultural Intelligence: its Measurement and Effects on Cultural Judgment and Decision Making, Cultural Adaptation and Task Performance." *Management and Organization Review* 3 (3): 335–371.

Antoncic, J., and B. Antoncic. 2011. "Employee Satisfaction, Intrapreneurship, and Firm Growth: a Model." *Industrial Management & Data Systems* 111 (4): 589–607.

Becker, G. S. 2002. "The age of Human Capital." In *Education, Globalization & Social Change*, edited by H. Lauder, P. Brown, J. Dillabough, and H. Halsey, 292–295. Oxford, UK: Oxford University Press.

Boone, C., B. Lokshin, H. Guenter, and R. Belderbos. 2019. "Top Management Team Nationality Diversity, Corporate Entrepreneurship, and Innovation in Multinational Firms." *Strategic Management Journal* 40 (2): 277–302.

Bosma, N. 2013. "The Global Entrepreneurship Monitor (GEM) and its Impact on Entrepreneurship Research." *Foundations and Trends in Entrepreneurship* 9: 143–248.

Bosma, N., S. Wennekers, M. Guerrero, J. E. Amorós, A. Martiarena, and S. Singer. 2013. *Global Entrepreneurship Monitor Special Report on Entrepreneurial Employee Activity*. London: GERA.

Brandes, U., J. Lerner, M. J. Lubbers, C. McCarty, J. L. Molina, and U. Nagel. 2010. "Recognizing Modes of Acculturation in Personal Networks of Migrants." *Procedia-Social and Behavioral Sciences* 4: 4–13.

Colombo, M. G., C. Rossi-Lamastra, and B. Matassini. 2015. "The Organizational Design of High-Tech Entrepreneurial Ventures." *Foundations and Trends® in Entrepreneurship* 11 (6): 427–523.

Cropley, D., and A. Cropley. 2017. "Innovation Capacity, Organisational Culture and Gender." *European Journal of Innovation Management* 20(3): 493-510.

Culpan, O., and G. H. Wright. 2002. "Women Abroad: Getting the Best Results from Women Managers." *International Journal of Human Resource Management* 13 (5): 784–801.

Díaz-García, C., A. González-Moreno, and F. J. Saez-Martinez. 2013. "Gender Diversity Within R&D Teams: Its Impact on Radicalness of Innovation." *Innovation* 15 (2): 149–160.

DiTomaso, N., C. Post, and R. Parks-Yancy. 2007. "Workforce Diversity and Inequality: Power, Status, and Numbers." *Annual Review of Sociology* 33: 473–501.

D'Netto, B., and A. S. Sohal. 1999. "Human Resource Practices and Workforce Diversity: an Empirical Assessment." *International Journal of Manpower* 20 (8): 530–547.

Fairlie, P. 2011. "Meaningful Work, Employee Engagement, and Other key Employee Outcomes: Implications for Human Resource Development." *Advances in Developing Human Resources* 13 (4): 508–525.

Friedman, J. J., and N. DiTomaso. 1996. "Myths About Diversity: What Managers Need to Know About Changes in the US Labor Force." *California Management Review* 38 (4): 54–77.

Garrett, R., S. Mattingly, J. Hornsby, and A. Aghaey. 2020. "Impact of Relatedness, Uncertainty and Slack on Corporate Entrepreneurship Decisions." *Management Decision*. https://doi.org/10.1108/MD-10-2019-1392

Gibson J. W., R. A. Greenwood, and E. F. Murphy Jr. 2009. "Generational Differences in the Workplace: Personal Values, Behaviors, and Popular Beliefs." Journal of Diversity Management 4 (3): 1.

Gilbert, J. A., B. A. Stead, and J. M. Ivancevich. 1999. "Diversity Management: A new Organizational Paradigm." *Journal of Business Ethics* 21 (1): 61–76.

Good, D., and E. J. Michel. 2013. "Individual Ambidexterity: Exploring and Exploiting in Dynamic Contexts." *The Journal of Psychology* 147 (5): 435–453.

Green, E., and L. Cohen. 1995. "Women's Business: Are Women Entrepreneurs Breaking new Ground or Simply Balancing the Demands of 'Women's Work' in a new way?" *Journal of Gender Studies* 4 (3): 297–314.

Guerrero, M., J. E. Amorós, and D. Urbano. 2019. "Do Employees' Generational Cohorts Influence Corporate Venturing? A Multilevel Analysis." *Small Business Economics*. https://doi.org/10.1007/s11187-019-00304-z

Guerrero, M., and I. Peña-Legazkue. 2013. "The Effect of Intrapreneurial Experience on Corporate Venturing: Evidence from Developed Economies." *International Entrepreneurship and Management Journal* 9 (3): 397–416.

Guerrero, M., and I. Peña-Legazkue. 2019. "Renascence After Post-Mortem: the Choice of Accelerated Repeat Entrepreneurship." *Small Business Economics* 52 (1): 47–65.

Guerrero, M., and D. Urbano. 2014. "Academics' Start-up Intentions and Knowledge Filters: An Individual Perspective of the Knowledge Spillover Theory of Entrepreneurship." *Small Business Economics* 43 (1): 57–74.

Guth, W., and A. Ginsberg. 1990. "Guest Editors Introduction: Corporate Entrepreneurship the Promise of Entrepreneurship as a Field of Research." *Strategic Management Journal* 11 (5): 5–11.

Hayton, J. C. 2005. "Competing in the new Economy: the Effect of Intellectual Capital on Corporate Entrepreneurship in High-Technology new Ventures." *R&D Management* 35 (2): 137–155.

Heavey, C., and Z. Simsek. 2013. "Top Management Compositional Effects on Corporate Entrepreneurship: The Moderating Role of Perceived Technological Uncertainty." *Journal of Product Innovation Management* 30 (5): 837–855.

Heavey, C., Z. Simsek, and B. C. Fox. 2015. "Managerial Social Networks and Ambidexterity of SMEs: The Moderating Role of a Proactive Commitment to Innovation." *Human Resource Management* 54 (S1): s201–s221.

Hornsby, J. S., D. F. Kuratko, and S. A. Zahra. 2002. "Middle Managers' Perception of the Internal Environment for Corporate Entrepreneurship: Assessing a Measurement Scale." *Journal of Business Venturing* 17 (3): 253–273.

Ireland, R. D., J. G. Covin, and D. F. Kuratko. 2009. "Conceptualizing Corporate Entrepreneurship Strategy." *Entrepreneurship Theory and Practice* 33 (1): 19–46.

Jahanshahi, A. A., K. Nawaser, and A. Brem. 2018. "Corporate Entrepreneurship Strategy: an Analysis of top Management Teams in SMEs." *Baltic Journal of Management* 13 (4): 528–543.

Jasso, G. 2001. "Studying Status: An Integrated Framework." *American Sociological Review* 66(1): 96–124.

Junni, P., R. M. Sarala, S. Y. Tarba, Y. Liu, and C. L. Cooper. 2015. "Guest Editors' Introduction: The Role of Human Resources and Organizational Factors in Ambidexterity." *Human Resource Management* 54 (S1): s1–s28.

Kim, P. H., H. E. Aldrich, and L. A. Keister. 2006. "Access (not) Denied: The Impact of Financial, Human, and Cultural Capital on Entrepreneurial Entry in the United States." *Small Business Economics* 27 (1): 5–22.

Kim, Y., S. S. Jeong, D. W. Yiu, and J. Moon. 2020. "Frequent CEO Turnover and Firm Performance: The Resilience Effect of Workforce Diversity." *Journal of Business Ethics*. https://doi.org/10.1007/s10551-020-04534-0.

Kostopoulos, K. C., N. Bozionelos, and E. Syrigos. 2015. "Ambidexterity and Unit Performance: Intellectual Capital Antecedents and Cross-Level Moderating Effects of Human Resource Practices." *Human Resource Management* 54 (S1): s111–s132.

Kuratko, D. F., J. S. Hornsby, and J. Hayton. 2015. "Corporate Entrepreneurship: the Innovative Challenge for a new Global Economic Reality." *Small Business Economics* 45 (2): 245–253.

Langer, Wolfgang. 2017. "How to assess the fit of multilevel logit models with Stata?," German Stata Users' Group Meetings 2017 05, Stata Users Group.

Lee, H. W., and E. Kim. 2020. "Workforce Diversity and Firm Performance: Relational Coordination as a Mediator and Structural Empowerment and Multisource Feedback as Moderators." *Human Resource Management* 59 (1): 5–23.

Lee, K., H. G. Woo, and K. Joshi. 2017. "Pro-innovation Culture, Ambidexterity and new Product Development Performance: Polynomial Regression and Response Surface Analysis." *European Management Journal* 35 (2): 249–260.

Li, C. R., C. J. Lin, and Y. H. Tien. 2016. "CEO Transformational Leadership and top Manager Ambidexterity." *Leadership & Organization Development Journal* 36 (8): 927–954.

March, J. G. 1991. "Exploration and Exploitation in Organizational Learning." *Organization Science* 2 (1): 71–87.

Marino, M., P. Parrotta, and D. Pozzoli. 2012. "Does Labor Diversity Promote Entrepreneurship?" *Economics Letters* 116 (1): 15–19.

Mickiewicz, T., M. Hart, F. Nyakudya, and N. Theodorakopoulos. 2019. "Ethnic Pluralism, Immigration and Entrepreneurship." *Regional Studies* 53 (1): 80–94.

Millan, J. M., E. Congregado, C. Roman, M. Van Praag, and A. van Stel. 2014. "The Value of an Educated Population for an Individual's Entrepreneurship Success." *Journal of Business Venturing* 29 (5): 612–632.

Mom, T. J., Y. Y. Chang, M. Cholakova, and J. J. Jansen. 2019. "A Multilevel Integrated Framework of Firm HR Practices, Individual Ambidexterity, and Organizational Ambidexterity." *Journal of Management* 45 (7): 3009–3034.

Mom, T. J., S. P. Fourné, and J. J. Jansen. 2015. "Managers' Work Experience, Ambidexterity, and Performance: The Contingency Role of the Work Context." *Human Resource Management* 54 (S1): s133–s153.

Mom, T. J., F. A. Van Den Bosch, and H. W. Volberda. 2009. "Understanding Variation in Managers' Ambidexterity: Investigating Direct and Interaction Effects of Formal Structural and Personal Coordination Mechanisms." *Organization Science* 20 (4): 812–828.

Monsen, E., H. Patzelt, and T. Saxton. 2010. "Beyond Simple Utility: Incentive Design and Trade-Offs for Corporate Employee-Entrepreneurs." *Entrepreneurship Theory and Practice* 34 (1): 105–130.

Narayanan, V. K., Y. Yang, and S. A. Zahra. 2009. "Corporate Venturing and Value Creation: A Review and Proposed Framework." *Research Policy* 38 (1): 58–76.

Parker, S. C. 2011. "Intrapreneurship or Entrepreneurship?" *Journal of Business Venturing* 26 (1): 19–34.

Parry, E., and P. Urwin. 2011. "Generational Differences in Work Values: A Review of Theory and Evidence." *International Journal of Management Reviews* 13 (1): 79–96.

Patel, P. C., J. G. Messersmith, and D. P. Lepak. 2013. "Walking the Tightrope: An Assessment of the Relationship Between High-Performance Work Systems and Organizational Ambidexterity." *Academy of Management Journal* 56 (5): 1420–1442.

Peroni, C., C. A. Riillo, and F. Sarracino. 2016. "Entrepreneurship and Immigration: Evidence from GEM Luxembourg." *Small Business Economics* 46 (4): 639–656.

Petrie, M., and P. M. Roman. 2004. "Race and Gender Differences in Workplace Autonomy: A Research Note." *Sociological Inquiry* 74 (4): 590–603.

Reynolds, P., N. Bosma, E. Autio, S. Hunt, N. De Bono, I. Servais, and N. Chin. 2005. "Global Entrepreneurship Monitor: Data Collection Design and Implementation 1998–2003″." *Small Business Economics* 24 (3): 205–231.

Rosing, K., and H. Zacher. 2017. "Individual Ambidexterity: the Duality of Exploration and Exploitation and its Relationship with Innovative Performance." *European Journal of Work and Organizational Psychology* 26 (5): 694–709.

Ruiz, L. E., J. E. Amoros, and M. Guerrero. 2019. "Does Gender Matter on Corporate Entrepreneurship? A Cross-Country Study." *Academy of Management Proceedings* 2019: 12908.

Scroggins, W. A. 2008. "Antecedents and Outcomes of Experienced Meaningful Work: A Person-job fit Perspective." *The Journal of Business Inquiry* 7 (1): 68–78.

Sessa, V. I. 1992. "Managing Diversity at the Xerox Corporation: Balanced Workforce Goals and Caucus Groups." In *Diversity in the Workplace*, edited by S. E. Jackson, 37–64 New York: The Guilford Press.

Sharma, P., and J. J. Chrisman. 1999. "Toward a Recognition of the Definitional Issues in the Field of Corporate Entrepreneurship." *Entrepreneurship: Theory & Practice* 23 (3): 11–28.

Stone, I., and C. Stubbs. 2007. "Enterprising Expatriates: Lifestyle Migration and Entrepreneurship in Rural Southern Europe." *Entrepreneurship and Regional Development* 19 (5): 433–450.

Sung, S. Y., and J. N. Choi. 2019. "Contingent Effects of Workforce Diversity on Firm Innovation: High-Tech Industry and Market Turbulence as Critical Environmental Contingencies." *The International Journal of Human Resource Management*. https://doi.org/10.1080/09585192.2019.1579243

Turner, N., H. Maylor, and J. Swart. 2015. "Ambidexterity in Projects: An Intellectual Capital Perspective." *International Journal of Project Management* 33 (1): 177–188.

Úbeda-García, M., E. Claver-Cortés, B. Marco-Lajara, and P. Zaragoza-Sáez. 2017. "Human Resource Flexibility and Performance in the Hotel Industry." *Personnel Review* 46 (4): 824–846.

Ucbasaran, D., P. Westhead, and M. Wright. 2009. "The Extent and Nature of Opportunity Identification by Experienced Entrepreneurs." *Journal of Business Venturing* 24 (2): 99–115.

Van Auken, H., F. L. Fry, and P. Stephens. 2006. "The Influence of Role Models on Entrepreneurial Intentions." *Journal of Developmental Entrepreneurship* 11 (02): 157–167.

Yadav, S., and U. Lenka. 2020. "Workforce Diversity: From a Literature Review to Future Research Agenda." *Journal of Indian Business Research.* https://doi.org/10.1108/JIBR-08-2019-0243

Yee, R. W., M. J. Miquel-Romero, and S. Cruz-Ros. 2020. "Work-life Management for Workforce Maintenance: A Qualitative Comparative Study." *Journal of Business Research* 121: 329–337.

Yeganegi, S., A. O. Laplume, P. Dass, and N. S. Greidanus. 2019. "Individual-Level Ambidexterity and Entrepreneurial Entry." *Journal of Small Business Management* 57 (4): 1444–1463.

Zacher, H., A. J. Robinson, and K. Rosing. 2016. "Ambidextrous Leadership and Employees' Self-Reported Innovative Performance: The Role of Exploration and Exploitation Behaviors." *The Journal of Creative Behavior* 50 (1): 24–46.

Zacher, H., and K. Rosing. 2015. "Ambidextrous Leadership and Team Innovation." *Leadership & Organization Development Journal* 36 (1): 54–68.

Appendix A1. Prevalence rates of labor force demographics per countries.

		Workforce demographics			
Country	Corporate venturing	Women workers	Migrant workers	Elderly workers	Low-income workers
South Africa	6.8%	41.4%	3.6%	19.3%	17.3%
Greece	0.0%	47.2%	5.3%	18.5%	0.0%
Belgium	3.6%	50.1%	4.2%	32.9%	10.7%
Hungary	7.3%	48.3%	2.7%	25.7%	24.8%
Romania	11.0%	44.4%	0.5%	21.3%	17.0%
United Kingdom	5.5%	54.1%	5.5%	34.1%	14.6%
Denmark	5.6%	49.0%	17.7%	24.6%	19.9%
Poland	6.2%	48.9%	0.2%	26.6%	25.8%
Peru	20.1%	32.1%	0.1%	14.3%	25.3%
Malaysia	2.9%	32.4%	3.7%	12.0%	24.4%
Philippines	12.0%	35.0%	0.1%	19.0%	34.6%
South Korea	5.0%	39.1%	0.2%	23.5%	27.8%
China	5.9%	48.0%	0.0%	13.5%	24.3%
Turkey	0.0%	36.6%	1.5%	11.0%	10.4%
Nigeria	32.2%	37.9%	0.4%	15.6%	16.1%
Namibia	23.2%	45.2%	3.6%	6.3%	26.1%
Finland	4.6%	51.3%	2.9%	32.6%	14.1%
Lithuania	7.6%	53.3%	2.8%	28.6%	22.3%
Estonia	9.5%	53.2%	9.2%	36.6%	25.3%
Croatia	8.2%	50.5%	11.4%	25.0%	10.2%

A gender study of principal investigator led public R&D centres and funding

James A. Cunningham, Alejandro Escribá-Esteve, María José Foncubierta-Rodríguez, Fernando Martín-Alcázar and José Luis Perea-Vicente

ABSTRACT

To survive and grow public Research and Development (R&D) centres need to raise competitive funds (Bazeley 1998; Lee and Om 1996; Muñoz 2007; Santamaría, Brage-Gil and Modrego 2010). The factors that can influence the capacity of national R&D teams within R&D centres to apply for and obtain competitive funding does not seem to have been studied in depth. The purpose of study is to firstly, to examine whether a consistent set of priorities defined by R&D centre lead principal investigators secures more competitive funding. Secondly, to examine whether the PI gender moderates the effect of the PI's priorities on the amount of competitive public funds that the R&D team of the PI obtains. Our study focuses on R&D activities carried out in Spanish public centres in the areas of Health and Biomedicine. Our results found that there were no gender differences in relation to the acquisition of competitive funding which is contrary to findings of other studies (Mayer and Rathmann 2018; Lerchenmueller and Sorenson, 2018).

1. Introduction

Increasingly, public institutions strive to increase the productivity of research funds, fostering research strategies, improving innovation and promoting policies to increase the effectiveness in securing funding (Nielsen 2016; Kaló et al. 2019). From a policy perspective, it is essential to ensure that the available funding is appropriately distributed, bearing in mind the needs of society and, the research areas that need to be developed further in order to improve people's quality of life (Gómez-García et al. 2014). For national governments, public R&D can realize several benefits such as increasing technological and scientific capacity, further wealth creation through patents, spin off firms and ensuring societal outcomes (Leyden and Link 2015). For public institutions and R&D centres, such funding is essential to build sustainable research relationships with stakeholders, to strengthen their existing research capacity as well as developing new scientific knowledge, deepening existing research areas or opening up new research avenues (see Cunningham et al. 2014). For scientists in the principal investigator (PI) role, securing public funding is essential and critical to furthering their research programmes and sustaining the research teams that depend on them (see Cunningham, Menter, and O'Kane 2018). As a consequence, to obtain public funding for research has become a highly competitive market (Grimpe 2012; Fang and Casadevall 2015).

Nevertheless, public funds scarcity intensifies the competition between R&D centres and the PIs that lead them. Only those highly competitive projects that can meet and realize several spheres of impact – scientific, economic, societal, technological – secures the necessary funds. This means decreasing the number of projects financed under public R&D programmes (see Muñoz 2007; Kaló et al. 2019). For this reason, the ability to attract funds on a competitive basis is a key factor for the survival of the research programmes (Wadman 2009) initiated by PIs within R&D centres. This natural selection of R&D projects ensures the most efficient distribution of the R&D public funds. Actually, competitive public funding processes frequently establish some minimum requirements such as on composition and size of the R&D team (Cummings and Kiesler 2005), because funding usually addresses groups rather than individual researchers (Beaudry and Allaoui 2012). It is the scientist in the PI role that leads the response these public funding calls with research programme grant applications and in doing so mobilizes industry and academic partners (Cunningham 2019). The existing literature has highlighted the importance of public funding programmes for research, even though relatively few studies have focused on identifying those factors which contribute to its acquisition (Ebadi and Schiffauerova 2015; Galsworthy and McKee 2013).

The R&D team is defined as 'a stable team formed by one or more scientific leaders, several researchers, young people on training internships and technical support personnel, that share technical-scientific goals, resources, infrastructure and equipment, with joint participation in research, development and innovation projects' (CICE 2006). The success of R&D teams in obtaining public competitive funding is influenced by a number of factors, whose better understanding is a key issue both for the public R&D system and R&D team's PI (Kaló et al. 2019; Ebadi and Schiffauerova 2015). One and the other can benefit from this knowledge and can improve opportunities to secure funds. In order to continue to secure competitive funding PIs constantly strategize and are open to collaborate with a range of stakeholders to realize their scientific mission (O'Kane et al. 2015). PIs capture value from public R&D through two value capture mechanisms, boundary spanning and brokering (O'Kane et al. 2020). However, PIs experience ongoing managerial challenges in leadings public R&D programmes and they learn how to manage and lead on the job as a PI (Cunningham et al. 2014). In essence, PIs are managers and need to have know-how capabilities particularly with respect to commercialization and technology transfer (Cunningham et al. 2020). Moreover, the PI role demands management capacity – which reflects 'the tacit management know-how' (Zorn et al. 2019, 1491) — and capability – which represents the responsibility to get things done effectively and efficiently (Boardman and Ponomariov 2014) and play a central role when developing certain types of activities in relation to competitive projects (see Barnett 2008; Barreto and Patient 2013; Cho and Hambrick 2006).

One of ongoing challenges scientists have in the PI role is how best to allocate their time in relation to dealing with a range of responsibilities such as research, technology transfer and commercialization (see Cunningham et al. 2016). Taking an attention-based view of the firm is as Ocasio (1997) states 'what decision-makers do depends on what issues and answers they focus their attention on'. Based on this, managers focus their attention on certain issues by observing and interpreting the stimulations present and the environmental features on which they focus and to which they respond (Ocasio 1997). The PI role identify – science networkers, project manager, research contractor and entrepreneurs – as posited by O'Kane et al. (2020) shapes how their decisions on which R&D activities they have to spend their resources on and in doing so they define their priorities. For this reason, it is proposed that their priorities can be one of the factors affecting the efficacy of R&D teams achieving public competitive funds.

Notwithstanding the increase in the number of women in science, gender differences still persists in relation to gender balance and research productivity (West et al. 2013; Mayer and Rathmann 2018; Beaudry and Larivière 2016). Some studies have found some differences in obtaining public funds when R&D teams' PIs are women (Burns et al. 2019; Hechtman et al. 2018). For example, Burns in a large-scale Canadian study the reviewed 55,700 grants involving 4087 researcher found women

31.1% of grant applications, experienced lower grant success rates and had lower personnel award success. Burns et al. (2019) conclude: Gender disparity existed overall in grant and personnel award success rates especially for grants directed to selected research communities. Funding agencies should monitor gender differences in grant success rates by content and explore possible explanations for gender disparity when identified. Similarly, Hechtman et al. (2018) found that women accounted for 31% of grantees of the National Institutes of Health in the US and that they had similar funding longevity compared to men. So not only are we studying the relationship between the priorities that the PIs establish in their R&D teams and the competitive public funds that they obtain but also the gender effect in this relationship. This also responds to the call to improve gender equality in research fields (Mayer and Rathmann 2018; Burns et al. 2019).

In this study, we have addressed the aforementioned gap in the research by proposing a model which analyses the effects that the priorities established by PI have on the success in obtaining competitive public funds, considering the moderation role of gender. We organize the paper as follows. After this introduction, our literature considerations focus on priorities in the R&D environment and gender differences in submitting and acquiring R&D competitive public funding. Then we develop an exploratory K-means cluster analysis to identify PI profiles in the sample and we also conducted a multiple regression analysis. Then the results are presented. After presenting the conclusion and discussion is developed, some limitations are presented along with further research avenues.

2. Background literature and research hypothesis

2.1. Priorities in the R&D environment

There is a growing pressure on R&D centres to maintain and grow their research activities, income and human capital. However, they face a constant lack of financial funds and intense competition in obtaining funds has increased (Kaló et al. 2019; Clausen, Fagerbergb, and Gulbrandsenb 2012; Nielsen 2016). The capacity and the ability to attract funds to finance their research projects have been highlighted as essential for them to ensure the viability of R&D centres and to foster their future sustainability (Wadman 2009; Cunningham et al. 2014). Obtaining competitive public funds not only rewards the hard work of the research that has been carried out but also provides the resources needed to continue with present and future lines of research (Larivière et al. 2011). The ability to obtain these funds is related to the number of projects submitted, which in turn will have a positive impact on the final amount of funding they will be able to receive (Burns et al. 2019). Furthermore, as more projects are submitted, more expertise is accumulated in the submission process that can benefit future project submissions. In this sense, those who incorporate past reviewers' recommendations in their next project submissions can enhance their proposal writing skills for funding programmes thereby, they can increase their probabilities of obtaining funds (Ebadi and Schiffauerova 2015).

To attain this level of competitiveness required by funders the priorities of R&D centres need to be clearly established, the objectives to be achieved need to be clearly defined (Ocasio 1997). The unique and particular nature of the research environment makes it even more important to have clear objectives and priorities for the R&D teams in order to achieve the desired objectives and maintaining the viability of the R&D centre and associated scientific and support personnel (Stock, Totzauer, and Zacharias 2014; Zhu and Chen 2016). Furthermore, it influences research development favourably (Shepherd, Mcmullen, and Ocasio 2017). Taking the attention-based premise (Ocasio 1997), R&D team's PI will establish the set of priorities depending on the competitive funding environment. In this sense, these priorities are designed to enhance the probability of obtaining competitive funding that meets the funders' expectations and that are aligned to the current and or future industry and market needs. The creation of priorities can depend on such issues as defining the scale and scope of disciplinary focus, the fields of use for the knowledge created along with the industrial sector setting and end customer application. Such clear priorities can then enable the R&D team to scope out and respond in a focused manner to public competitive funding calls. Moreover, having a consistent set of priorities provides clarity of purpose and focus for the R&D team and certainty overtime. It also not alone the PI but also the R&D team to adapt a proactive strategic posture rather than a reactive one that can lead to poorer outcomes (see O'Kane et al. 2015). Priorities also make it easier for R&D centre researchers and PIs and key stakeholders to be clear about the strategic direction and scope of R&D activities. As long as the PI clearly identifies the priorities of the R&D team in order to achieve the established objectives, it contributes to the process obtaining funding in such a competitive environment as the research environment has become (Bazzoli et al. 2000; Cunningham et al. 2015; O'Kane et al. 2015). By doing this, PIs establish R&D teams' priorities over a specified period of time as part of a proactive strategy that is designed to support the probability of obtaining funding. The PI determines those activities that will be undertaken earlier than others, establishing an order, and sending a clear message about the activities on which efforts and resources should be focused (Lin et al. 2005).

There are a sparse number of studies that have focused on the factors that determine which teams obtain funding with respect to others (Ebadi and Schiffauerova 2015). Although none have focused on studying the influence that an internally consistent set of priorities defined by PI has over the funding of R&D team projects. So, knowing the priority of the PI will be crucial to a better understanding on how R&D teams obtain competitive public funds and what makes them different from the others. For that reason, the following hypothesis is proposed:

H1: A more consistent set of priorities defined by PIs, more funds are obtained by competitive public funds.

2.2. Gender differences in submitting and acquiring R&D competitive public funding

Notwithstanding the appearance of similarity in the possibilities for men and women, throughout the literature there is a significant evidence of the difference between them still persists (Burns et al. 2019; Lynn et al. 2019). Even though women representativeness has increased in recent years in science, there are evidences that still deep gender differences remain in a number of spheres as scientific production, career progression, commercialization, number of submission applications and acquiring competitive public funds or successfully maintaining their line of research (see Bordons et al. 2003; Rosa and Dawson 2006; Mayer and Rathmann 2018; Lerchenmueller and Sorenson 2018). All these drawbacks, seriously inhibit the progression of women into more senior positions (Abramo, Cicero, and D'Angelo 2015).

From the existing literature, it has been demonstrated that for a female scientist is tougher to get to a leader position, so they have to break through a lot of barriers (Fox 2005; Howe-Walsh and Turnbull 2016). Fox (1991) asserted that formal network – institutional support – or/and informal network – interaction with colleagues inside and outside their organisation – affect their likelihood of receiving information about funding processes. Even though, recently it has been suggested that gender inequality has been decreasing (Ceci and Williams 2011), differences still persist if we compare scholarly authorships (West et al. 2013). In some research areas, it is even harder, such as science, technology and engineering (West et al. 2013). In some cases, it has been identified as *boys club* in these disciplines (Barnard et al. 2010). Thus, gendered cultural within academia go against women progression in particular within science, technology and engineering seniority positions, for instance, the predominance of men among recruiters, selectors and promoters (Howe-Walsh and Turnbull 2016). This reinforces the notion that there is a need for role models in which women can be identified (Ecklund, Lincoln, and Tansey 2012; Stout et al. 2011).

Previous studies have highlighted lower presence of women in peer-review journals which inhibits them from making the requisite advancement in their scientific career to achieve the necessary prestige (West et al. 2013; Mayer and Rathmann 2018). Moreover, becoming a project PI and managing R&D teams is seen as a prestigious scholarship standing indicator and a milestone achievement in a professional career (Cunningham et al. 2014). There are more male PIs than female PIs, in some cases, this difference reaches 20% (see Bornmann, Mutz, and Hans-Dieter 2007; Lerchenmueller and Sorenson 2018).

There are academic career differences in accessing and developing their academic careers (Ding, Murray, and Stuart 2006; Probert 2005; Leahey, Crockett, and Hunter 2008). Moreover, Cunningham et al. (2017, 239) found that gender differences among PIs: 'with respect to commercial experiences, sources of funding, numbers of projects and career planning' and male PI had secured more international funding than women PIs. Previous studies have also found the level of specialization, the research collaborations and the limitations associated with the pivotal role of women in the family unit as causes of gender difference in scientific productivity and academic career progression (Fox 2005; Leahey 2006; Abramo, D'Angelo, and Murgia 2013). Witteman et al. (2019) suggested three main ideas to explain the reasons why women are poorly evaluated than men when they submit for competitive public funds: reviewers' subjective evaluations, the unfairly evaluations favouring male PIs and less compellingly applications.

Despite these gender differences and inhibitors found in previous studies, the success rate of women and men acquiring funds is similar, although men submitted much more applications than women (Van den Besselaar and Sandström 2017). Nevertheless, there are no studies that have investigated the moderating effect of gender on the impact of the R&D teams' PI priorities in obtaining competitive public funding. Being able to obtain competitive public funds is one of the requirements academic career progession (West et al. 2013). Therefore, women who want to develop a career and aspire to be promoted to senior positions must demonstrate their ability doing it (Howe-Walsh and Turnbull 2016). Even though, in literature there is a majority of researchers who posit that there are disadvantages for women (Head et al. 2013; Witteman et al. 2019), some other researchers state that women in PI roles achieve similar results. In this case, the difference is in number of competitive public funding submissions (Van den Besselaar and Sandström 2017; Sotudeh and Khoshian 2014; Ceci et al. 2014). In this study, we address Burns' call (2019) to find an explanation for the gender gap in the acquisition of competitive public funds, examining the moderating effect of gender on the relationship between the R&D team's PI priorities and the funds obtained. So, we propose the following hypothesis:

H2: The PI gender moderates the effect of the PI's priorities on the amount of competitive public funds that the R&D team of the PI obtains.

3. Methodology

3.1. Background, data and sample

The study was conducted in R&D teams of Spanish R&D public centres which research is focused in the areas of Biomedicine and Health. In the Spanish context, during the process of submitting funding applications, R&D teams can rely on Research Management Office. Actually, one of the most common functions of Research Management Offices is to support R&D teams in the process of searching for funding sources. Furthermore, they offer advice on the verification of funding applications. In addition, not only do they provide support in the process of submitting applications to the relevant funding agencies, but also in the reception and acceptance processes. Therefore, even though they review the formal aspects of the submitting applications, they do not review the quality of the proposal (Red OTRI de universidades). Furthermore, in Spain, the directors of the research centres, where the R&D teams are, do not review the quality of the proposal either. One reason for this is because in many cases they are not experts in all fields, and another is that in many cases they are designated by political rather than scientific criteria. Nevertheless, there are many authors that disagree with the benefits proclaimed by Research Management Offices, and define them in some cases as hampers in these processes, in which they should be facilitators (Siegel et al. 2007; Grimaldi et al. 2011; Belitski, Aginskaja, and Marozau 2019).

Several secondary sources of information were considered to identify the population. Our study was limited to those R&D teams who had applied for competitive funding projects from national or international programmes from 2011 to 2016. In this period of time, there were not any kind of dedicated equality support for female scientists in the PI role, in the Spanish context – national or regional level – (European Regional Development Fund 2017). The resulted list of R&D public centres was consulted to a panel of experts from the ISCIII European Office and the European Office of the Spanish Ministry of Economy, Industry and Competitiveness through the Secretary of State for Research, Development and Innovation to evaluate its suitability and relevance. They agree with the final list, and they also recommended to include some other important R&D centres and associated PIs to the population list. Therefore, the population is comprised of 68 Spanish R&D public centres. We sent e-mails to the whole population. In fact, emails were sent to every single director of the 68 R&D public centres. In the email, we explained in detail the procedure we planned for collecting the data and requested her/him to inform each of the R&D teams' PIs that existed in her/his centre that we would be contacting them. Finally, we received answered questionnaires from a total of 47 R&D public centres (69.11%). In these R&D public centres are 128 R&D team's PIs. We received a valid answered questionnaire from a total of 97 R&D team's PIs (75.78%), where 23.71% are women. Therefore, the final sample is comprised of 97 R&D team's PIs which research is focused in Biomedicine and Health areas.

Previous to sending the questionnaire, a pre-test analysis was developed. A draft questionnaire was sent to a group of experts in the fields of Biomedicine and Health and Management Research. This allowed us to review some typo and rewrite some information on the presentation of the questionnaire. Then the questionnaire was sent to the target population through the SocialSci platform to be answered directly through its online platform. A total of 128 answered questionnaires of the R&D teams' PIs were received. The questionnaire included some demographic questions both of PI such as gender, experience (years in PI position) and of the R&D team like size. Experience of the PI, which was measured by the number of years in an R&D team's PI position; and the size of the R&D team, which was measured by the number of members who comprise the R&D team, were utilized as control variables. Also, a 17-items scale of five-point Likert scale by Clausen, Fagerbergb, and Gulbrandsenb (2012) was included asking in order to identified R&D team's PI priorities (Table 1). The dependent variable in this study is national competitive public fund which is measured by the amount of public competitive funds that the R&D teams of the PIs obtained from national calls.

3.2. Method 1: cluster analysis

For our analysis, a K-means cluster analysis was developed to identify the different PI profiles. Previously, a hierarchical cluster analysis was carried (Ketchen and Shook 1996) to determine the number of profiles depending on the sample. Based on the resulting dendrogram, two profiles were the most accurate number of profiles for this sample. After developing a K-means cluster analysis, two different profiles of PIs were identified with 41 and 56 cases each that were based on the priorities that the PIs chose. ANOVA indicated that all items were significant for clustering except one 'to get higher long-term financing associated to projects' (Table 2).

3.3. Method 2: multiple regression analysis

A new variable was defined to capture belonging of respondents to a profile 1 – *Supporting and Empowering R&D Focused PIs* or 2 – *Prioritized R&D Team Focused PI*, which we termed based on our analysis. Multiple regression analysis was utilized to check the hypotheses. Three models were estimated. Model 1 only contains the effect of the control variables (experience of the PI and size of the team) on the national competitive public funds acquired. In the Model 2 and Model 3, the

Table 1. Priorities of the R&D teams' PIs.

To get higher long-term financing associated to projects
To get more basal funds not coming from national or international projects
To increase the number of international scientific publications
To attract good researchers
To improve the international collaborations
To develop a better scientific program
To get more support from the CEO and TMT
To improve the scientific leadership of the R&D area
To achieve better support from the policy makers institutions
To improve the researchers' employment opportunities
To increase collaborations with industry
To develop education & training programmes
To get practical and applicable results from the developed research projects
To get more support from other R&D areas
To improve the research culture of the area and the centre
To increase the support from other local or regional R&D areas
To face communication or collaboration internal problems

Source: Clausen, Fagerbergb, and Gulbrandsenb (2012).

two hypotheses were tested. In Table 3 are represented the descriptive statistics – minimum and maximum values, means and standard deviations – and the correlation matrix of variables of the proposed model. Multiple regression analysis runs fine when independent variables have weak correlations, as is the case in this study, where the variance inflation factor of all independent variables are close to 1. Therefore, it does not exist a problem of multicollinearity (Stock and Watson 2015; Greene 2000). Having applied the Welch and Brown-Forsythe test, it is confirmed that there is a relationship between all the variables in the model, even though the standard errors are robust for heteroscedasticity (Vallejo y Ato 2012).

4. Analysis

Supporting and Empowering R&D Team Focused PIs is comprised of 41 R&D team's PIs. Just 7 out of 41 are women, thus 17% of this profile are female PIs. They are those PIs that have ranked each of the priorities with the lowest average scores of the sample. This group represents a profile of PIs who are aware of supporting and empowering the R&D team, but it is not such a priority. They demonstrate a

Table 2. Cluster analysis.

	ANOVA	
Grouping variables	*F*	Sig.
To get higher long-term financing associated to projects	3901	0.051
To increase the number of international scientific publications	14,018	0.000
To attract good researchers	21,134	0.000
To improve the international collaborations	11,612	0.001
To get more basal funds not coming from national or international projects	44,49	0.000
To develop a better scientific programme	53,411	0.000
To get more support from the CEO and TMT	29,392	0.000
To improve the scientific leadership of the R&D area	23,307	0.000
To achieve better support from the policy makers institutions	27,742	0.000
To improve the researcher's employment opportunities	22,838	0.000
To increase collaborations with industry	24,625	0.000
To develop education & training programmes	36,252	0.000
To get practical and applicable results from the developed research projects	52,159	0.000
To get more support from other R&D areas	44,649	0.000
To improve the research culture of the area and the centre	40,287	0.000
To increase the support from other local or regional R&D areas	49,629	0.000
To face communication or collaboration internal problems	26,529	0.000

Table 3. Descriptive statistics and correlation matrix.

	Variable	Min	Max	Mean	SD	1	2	3	4	5
1	National Competitive Public Funds (dependent variable)	0	4	2.180	1.211	1				
2	Experience of the PI (control variable)	1	3	1.990	0.777	0.028	1			
3	Size of the Team (control variable)	0.69	5.71	2.689	1.269	0.644**	0.163	1		
4	Profiles	1	2	1.58	0.497	0.284*	−0.205	0.074	1	
5	Gender of the PI	0	1	0.75	0.434	−0.08	−0.034	0.12	0.015	1

**Correlation is significant at the 0.01 level; *Correlation is significant at the 0.05 level.

moderated intensity in priorities towards achieving competitive public funds. For them attracting good researchers and retaining them by improving employment opportunities are the two most valued priorities, but not as high as in prioritized R&D team focused PI profile. As in prioritized R&D team focused PI profile, the group ranked 6 priorities the same, although in a different order and with a difference of one point between the averages of the scores (Table 4). Therefore, we have considered that the PIs comprising this group are aware that they should support and enhance the R&D team, but not what they focus on most.

Prioritized R&D Team Focused PI profile is comprised of 56 R&D team's PIs. About 17 out of 56 are women, thus 30% of this profile are female PIs, almost the double than profile 1. PIs within this group present a profile that demonstrates an intense focus in supporting and empowering the R&D team. They are those PIs that have valued each of the priorities with the highest average scores of the sample. These PIs demonstrate a higher intensity in priorities towards achieving competitive public funds. In this case, the set priorities with the highest average score are also those oriented to strengthening the resources of the R&D team, but with a higher average of the scores. For instance, the two most valued priorities are focused on supporting and fostering the R&D team's human resources. The first of them refers to attracting good researchers and the other to retaining them, both of which are basic principles in HR policies (Nyberg et al. 2018).

Table 4. Cluster supporting and empowering R&D team focused PIs and prioritized R&D team focused PIs.

Grouping variables	Supporting and empowering R&D team focused PIs (Means)	Prioritized R&D team focused PIs (Means)
To get higher long-term financing associated to projects	4.71	4.89
To increase the number of international scientific publications	3.66	4.37
To attract good researchers	3.63	4.59
To improve the international collaborations	4.1	4.7
To get more basal funds not coming from national or international projects	3.56	4.62
To develop a better scientific programme	3.37	4.61
To get more support from the CEO and TMT	2.73	3.95
To improve the scientific leadership of the R&D area	3.05	4.09
To achieve better support from the policy makers institutions	3	4.11
To improve the researcher's employment opportunities	3.95	4.71
To increase collaborations with industry	3.24	4.18
To develop education & training programmes	2.56	3.73
To get practical and applicable results from the developed research projects	3.41	4.61
To get more support from other R&D areas	2.71	3.95
To improve the research culture of the area and the centre	2.63	3.84
To increase the support from other local or regional R&D areas	2.51	3.84
To face communication or collaboration internal problems	2.17	3.38

From the following six most valued priorities, five are variables that are highly valued in the assessment processes to achieve competitive public funding. These are scientific production variables such as number of publications and applicability of research project results. Moreover, improving international collaborations and collaborations with industry are key to obtain public competitive funds (Beaudry and Allaoui 2012; Ebadi and Schiffauerova 2015). In addition, another variable is to develop a better scientific programme, which indirectly has a positive effect on the quality and consistence of the submissions.

As Table 5 depicts, hypothesis 1 is supported, but it is not the same with hypothesis 2. Contrary to expected H2, the PI gender does not moderate the effect of the PI's priorities on the amount of competitive public funds that the R&D team of the PI obtains. The estimation of the third model was not significant. This result is contrary to the extended idea that there is a gender difference in acquiring competitive public funds (Mayer and Rathmann 2018; Lynn et al. 2019).

5. Discussion

In the career of PIs, acquiring competitive public funding has become an essential feature (Kaló et al. 2019; Larivière et al. 2011). Because obtaining funding is crucial in the promotion process to higher career positions of the scientists in the PI role. Previous empirical studies found gender differences persists in acquiring competitive public funds (Mayer and Rathmann 2018; Lerchenmueller and Sorenson 2018), hence our study was to analyse gender differences in the process of obtaining funds. Therefore, it is important to understand the factors that influence on the amount of funds that PIs of the R&D teams acquire, as well as knowing the moderating effect of gender on this relationship (Ebadi and Schiffauerova 2015).

There are few studies in the literature so far which have focused on the factors that can demonstrate the acquisition of competitive public funds (see Kaló et al. 2019; Ebadi and Schiffauerova 2015; Galsworthy and McKee 2013). This study proposes a new factor that explains it based on the attention-based theory (Li et al. 2010). From an exploratory cluster analysis, two different profiles of R&D teams' PIs establishing priorities of their teams were defined. This identification of the different profiles of the PIs contributes to clarify the influence that priority setting has on the amount of competitive public funding, which is crucial in the career progress of the PIs and on the survival of the R&D team (Wadman 2009; West et al. 2013).

We approached this theme by studying the relationship between the priorities of R&D teams' PIs and the amount of competitive public funding obtained by those PIs, in a sample of R&D teams in the fields of Biomedicine and Health Sciences from Spanish R&D public centres. Results have revealed that those R&D teams' PIs who, through the establishment of their priorities, have an intense focus on supporting and empowering the R&D team will obtain a greater amount of national competitive public funds. However, as the priorities of the R&D teams' PIs become less focused on supporting and empowering the R&D team, the number of national competitive public funds will decrease. Therefore, hypothesis 1 is supported (Table 5). From the cluster analysis, we can conclude that the profile in which there is the highest female representation – actually the prioritized R&D

Table 5. Results of multiple regression analysis.

Variables	Model 1		Model 2		Model 3	
Constant		(0.37)		(0.543)		(0.536)
Experience of the PI (control variable)	−0.079	(0.158)	−0.028	(0.156)	−0.048	(0.155)
Size of the team (control variable)	0.657***	(0.091)	0.631***	(0.088)	0.651***	(0.088)
Profiles			0.232*	(0.23)	0.313*	(0.256)
Profiles × Gender of the PI					−0.175	(0.158)
R^2	0.421		0.472		0.494	
Durbin-Watson					2.203	
Overall F	24,342***		19,645***		15,872***	

$N = 70$. Standardized regression coefficients are report, standard errors are in parentheses. $^*p < 0.05$, $^{**}p < 0.01$, $^{***}p < 0.001$.

team focused PI profile it is almost double that of supporting and empowering R&D team focused PI, 30% versus 17%, respectively – is the one where exists an intensity of priorities more ambitious and determinate to improve R&D teams' opportunities of achieving more competitive public funds. Therefore, prioritized R&D team focused PI profile is more successful in obtaining funding in national calls.

Moreover, it is interesting to reflect on the difference between the experience average of the profiles and its average of the sample. In prioritized R&D team focused PI profile, the average number of years in the same position is lower than the sample average. Surprisingly, something that may seem negative at first and according to Ebadi and Schiffauerova (2015), in this case, we observe that it is not. This may be the result of a new vision of how an R&D team should be managed, renewed strength or the enthusiasm for reaching a needed objective in their career progress (Robson, Schlegelmilch, and Bojkowszky 2012). This is the opposite for supporting and empowering R&D team focused PIs where the average experience is higher than the sample average. It might be because this profile is mainly comprised of PIs who have already reached the desired career level and they are in their later stages of their careers, so their ambitions have been already fulfilled (Robson, Schlegelmilch, and Bojkowszky 2012). Therefore, their efforts in the acquiring competitive public funds are decreasing and focusing on other types of priorities. The variable measuring the size of the R&D teams are significant and positively related to competitive public funds acquire. This result can be explained by the fact that with more people on the team, there is a higher probability of submissions for national public competitive funds, and their subsequent obtainment (Burns et al. 2019).

Even though, the representation of women in higher education in the last few years has increased (Mayer and Rathmann 2018) and the number of female and male scientists is almost similar (Spanish Universities Rectors Conference 2017). In our sample, female PIs are underrepresented in comparison to male colleagues so, there is a structural underrepresentation of female PIs. This is not uncommon and similar to what Cunningham et al. (2020) of their large-scale study of PIs that successfully secured EC structural funding. Unfortunately, this ratio is more common than it should be (Howe-Walsh and Turnbull 2016; Lerchenmueller and Sorenson 2018).

Nevertheless, the study does not demonstrate the moderate effect of gender differences in the relationship of the model proposed (Figure 1), in our sample, most female PIs are committed to establish an intense focus of priorities oriented towards improving the R&D team to enhance their chances of obtaining more competitive public funds. That profile is more efficient than the first one. These results lead us to assume that although hypothesis 2 has not been supported, it is necessary for a further understanding of gender differences.

6. Conclusions and implications

Based on the results, we can conclude that the priorities established by PIs in their R&D teams have a positive influence on the acquisition of competitive public funding and that the PI profile that is most efficient in achieving these objectives – prioritized R&D team focused PI profile is where there is a

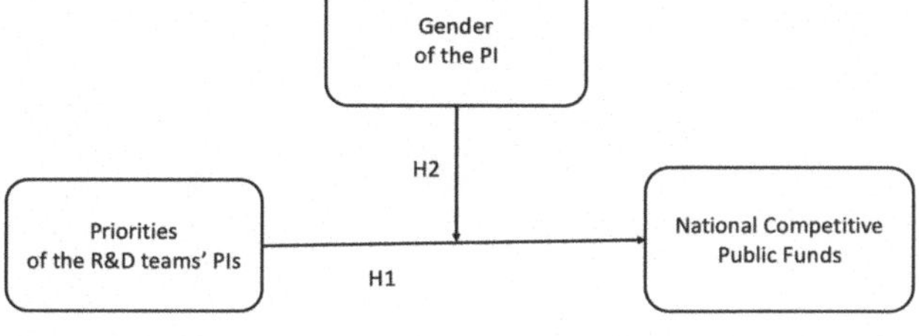

Figure 1. Model proposed.

greater female presence (see Figure 2). Furthermore, we can also conclude that gender does not have a moderating effect on the relationship priorities of the R&D teams' PIs and the amount of public competitive funds that the R&D teams of the PIs obtained from national calls. Even though there is not a gender moderating effect in the relationship between PI's priorities and the amount of competitive public funds that the R&D team of the PI obtains, one may conclude that although in absolute numbers men are able to submit more applications for national public funding, women obtain the same success percentage when submitting in relative terms. Thus, when they reach the position of PI of an R&D team, they are as successful as men can be. One might even say that they are more efficient, because although they present fewer applications and accumulate less experience in these processes, they are still able to achieve the same success rate (Van den Besselaar and Sandström 2017).

Therefore, it might not be so much a question of the quality of the application submitted, but a question of the capacity to lead teams able to submit a higher number of proposals and about the knowledge of these competitive public funding applications, and the composition of their network and relevant sources of information (Whittington and Smith-Doerr 2005; Lutter 2015; Woehler et al. 2020). This might be explained on the basis that the quality of the projects submitted may not differ in terms of gender, but there are still some obstacles in the race to reach PI positions for women

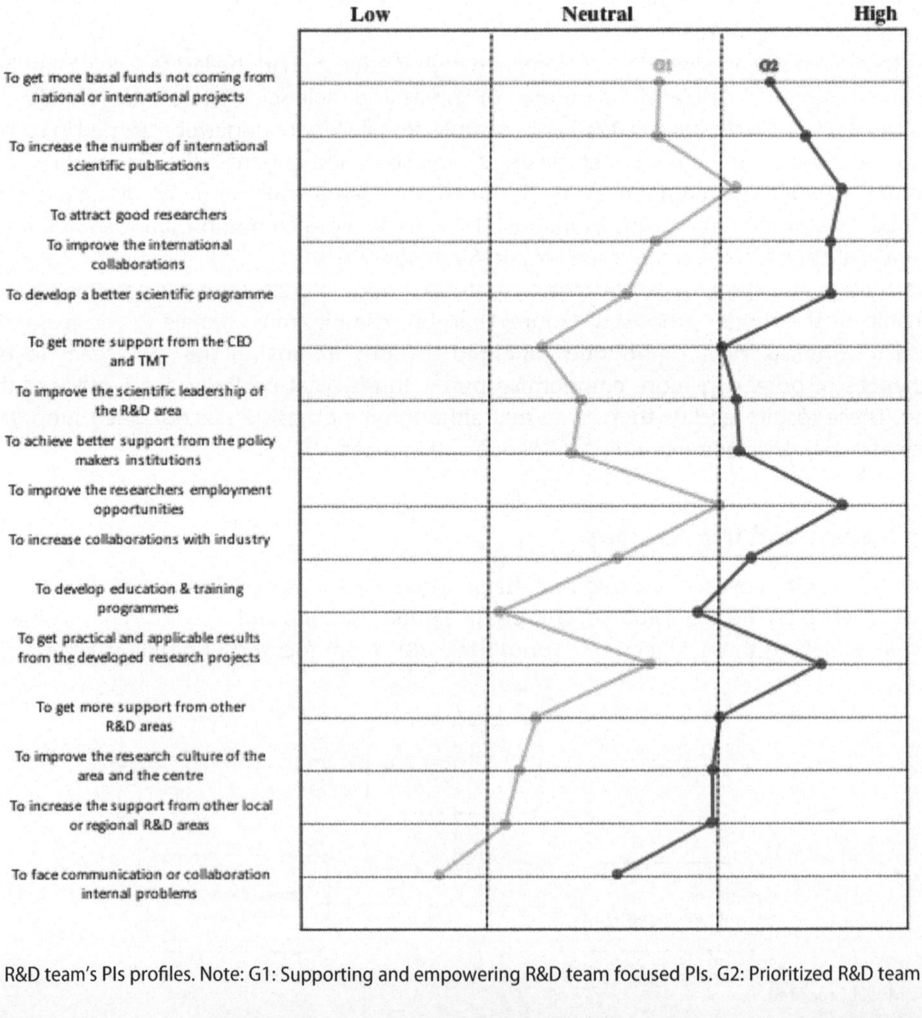

Figure 2. R&D team's PIs profiles. Note: G1: Supporting and empowering R&D team focused PIs. G2: Prioritized R&D team focused PIs

(Grimaldi et al. 2011; Belitski, Aginskaja, and Marozau 2019). In this sense, women are at a disadvantage compared to men, which slows them down and often even prevents them from reaching for higher career positions, such as PI roles (Lutter 2015). Moreover, since many decision panels and managerial levels have a higher percentage of men than women, it does not benefit their progression in the academic career (Lutter 2015; Howe-Walsh and Turnbull 2016). Nevertheless, it remains interesting that there is an underrepresentation of females in PI roles, while the percentages of men and women among researchers are much more balanced, especially in certain knowledge areas such as health research.

Our research is not without limitations given the narrow scope of this study. One of the limitations is related to the self-reporting bias with both of the variables involved in the proposed model: priorities of the R&D teams' PIs and the amount of public competitive funds that the R&D teams of the PIs obtained from national calls. However, in all cases, we asked, in a complementary survey to the Research Management Office representatives, about the number of total projects submitted and achieved by each research centre, and the data are consistent with the numbers and percentages of success reported by the PIs. In any case, future studies might ask to the co-PIs or the director of the R&D department to assess the former variable and might ask for corroboration of the latter variable, such as a confirmation of the amount of public competitive funds that the R&D teams of the PIs obtained from national calls. Another limitation is related to the size of the studied population. Even though the Spanish R&D public centres of the fields of Biomedicine and Health Sciences were chosen because research in this area is frequently considered to demonstrate how knowledge is produced and often leads to important results in research policy, the population is not as large as would be desirable. An additional limitation is the contextual and constraints characteristics of the Spanish public research system. Defining our dependent variable as the amount of public competitive funds that the R&D teams of the PIs obtained from national calls is another limitation, because we are limiting the effect of the priorities of the R&D teams' PIs to that specific competitive public funding. However, all public research centres in Spain pay a lot of attention to the national research program, and all of them apply regularly to these funding calls, and consequently we think that this measure may be a good indicator of the proactivity and efficiency of research teams in terms of getting funds for research.

Since the difference between the two profiles was the intensity in which PIs determined each of the different priorities, it offers the possibility of broaden the investigation of the factors that influence the acquisition of competitive public funds from a gender perspective. Therefore, a possible future research can be based on the self-determination theory, since the contextual characteristics and individual differences of each of the PIs from a gender perspective and their motivations can be factors that influence to increase the competitive public funding obtained (Dewett 2007; Harris 2019). Future research should be focused on widening the range of financing instruments as well as including international competitive public funding calls. It could be interesting to study the influence on the acquisition of competitive public funds of the relational capital of the PIs within their R&D team members, with R&D team's members of other areas and also with the research management office's members and manager who manage their funds submission. Does gender influence matter? Studying the direct effect of gender of the R&D team's PI on the amount of public competitive funds that the R&D teams obtained is an interesting future research line (Stock and Watson 2015).

Another limitation might be that gender may include internal elements that may overlap the actual effect. It would have to be considered whether or not, on a contingent basis, there is gender discrimination, and therefore whether or not the same results are obtained. In our research, we have not asked for contingent circumstances of the PI – for example, cultural circumstances, family circumstances, surrounding circumstances –, in order to compare whether these issues explain the differences in funding results instead of the gender itself. However, differences in the roles assumed by men and women in all occidental societies are still different and these aspects have been frequently documented as factors that hinder the possibilities for women to develop a more successful professional career in comparison with men (Ely, Stone, and Ammerman 2014). Hence, a future line of research could be to undertake a more in-depth study on the contextual differences between genders, which would capture that information and allow for a broader analysis.

Finally, our study raises an important issue for policy makers in relation to the under-representation of women PIs being in a position to compete for and ultimately secure public funding for large-scale research programmes. New support and funding instruments, different career and funding evaluation criteria and other appropriate equality and diversity measures need to be considered by policy makers in the design of public research programmes. Our study clearly demonstrates that there is not a moderating effect of gender in the relationship between priorities of the R&D teams' PIs and the amount of public competitive funds that the R&D teams of the PIs obtained from national calls and since women PIs are in position to acquire public competitive funding they can be as successful as male PIs, which is contrary to what Mayer and Rathmann (2018) and Lerchenmueller and Sorenson (2018) found in their studies. However, the ongoing challenges are a systemic one that requires proactive measures and policies to deal effectively with women under representation and to ensure as Link (2017, 2) succinctly notes so to: 'ensure opportunities for underrepresented minorities and women in the entrepreneurial ecosystem'.

Acknowledgements

The authors appear in alphabetical order and have contributed equally to this work. This study has benefited from financing from Research Project ECO2014-56580-R and ECO2016-80002-R of the Spanish Ministry of Economy and Competitiveness. The authors wish to thank Professor Albert N. Link and aynomomous reviewers for their constructive feedback.

Disclosure statement

No potential conflict of interest was reported by the authors.

Funding

This study has benefited from financing from Research Project ECO2014-56580-R and ECO2016-80002-R of the Spanish Ministry of Economy and Competitiveness.

References

Abramo, Giovanni, Tindaro Cicero, and Ciriaco Andrea D'Angelo. 2015. "Should the Research Performance of Scientists be Distinguished by Gender?" *Journal of Informetrics* 9 (1): 25–38. doi:10.1016/j.joi.2014.11.002.

Abramo, G., C. A. D'Angelo, and G. Murgia. 2013. "Gender Differences in Research Collaboration." *Journal of Informetrics* 7 (4): 811–822. doi:10.1016/j.joi.2013.07.002.

Barnard, S., A. Powell, B. Bagilhole, and A. Dainty. 2010. "Researching UK Women Professionals in SET: A Critical Review of Current Approaches." *International Journal of Gender, Science and Technology* 2 (3): 362–381.

Barnett, M. L. 2008. "An Attention-Based View of Real Options Reasoning." *Academy of Management Review* 33 (3): 606–628. doi:10.5465/amr.2008.32465698.

Barreto, I., and D. L. Patient. 2013. "Toward a Theory of Intraorganizational Attention Based on Desirability and Feasibility Factors." *Strategic Management Journal* 34 (6): 687–703. doi:10.1002/smj.2029.

Bazeley, P. 1998. "Peer Review and Panel Decisions in the Assessment of Australian Research Council Projects Grant Applications: What Counts in a Highly Competitive Context?" *Higher Education* 35 (4): 435–452. doi:10.1023/A:1003118502318.

Bazzoli, G. J., B. Chan, S. M. Shortell, and T. D'Aunno. 2000. "The Financial Performance of Hospitals Belonging to Health Networks and Systems." *Inquiry* 37 (3): 234–252.

Beaudry, C., and S. Allaoui. 2012. "Impact of Public and Private Research Funding on Scientific Production: The Case of Nanotechnology." *Research Policy* 41 (9): 1589–1606. doi:10.1016/j.respol.2012.03.022.

Beaudry, C., and V. Larivière. 2016. "Which Gender Gap? Factors Affecting Researchers' Scientific Impact in Science and Medicine." *Research Policy* 45 (9): 1790–1817. doi:10.1016/j.respol.2016.05.009.

Belitski, M., A. Aginskaja, and R. Marozau. 2019. "Commercializing University Research in Transition Economies: Technology Transfer Offices or Direct Industrial Funding?" *Research Policy* 48 (3): 601–615.

Boardman, C., and B. Ponomariov. 2014. "Management Knowledge and the Organization of Team Science in University Research Centers." *The Journal of Technology Transfer* 39 (1): 75–92. doi:10.1007/s10961-012-9271-x.

Bordons, M., F. Morillo, M. T. Fernández, and I. Gómez. 2003. "One Step Further in the Production of Bibliometric Indicators at the Micro Level: Differences by Gender and Professional Category of Scientists." *Scientometrics* 57 (2): 159–173.

Bornmann, Lutz, Rüdiger Mutz, and D. Hans-Dieter. 2007. "Gender Differences in Grant Peer Review: A Meta-Analysis." *Journal of Informetrics* 1 (3): 226–238. doi:10.1016/j.joi.2007.03.001.

Burns, K. E., S. E. Straus, K. Liu, L. Rizvi, and G. Guyatt. 2019. "Gender Differences in Grant and Personnel Award Funding Rates at the Canadian Institutes of Health Research Based on Research Content Area: A Retrospective Analysis." *PLoS Medicine* 16 (10): e1002935. doi:10.1371/journal.pmed.1002935.

Ceci, S. J., D. K. Ginther, S. Kahn, and W. M. Williams. 2014. "Women in Academic Science: Explaining the Gap." *Psychological Science in the Public Interest* 15 (3): 75–141. doi:10.1177/1529100614541236.

Ceci, S. J., and W. M. Williams. 2011. "Understanding Current Causes of Women's Underrepresentation in Science." *Proceedings of the National Academy of Sciences* 108 (8): 3157–3162.

Cho, T. S., and D. C. Hambrick. 2006. "Attention as the Mediator Between Top Management Team Characteristics and Strategic Change: The Case of Airline Deregulation." *Organization Science* 17 (4): 453–469. doi:10.1287/orsc.1060.0192.

CICE. 2006. *Plan andaluz de investigación, desarrollo e innovación tecnológica*. Sevilla: Servicio de Publicaciones, Consejería de Innovación, Ciencia y Empresa.

Clausen, T., J. Fagerbergb, and M. Gulbrandsenb. 2012. "Mobilizing for Change: A Study of Research Units in Emerging Scientific Fields." *Research Policy* 41 (7): 1249–1261. doi:10.1016/j.respol.2012.03.014.

Cummings, J. N., and S. Kiesler. 2005. "Collaborative Research Across Disciplinary and Organizational Boundaries." *Social Studies of Science* 35 (5): 703–722. doi:10.1177/0306312705055535.

Cunningham, J. A. 2019. "Principal Investigators and Boundary Spanning Entrepreneurial Opportunity Recognition: A Conceptual Framework." In *A Research Agenda for Entrepreneurship and Innovation*, edited by David B. Audretsch, Erik E. Lehmann, and Albert N. Link, 55–73. Edward Elgar Publishing.

Cunningham, J. A., D. Hooper, D. Nepelski, and V. Van Roy. 2020. *The Role of Project Coordinators in European Commission Framework Programme Projects. Results of the Innovation Radar PC Survey in FP R&I Projects* (No. JRC120015). Joint Research Centre (Seville site).

Cunningham, J. A., M. Menter, and C. O'Kane. 2018. "Value Creation in the Quadruple Helix: A Micro Level Conceptual Model of Principal Investigators as Value Creators." *R&D Management* 48 (1): 136–147.

Cunningham, James A., P. O'Reilly, B. Dolan, C. O'Kane, and V. Mangematin. 2016. "Publicly Funded Principal Investigators Allocation of Time for Public Sector Entrepreneurship Activities." *Economia e Politica Industriale* 43 (4): 383–408. doi:10.1007/s40812-016-0054-5.

Cunningham, J. A., P. O'Reilly, B. Dolan, C. O'Kane, and V. Mangematin. 2017. "Gender Differences and Academic Entrepreneurship: A Study of Scientists in the Principal Investigator Role." In *Gender and Entrepreneurial Activity*, edited by Albert N. Link, 221–251. Edward Elgar Publishing.

Cunningham, J. A., P. O'Reilly, C. O'Kane, and V. Mangematin. 2014. "The Inhibiting Factors That Principal Investigators Experience in Leading Publicly Funded Research." *The Journal of Technology Transfer* 39 (1): 93–110. doi:10.1007/s10961-012-9269-4.

Cunningham, J. A., P. O'Reilly, C. O'Kane, and V. Mangematin. 2015. "Managerial Challenges of Publicly Funded Principal Investigators." *International Journal of Technology Management* 68 (3-4): 176–201.

Dewett, T. 2007. "Linking Intrinsic Motivation, Risk Taking, and Employee Creativity in an R&D Environment." *R&D Management* 37 (3): 197–208. doi:10.1111/j.1467-9310.2007.00469.x.

Ding, W. W., F. Murray, and T. E. Stuart. 2006. "Gender Differences in Patenting in the Academic Life Sciences." *Science* 313 (5787): 665–667.

Ebadi, A., and A. Schiffauerova. 2015. "How to Receive More Funding for Your Research? Get Connected to the Right People!." *PLoS One* 10 (7): e0133061. doi:10.1371/journal.pone.0133061.

Ecklund, E. H., A. E. Lincoln, and C. Tansey. 2012. "Gender Segregation in Elite Academic Science." *Gender & Society* 26 (5): 693–717.

Ely, Robin J., Pamela Stone, and Colleen Ammerman. 2014. "Rethink What You 'Know' About High-Achieving Women." *Harvard Business Review* 92 (12): 100–109.

European Regional Development Funds (2011-2016). 2017. Accessed 21 September 2020. http://www.fondos.ciencia.gob.es/portal/site/fondos/menuitem.8a9882a3d308c892c5bcb410026041a0/?vgnextoid=b460bc05f418b510VgnVCM1000001d04140aRCRD&vgnextchannel=c58b4e15e97e1610VgnVCM1000002006140aRCRD&vgnextfmt=formato2&id3=f060bc05f418b510VgnVCM1000001d04140a____&lang_choosen=en.

Fang, F. C., and A. Casadevall. 2015. "Competitive Science: is Competition Ruining Science?" *Infection and Immunity* 83 (4): 1229–1233. doi:10.1128/IAI.02939-14.

Fox, M. F. 1991. "Gender, Environmental Milieu, and Productivity in Science." In *The Outer Circle: Women in the Scientific Community*, edited by H. E. Zuckerman, J. R. Cole, and J. T. Bruer, 188–204. New York: WW Norton & Co.

Fox, M. F. 2005. "Gender, Family Characteristics, and Publication Productivity Among Scientists." *Social Studies of Science* 35 (1): 131–150. doi:10.1177/0306312705046630.

Galsworthy, M., and M. McKee. 2013. "Europe's 'Horizon 2020' Science Funding Programme: How is it Shaping Up?" *Journal of Health Services Research & Policy* 18 (3): 182–185. doi:10.1177/1355819613476017.

Gómez-García, T., T. Moreno-Casbas, E. González-María, and C. Fuentelsaz-Gallego. 2014. "Relationship Between Disease Burden and Research Funding Through the Health Research Foundation in Spain." *Enfermería Clínica* 24 (4): 219–232. doi:10.1016/j.enfcli.2014.04.001.

Greene, W. H. 2000. *Econometric Analysis*. Upper Saddle, NJ: Prentice Hall.

Grimaldi, R., M. Kenney, D. S. Siegel, and M. Wright. 2011. "30 Years After Bayh–Dole: Reassessing Academic Entrepreneurship." *Research Policy* 40 (8): 1045–1057.

Grimpe, C. 2012. "Extramural Research Grants and Scientists' Funding Strategies: Beggars Cannot be Choosers?" *Research Policy* 41 (8): 1448–1460. doi:10.1016/j.respol.2012.03.004.

Harris, A. 2019. *Psychoanalytic Perspectives on Women and Their Experience of Desire, Ambition and Leadership*, edited by Stephanie R. Brody and Frances Arnold, Vol. 35. Routledge.

Head, M. G., J. R. Fitchett, M. K. Cooke, F. B. Wurie, and R. Atun. 2013. "Differences in Research Funding for Women Scientists: A Systematic Comparison of UK Investments in Global Infectious Disease Research During 1997–2010." *BMJ Open* 3 (12): 1–10. doi:10.1136/bmjopen-2013- 003362.

Hechtman, L. A., N. P. Moore, C. E. Schulkey, A. C. Miklos, A. M. Calcagno, R. Aragon, and J. H. Greenberg. 2018. "NIH Funding Longevity by Gender." *Proceedings of the National Academy of Sciences* 115 (31): 7943–7948. doi:10.1073/pnas.1800615115.

Howe-Walsh, Liza, and Sarah Turnbull. 2016. "Barriers to Women Leaders in Academia: Tales from Science and Technology." *Studies in Higher Education* 41 (3): 415–428. doi:10.1080/03075079.2014.929102.

Kaló, Z., L. H. M. van den Akker, Z. Vokó, M. Csanádi, and J. G. Pitter. 2019. "Is There a Fair Allocation of Healthcare Research Funds by the European Union?" *PLoS ONE* 14 (4): 1–13. doi:10.1371/journal.pone.0207046.

Ketchen, D. J., and C. L. Shook. 1996. "The Application of Cluster Analysis in Strategic Management Research: An Analysis and Critique." *Strategic Management Journal* 17: 441–458. doi:10.1002/(SICI)1097-0266(199606)17:6 < 441::AID-SMJ819 > 3.0.CO;2-G.

Larivière, V., E. Vignola-Gagné, C. Villeneuve, P. Gélinas, and Y. Gingras. 2011. "Sex Differences in Research Funding, Productivity and Impact: An Analysis of Québec University Professors." *Scientometrics* 87 (3): 483–498. doi:10.1007/s11192-011-0369-y.

Leahey, E. 2006. "Gender Differences in Productivity: Research Specialization as a Missing Link." *Gender and Society* 20 (6): 754–780. doi:10.1177/0891243206293030.

Leahey, E., J. L. Crockett, and L. A. Hunter. 2008. "Gendered Academic Careers: Specializing for Success?" *Social Forces* 86 (3): 1273–1309.

Lee, M., and K. Om. 1996. "Different Factors Considered in Project Selection at Public and Private R&D Institutes." *Technovation* 16 (6): 271–275.

Lerchenmueller, M. J., and O. Sorenson. 2018. "The Gender Gap in Early Career Transitions in the Life Sciences." *Research Policy* 47 (6): 1007–1017. doi:10.1016/j.respol.2018.02.009.

Leyden, D. P., and A. N. Link. 2015. *Public Sector Entrepreneurship: US Technology and Innovation Policy*. Oxford University Press, USA.

Li, Q., P. G. Maggitti, K. G. Smith, P. E. Tesluk, and R. Katila. 2010. "Top Management Attention to Innovation: The Role of Search Selection and Intensity in New Product." *Academy of Management Journal* 56 (3): 893–916. doi:10.5465/amj.2010.0844.

Lin, Z., H. B. Yang, B. Arya, Z. Huang, and D. Li. 2005. "Structural Versus Individual Perspectives on the Dynamics of Group Performance: Theoretical Exploration and Empirical Investigation." *Journal of Management* 31 (3): 354–380. doi:10.1177/0149206304272150.

Link, A. N., ed. 2017. *Gender and Entrepreneurial Activity*. Cheltenham: Edward Elgar Publishing.

Lutter, M. 2015. "Do Women Suffer from Network Closure? The Moderating Effect of Social Capital on Gender Inequality in a Project-Based Labor Market, 1929 to 2010." *American Sociological Review* 80 (2): 329–358.

Lynn, F. B., M. C. Noonan, M. Sauder, and M. A. Andersson. 2019. "A Rare Case of Gender Parity in Academia." *Social Forces* 98 (2): 518–547. doi:10.1093/sf/soy126.

Mayer, S. J., and J. M. Rathmann. 2018. "How Does Research Productivity Relate to Gender? Analyzing Gender Differences for Multiple Publication Dimensions." *Scientometrics* 117 (3): 1663–1693. doi:10.1007/s11192-018-2933-1.

Muñoz, E. 2007. "New Socio-Political Environment and the Dynamics of European Public Research Systems". *Consejo Superior de Investigaciones Científicas. Grupo de Ciencia, Tecnología y Sociedad (Unidad de Políticas Comparadas)*, Working Paper: 02–20.

Nielsen, M. W. 2016. "Gender Consequences of a National Performance-Based Funding Model: New Pieces in an Old Puzzle." *Studies in Higher Education* 42 (6): 1033–1055. doi:10.1080/03075079.2015.1075197.

Nyberg, A., G. Reilly, S. Essman, and J. Rodrigues. 2018. "Human Capital Resources: A Call to Retire Settled Debates and to Start a Few New Debates." *The International Journal of Human Resource Management* 29 (1): 68–86. doi:10.1080/09585192.2017.1381138.

Ocasio, W. 1997. "Towards an Attention-Based View of the Firm." *Strategic Management Journal* 18 (S1): 187–206.

O'Kane, C., J. Cunningham, V. Mangematin, and P. O'Reilly. 2015. "Underpinning Strategic Behaviours and Posture of Principal Investigators in Transition/Uncertain Environments." *Long Range Planning* 48 (3): 200–214.

O'Kane, Conor, Jing A. Zhang, James A. Cunningham, and Lawrence Dooley. 2020. "Value Capture Mechanisms in Publicly Funded Research." *Industrial Marketing Management* 90: 400–416. doi:10.1016/j.indmarman.2020.08.006.

Probert, B. 2005. "'I Just Couldn't Fit it in': Gender and Unequal Outcomes in Academic Careers." *Gender, Work & Organization* 12 (1): 50–72.

Robson, M. J., B. B. Schlegelmilch, and B. Bojkowszky. 2012. "Resource Deployment Stability and Performance in International Research-and-Development Alliances: A Self-Determination Theory Explanation." *Journal of International Marketing* 20 (1): 1–18. doi:10.1509/jim.11.0072.

Rosa, P., and A. Dawson. 2006. "Gender and the Commercialization of University Science: Academic Founders of Spinout Companies." *Entrepreneurship and Regional Development* 18 (4): 341–366.

Santamaría, L., A. Brage-Gil, and A. Modrego. 2010. "Public Selection and Financing of R&D Cooperative Projects: Credit Versus Subsidy Funding." *Research Policy* 39 (4): 549–563. doi:10.1016/j.respol.2010.01.011.

Shepherd, D. A., J. S. Mcmullen, and W. Ocasio. 2017. "Is That an Opportunity? An Attention Model of Top Managers' Opportunity Beliefs for Strategic Action." *Strategic Management Journal* 38 (3): 626–644. doi:10.1002/smj.2499.

Siegel, D. S., M. Wright, and A. Lockett. 2007. "The Rise of Entrepreneurial Activity at Universities: Organizational and Societal Implications." *Industrial and Corporate Change* 16 (4): 489–504.

Sotudeh, H., and N. Khoshian. 2014. "Gender Differences in Science: The Case of Scientific Productivity in Nano Science & Technology During 2005–2007." *Scientometrics* 98 (1): 457–472. doi:10.1007/s11192-013-1031-7.

Spanish Universities Rectors Conference. 2017. Accessed March 15, 2020. https://www.crue.org/wp-content/uploads/2020/02/Resumen-ITC-2019_V5.pdf.

Stock, R. M., F. Totzauer, and N. A. Zacharias. 2014. "A Closer Look at Cross-Functional R&D Cooperation for Innovativeness: Innovation-Oriented Leadership and Human Resource Practices as Driving Forces." *Journal of Product Innovation Management* 31 (5): 924–938. doi:10.1111/jpim.12132.

Stock, J. H., and M. W. Watson. 2015. *Introduction to Econometrics*. London: Pearson Education Limited.

Stout, J. G., N. Dasgupta, M. Hunsinger, and M. A. Mcmanus. 2011. "STEMing the Tide: Using Ingroup Experts to Inoculate Women's Self-concept in Science, Technology, Engineering, and Mathematics (STEM)." *Journal of Personality and Social Psychology* 100: 255–270. doi:10.1037/a0021385.

Vallejo, G., and M. Ato. 2012. "Robust Tests for Multivariate Factorial Designs Under Heteroscedasticity." *Behavior Research Methods* 44 (2): 471–489.

Van den Besselaar, Peter, and Ulf Sandström. 2017. "Vicious Circles of Gender Bias, Lower Positions, and Lower Performance: Gender Differences in Scholarly Productivity and Impact." *PLoS One* 12 (8): e0183301. doi:10.1371/journal. pone.0183301.

Wadman, M. 2009. "Research Funding: Closing Arguments." *Nature* 457 (7230): 650–655.

West, J. D., J. Jacquet, M. M. King, S. J. Correll, and C. T. Bergstrom. 2013. "The Role of Gender in Scholarly Authorship." *PLoS ONE* 8 (7): e66212. doi:10.1371/ journal.pone.0066212.

Whittington, K. B., and L. Smith-Doerr. 2005. "Gender and Commercial Science: Women's Patenting in the Life Sciences." *The Journal of Technology Transfer* 30 (4): 355–370.

Witteman, H. O., M. Hendricks, S. Straus, and C. Tannenbaum. 2019. "Are Gender Gaps Due to Evaluations of the Applicant or the Science? A Natural Experiment at a National Funding Agency." *The Lancet* 393 (10171): 531–540. doi:10.1016/S0140-6736(18)32611-4.

Woehler, M. L., K. L. Cullen-Lester, C. M. Porter, and K. A. Frear. 2020. "Whether, How, and Why Networks Influence Men's and Women's Career Success: Review and Research Agenda." *Journal of Management*, doi:10.1177/0149206320960529.

Zhu, Y. Q., and H. G. Chen. 2016. "Empowering Leadership in R & D Teams: A Closer Look at its Components, Process, and Outcomes." *R&D Management* 46 (4): 726–735. doi:10.1111/radm.12114.

Zorn, M. L., J. C. Sexton, M. S. Bhussar, and B. T. Lamont. 2019. "Unfinished Business: Nested Acquisitions, Managerial Capacity, and Firm Performance." *Journal of Management* 45 (4): 1488–1516. doi:10.1177/0149206317708855.

Does blockchain technology democratize entrepreneurial finance? An empirical comparison of ICOs, venture capital, and REITs

Christian Fisch, Michele Meoli and Silvio Vismara

ABSTRACT

Initial coin offerings (ICOs) are one of the major innovations that characterize the digital revolution of financial markets. Among the expectations created by the digital revolution is the democratization of entrepreneurial finance, defined in terms of the creation of more equality regarding the access to financial resources by categories known to be underrepresented among potential entrepreneurs. Following this line of research, we investigate, through two complementary empirical studies, whether gender, ethnicity, and geography affect the choice of ICOs vs. traditional financing alternatives. Additionally, we assess whether these characteristics increase the amount of money an entrepreneur can raise. In Study I, we compare 390 ICO ventures to a sample of 1,078 VC-backed blockchain ventures, identifying a negative correlation between the choice of an ICO (vs. VC-backing) and a location in an urban area. In Study II, we compare 160 ICO ventures to 163 real estate investment trusts (REITs), reaffirming the results of Study I. The findings show significant participation and likelihood of successful campaigns for ethnical minorities in ICOs, with the latter also being able to collect, ceteris paribus, larger amounts of funding. In contrast, female entrepreneurs do not have higher chances to participate nor raise funds in ICOs.

1. Introduction

Most recently, initial coin offerings (ICOs) have emerged as a new form of entrepreneurial finance that is discussed vividly by practitioners, researchers, and policymakers (Fisch 2019; Howell, Niessner, and Yermack 2020; Huang, Meoli, and Vismara 2020; Momtaz 2020a, 2020b). ICOs leverage blockchain technology to collect financing without intermediaries. This has large implications for corporate governance from the perspective of corporate managers, institutional investors, debt investors, auditors, and other groups (Yermack 2017). Since the first ICO was conducted in July 2013, thousands of ICOs have followed with funding volumes surpassing those realized in crowdfunding (e.g. Fisch 2019; Lyandres, Palazzo, and Rabetti 2019).

A specific aspect of new forms of entrepreneurial finance that build on digital information and communication technologies (ICT) is that they have vast potentials to democratize entrepreneurial finance. We define the democratization of entrepreneurial finance in terms of the creation of more equality regarding the access to financial resources by categories known to be underrepresented among potential entrepreneurs. While traditional deals in entrepreneurial finance are limited to a relatively small group of private investors, digital finance allows issuers to broadly solicit and advertise their securities to the general public, thereby increasing the diversification of potential investors (Block et al. 2018). This opportunity has attracted the attention of policymakers. For instance, when signing the JOBS Act, former US President Obama proclaimed that 'for the first time, ordinary Americans will be able to go online and invest in entrepreneurs that they believe in'.[1] The expectation is that technological advancements will enlarge the number of participants in digital finance markets by delivering more investment opportunities to investors as well as more financing opportunities to entrepreneurs. In this study, we take the latter perspective and focus on an increasing diversification for entrepreneurs that seek funding.

Traditionally, the issuance and exchange of shares in private companies is a paper-based process. This can be cumbersome, time-consuming, and error-prone. Digital finance has the potential to make these markets more efficient, bypassing traditional intermediaries such as banks and venture capitalists (VCs). While crowdfunding's role in democratizing entrepreneurial finance has been addressed (e.g. Cumming, Meoli, and Vismara 2019a), little is known about the role of ICOs in democratizing entrepreneurial finance (see Block et al. 2020 for a comparison between equity crowdfunding and ICOs).

We investigate whether blockchain technology is as inclusive as often portrayed. Tokens (i.e. the unit of value sold to investors in ICOs) can be created using blockchain technology and can represent a wide range of scarce assets (Fisch 2019). Blockchain technology is required for issuing and selling tokens and is a necessary component of ICOs as a funding mechanism. Often, blockchain technology is also a part of the business models of the ventures that engage in ICOs (e.g. Fisch 2019; Momtaz 2020a). ICOs are inherently global and can raise funds more easily (Huang, Meoli, and Vismara 2020). Because tokens are highly divisible, each token can represent a small percentage of the overlying asset. This enables fractional ownership, increasing accessibility to the securities market by allowing for a wider scope of eligible investors due to pared-down minimum investment amounts. Therefore, the expectation is that by replacing a small set of homogeneous experts with a diverse crowd, the significance of a CEOs' gender or race will decline. There is, however, disagreement. The democratization potential of blockchain is sometimes criticized by being described as

> a few self-serving white men (there are hardly any women or minorities in the blockchain universe) pretending to be messiahs for the world's impoverished, marginalized and unbanked masses claim to have created billions of dollars of wealth out of nothing. (Roubini 2018)

Does blockchain technology democratize entrepreneurial finance? To answer this question, we compare how companies raise primary capital through blockchain technology (i.e. ICOs) with traditional alternatives (e.g. VC). This is challenging and, to the best of our knowledge, has not been done yet. A critical issue in this regard is the identification of such a matched sample of innovative blockchain-based ventures. For this reason, we assess our research question in two distinct empirical studies that complement each other.

In Study I, we compare 390 ICO ventures to a sample of 1,078 VC-backed blockchain ventures to enable comprehensive insights on how ICO ventures differ from VC-backed ventures. Study I provides evidence on how democratization variables correlate with the pursuit of an ICO (vs. VC-backing) and ICO success. While this investigation enables a comprehensive overview of the field of ICO ventures in comparison to VC-backed firms, Study I neglects potential differences relating to the industrial setting. Indeed, while ICOs are often pursued by ventures whose business is based on blockchain technology, VCs existed before the advent of blockchain technology and invest more broadly in high tech ventures (e.g. Fisch and Momtaz 2020). Hence, a possible limitation of Study I stems from the potential industry-specific differences across the two samples.

In Study II, we compare 160 ICO ventures to 163 real estate investment trusts (REITs). A REIT is an investment trust that manages real estate or related assets and allows individuals to earn a share of the income produced through commercial real estate ownership (SEC 2019). Recently, the real estate industry saw an increased digital representation of asset ownership (Baum 2020). The process of representing a fractional ownership interest in an asset with a blockchain-based token ('fractionalization' and 'tokenization') is exploited through ICOs. According to icobench.com, the real estate industry runs fourth in terms of total funds raised in 2019 (after cryptocurrency, platform, and business services) but is the industry with the highest average amount of funds raised per ICO (17.7 m USD per project). Since the financing object is very similar in traditional REITs and real-estate ICOs, the comparability of their business is high. This addresses Study I's lack of accounting for industry-specific differences.

Study I identifies a negative correlation between the choice of an ICO (vs. VC-backing) and a venture's location in an urban area. Hence, the results of Study I suggest that ICOs lead to a democratization of entrepreneurial finance in terms of geography since they are more often used by ventures in more rural regions. In contrast, we find that the presence of female founders is associated with lower ICO success. Complementing these results, Study II provides evidence on a higher likelihood of ICOs for rural ventures, reaffirming the findings of Study I. Also, the results suggest increasing participation of ethnical minorities. Moreover, our results show that younger teams and teams with the participation of ethnic minorities are more likely to succeed in their funding initiative, with the latter also being able to collect, ceteris paribus, larger amounts.

Our analysis contributes to the growing literature that explores whether the digitalization of entrepreneurial finance democratizes the access to financing for under-represented categories, such as women, ethnic minorities, and remote regions (e.g. Cumming, Meoli, and Vismara 2019a; Dy, Marlow, and Martin 2017). In particular, given that the specific role of ICOs has not yet been addressed in this respect, scholars, practitioners, and policymakers may find in our results evidence on how ICOs mitigate the financing gaps for different categories of typically under-represented entrepreneurs. Complementary to the demand-side approach of our analysis, the supply-side of democratization regards investors in terms of allowing a wider range of individuals to invest in diverse ventures with different motivations (Fisch et al. 2019). Fractional ownership and micro-investments might indeed become increasingly popular and increase the financial inclusion across demographics of low-income sections of society. However, chances are that the tokens of some ICOs remain illiquid. This would undermine the efficiency of blockchain finance in reaching the 'bottom of the pyramid'.

The paper is organized as follows. Section 2 presents the theory, while Section 3 illustrates the research design of this study. Section 4 is dedicated to Study 1 and Section 5 to Study 2. Conclusions are provided in Section 6.

2. Digital finance and emancipation

The expectations for digital technology as an enabler of democratization are high (e.g. Dy, Marlow, and Martin 2017). For example, Daniels (2009) describes digital cyberspace as a 'disembodied realm where gendered and racialized bodies can be left behind'. However, a significant gap between expectations and reality persists in small businesses concerning the usage of ICTs (Morgan-Thomas 2016). In particular, little is known about the emancipatory possibilities offered by digital finance. Compared to traditional finance, digital finance has lower barriers to entry and easier access to information. Consequently, digital finance is expected to improve the financing opportunities for those groups who were previously excluded or limited.

Following Cumming, Meoli, and Vismara (2019a), democratization in entrepreneurial finance is investigated in this study along three dimensions, namely geography, gender, and ethnicity. If ICOs (and blockchain technology) are effectively democratizing access to funding, they should provide financing to these three categories which are typically referred to as financially constrained.

A large number of studies have indeed found that differences in access to capital markets exist. This is partly due to demand-side (*entrepreneurs*) issues, which refer to differences in human capital or aspirations between men's and women's ventures, or between races. For example, Audretsch,

Lehmann, and Wirsching (2017) find that barriers based on personal characteristics, attitudes, cultural background, and the entrepreneurial environment hinder latent and nascent female entrepreneurs from starting new ventures. Women are less likely to have prior entrepreneurial or/and managerial experience and to participate in networks with high net worth individuals (Verheul and Thurik 2001). Hence, an explanation for the underrepresentation of women and minorities in finance markets is that resource providers are biased against minority and female founders, thereby ascribing the bias also to pre-entry constraints. The theory of statistical discrimination (Arrow 1998) suggests that prospective supporters use race or gender as a proxy for unobserved traits that indicate the investment is more likely to fail (Morse 2015).

Additionally, supply-side (*investors*) issues apply, such as male and white dominance among VCs and investment bankers (Greene et al. 2001). For instance, Amatucci and Sohl (2004) point to investor assumptions or stereotyping towards women owners' management potential despite extensive business backgrounds, which impact the gender bias in entrepreneurial finance. Brush et al. (2004) document that although women own more than 30 percent of US businesses, they receive less than 5 percent of venture capital funds distributed annually. Hence, taste-based discrimination (Becker 1957) implies that prospective supporters reject minority founders, irrespective of their qualifications, out of their aversion for minorities or females more broadly.

The literature on female entrepreneurship has boomed in recent years and has largely pointed to the challenges that women face in establishing and running a business. A particular focus is on access to information, finance, and networks (see, for instance, Link 2017; Ughetto et al. 2020). Using the US Small Business Innovation Research SBIR project data program, Bednar, Gicheva, and Link (2019) find that Phase II projects led by a female principal investigator have a greater probability of being commercialized in female-owned firms than in male-owned firms. However, Gicheva and Link (2013) find that women-owned firms are as much as 16 percentage points less likely to attract private investment dollars compared to male-owned firms, factors excluding the size of the SBIR award held constant. Gicheva and Link (2015) confirm that female-owned firms are disadvantaged in their access to private investment. To address this problem, several women-focused capital funds were recently launched in the USA and Canada. However, preliminary evidence provided by Orser, Coleman, and Li (2020) reveals that only a minority of these funds seek to address structural barriers associated with women entrepreneurs' access to financial capital, thus falling short of supporting a broader feminist agenda.

A few studies focus on gender discrimination in digital finance. In a study of UK equity crowdfunding, Vismara, Benaroio, and Carne (2017) find that female investors in female-led businesses are twice those in male-led businesses. Using projects listed on German platforms, Prokop and Wang (2018) find that equity crowdfunding campaigns initiated by women attract fewer investors and lower funding amounts than those initiated by men. Using a sample of 167 UK equity crowdfunding offerings, Cumming, Meoli, and Vismara (2019a) find that those launched by female entrepreneurs do not have higher chances to raise funds relative to traditional initial public offerings. Finally, Giudici, Guerini, and Rossi-Lamastra (2020) study 13 equity crowdfunding campaigns in Italy and confirm no significant effect related to gender.

The underrepresentation of minorities in entrepreneurial finance is another subject of increasing attention. For instance, Fairlie and Robb (2007) show that the availability of startup capital is conditioned by race. More recent studies find mixed results about minorities' access to finance in peer-to-peer markets. Indeed, Pope and Sydnor (2011) find evidence of significant racial disparities in peer-to-peer lending. Loan listings by black people are 25–35 percent less likely to receive funding those of whites with similar credit profiles. In contrast, Herzenstein et al. (2008) find no racial bias. The effect of ethnicity is indeed very small in comparison to the effects of borrowers' financial strength and their effort when listing and publicizing the loan. They conclude that individual digital lenders lend more fairly and are less influenced by racial stereotypes than are banks. Finally, Cumming, Meoli, and Vismara (2019a) find that minority entrepreneurs do not have higher chances of successfully raising capital in equity crowdfunding. However, they can attract a higher number of small investors.

Traditionally, investors tend to prefer geographically close investment opportunities (e.g. French and Poterba 1991). For instance, the probability of investment by VCs decreases with geographic distance (Sorenson and Stuart 2001). The arguments for this preference, and a resulting 'home bias', are related to lower information asymmetries, better monitoring capabilities, and lower associated costs. However, in a digitalized world, geographic distance should matter less to investors. Indeed, digitalization enables remote forms of organization and disintermediation (Nambisan et al. 2017), especially in the area of entrepreneurial finance (Coval and Moskowitz 2001). Coherently, Cumming, Meoli, and Vismara (2019a) find that remotely located companies are more likely to launch equity crowdfunding offerings than an initial public offering and have higher chances to complete an equity crowdfunding offering. The first evidence about the geographical implications of ICOs is provided by Huang, Meoli, and Vismara (2020), which reveals that ICOs take place more frequently in countries with developed financial systems, public equity markets, and advanced digital technologies.

3. Research design

Our research design comprises two empirical exercises that complement each other and enable a coherent assessment of ICOs' role in the democratization of entrepreneurial finance. The first aspect that we investigate is the choice to raise entrepreneurial funding through an ICO in contrast to other alternatives. This implies that we need to set up a database comprising ICO deals and comparable capital raising through traditional instruments. In doing so, we consider that an ICO is feasible only for blockchain ventures and that ICOs are a sizeable phenomenon that started in 2017. This is why we use Crunchbase to retrieve a sample of blockchain ventures that received funding from 2017 onwards. Crunchbase is an established database in the field of entrepreneurial finance and is frequently used to assess the funding of innovative companies (e.g. Bernstein, Korteweg, and Laws 2017). In particular, Crunchbase is known for its wide coverage and high recency (e.g. Fisch and Block 2020; Ter Wal et al. 2016), which are critical for our study. Also, Crunchbase is one of the few databases that also contains ICOs alongside more traditional forms of entrepreneurial finance (e.g. VC, BAs), which are crucial for funding for blockchain ventures.

We are aware that features increasing the likelihood to choose an ICO versus traditional entrepreneurial finance may overlap with the determinants of funding success. We deal with this potential sample selection bias by estimating a system of two equations: a probit model on the probability to choose ICOs over traditional funding, and a probit model on the probability of success in the ICO. This system is a probit model with sample selection and can be estimated according to Van de Ven and Van Praag (1981). The identification condition will be granted by the inclusion of industry dummies in the first equation.

Study I compares ICO ventures and VC-backed blockchain ventures and provides insights on whether ICOs contribute to a democratization of entrepreneurial finance vis-à-vis VC. We choose VC-backed ventures as a comparison group because VC is used to finance highly innovative entrepreneurial ventures in the presence of high uncertainty (e.g. Gompers and Lerner 2001; Puri and Zarutskie 2012). This is similar to ICO ventures, which are typically characterized by high innovative potential and high uncertainty (e.g. Fisch 2019; Momtaz 2020a). Also, similar to VC-backed companies, ICO ventures are typically in very early stages of their life cycle (e.g. Fisch and Momtaz 2020). In contrast, other forms of entrepreneurial finance occur in later stages, such as initial public offerings or leveraged buyouts. Finally, to establish our comparison group, we focus on ventures active in the blockchain sector because blockchain technology is a core feature of ICOs (e.g. Fisch 2019; Howell, Niessner, and Yermack 2020; Momtaz 2020a).

Study II complements our analysis with an industry focus and investigates whether and how ICOs contribute to the democratization of fundraising in the real estate industry. High entry barriers, the presence of transaction costs due to intermediation, lack of transparency, asymmetric information, and geographical distance could represent serious issues to overcome for any global investor that could be interested in the real estate market resulting in a possible disruption of value. A tokenization of real estate could offer a solution to the high costs of transactions and allow online investors to diversify their asset portfolio by capitalizing on fractional properties (Smith et al. 2019).

To assess whether ICOs have created opportunities for democratization in this sector, we analyze them vis-à-vis the closest term of comparison in terms of entrepreneurial fundraising, REITs. REITs manage real estate or related assets and allow individuals to invest in large-scale, income-producing real estate, thus providing a way for individual investors to earn a share of the income produced through commercial real estate ownership (SEC 2019). Publicly traded REITs allow individuals to invest in real estate properties. Hence, REITs represent a channel for both retail and institutional investors to gain income from commercial real estate, while avoiding the nuances of direct real estate exposure, such as extended lock-up periods, large minimum investments, and responsibility for property management (Smith et al. 2019). Thanks to the detailed information available for REITs, Study II allows us to extend the list of factors that we consider as determinants of the choice of funding and funding success, covering gender, age, ethnicity, and geographical location.

Notice that both studies only observe ventures that were eventually funded. Therefore, our empirical analysis investigates the realized choice of funding, not whether funding was obtained or not, which needs to be considered when interpreting our findings.

4. Study I: comparison of ICO ventures and VC-backed ventures

4.1. Sample

In Study I, we use Crunchbase to retrieve our sample of ICO ventures and VC-backed ventures. We retrieved our initial sample of ventures from Crunchbase in January 2020. First, we identified all ventures that had received funding in the form of an ICO, resulting in an initial sample of 578 ICO ventures. In addition to retrieving all venture- and funding level information for these ventures, we identified the ventures' founders/CEOs (N = 959). We extracted all founder-level information included in Crunchbase, which includes information used to construct our democratization variables, such as the CEO's location and gender. Second, we identified all ventures listed in Crunchbase that are active in the blockchain sector (category indicated in Crunchbase) and did not conduct an ICO. To establish temporal comparability, we only selected those ventures that received their initial round of funding after 31 December 2014. Before this date, ICOs were virtually non-existent (Howell, Niessner, and Yermack 2020). This sampling approach resulted in an initial sample of 1,752 blockchain ventures that received funding in ways other than an ICO.

We were forced to exclude observations due to a range of missing values, which is a common problem in ICO research in which data is often scarcely available (Momtaz 2020a). Missing values occurred concerning the personal information included in Crunchbase (e.g. location data), venture-level information (e.g. founding date), and funding data (funding raised). For the sake of internal consistency and argumentative clarity, we aim to compare ICO ventures to VC-backed ventures. Since Crunchbase includes all types of private equity financing, we thus excluded firms that (only) received funding in the form of IPOs, debt funding, or crowdfunding.

Ultimately, our final sample includes 1,468 ventures, of which 390 received funding in the form of an ICO, while 1,078 received financing in the form of VC (including business angel investments).

4.2. Model, data, and variables

Our analysis implements a Cragg's double hurdle model, to take into account a selection issue (namely, a company opting for an ICO over a VC financing) and a possible corner solution (i.e. the ICO not reaching the minimum amount to raise money). The Cragg's model implies a two-equation approach, estimated through Maximum Likelihood, under assumption of a joint distribution of the unobservable. In the first equation, our dependent variable is '*ICO venture*', which takes a value of 1 if the venture conducted an ICO and 0 otherwise. The reference group mainly comprises VC investments and investments by business angels. The second equation exclusively considers ICO ventures and assesses ICO success as the dependent variable. We capture ICO success by the amount of funding raised in the respective ICO (*'funds raised (log.)'*), which is a standard success measure in ICO research (e.g. Fisch 2019; Momtaz 2020b). We use the natural logarithm of the amount raised to account for the variable's skewness.

To assess potential democratization effects with regard to gender, we construct a variable ('# *female founders*') that captures the number of female founding team members for each venture The data is obtained from Crunchbase. To investigate democratization effects related to the venture's location, we construct a variable that captures whether the venture is located in an urban area (*'urban area'*) or not. We consider a founder's location as urban according to the definition of Functional Urban Areas by the OECD, which defines metropolitan areas as areas with more than 500,000 inhabitants (OECD 2020).

We include a variety of control variables that might influence a venture's decision to pursue funding in the form of an ICO vs. VC (first equation) as well as ICO success (second equation). Our first set of control variables captures the GDP per capita of the country in which the venture is located. We also control for the venture's number of TMT members (*'TMT size'*)), which has been associated with funding outcomes in prior research in entrepreneurial finance (e.g. Baum and Silverman 2004; Hsu 2007). For example, a larger number of founders can reflect a broader experience of the venture team, which might translate to higher success later on.

To control for differences related to how established a venture is, we include the venture's age in years (*'venture age'*). For example, older ventures might possess more meaningful track records, which could influence the likelihood of obtaining VC or the success in an ICO. In a similar vein, we include the venture's number of employees. This variable serves as another indicator of venture development or venture size that could impact funding outcomes (*'employees'*). Employee data is recorded in a categorical format in Crunchbase and increases from 1 to 10 employees (coded as 1) to more than 1,000 employees (coded as 7) (Block et al. 2019). We coded ventures without employee data as 0. Finally, we include the number of funding rounds the venture received (*'funding rounds'*). Similar to the number of employees, a higher number of funding rounds indicates a larger resource endowment. Also, a higher number of funding rounds usually suggests that the venture is in a more advanced life cycle stage, which can influence funding outcomes (e.g. Block et al. 2019). Moreover, we control for the venture's presence in social media by capturing whether the venture lists a LinkedIn account (*'LinkedIn account'*) and/or a Twitter account (*'Twitter account'*) on their Crunchbase profile. Presence on professional social networks such as LinkedIn might be related to the pursuit of professional investors (e.g. VC). Also, ventures' social media activity is linked to increased ICO success (e.g. Fisch 2019).

Our final set of control variables refers to the venture's industry. On Crunchbase, ventures can self-select an unspecified amount of industry categories. We use the number of different categories specified as a control variable (*'industries'*) to account for the venture's industrial diversity. A greater variety might influence the likelihood and success of an ICOpositively or negatively. Similarly, industrial differences might exist between ICO venture and ventures that are VC-backed blockchain ventures, as indicated by (Howell, Niessner, and Yermack 2020). To account for these differences, we include a set of dummy variables that capture whether the venture is active in financial services, data, and analytics, hardware, IT, internet services, lending and investments, payments, or software.

The variables, definitions, and data sources use din Study I are summarized in Table 1.

4.3. Descriptive statistics

Table 2 provides descriptive statistics on the firms in our samples and enables an initial comparison of ICO ventures and VC-backed ventures. Overall, the sample used in Study I includes 1,468 ventures. 390 (26.6%) of these ventures conducted an ICO, while the remaining 1,078 ventures (73.4%)

Table 1. Study I: variables.

Variable	Definition	Data source
Democratization variables		
# Female founders (*)	Number of female founders.	Crunchbase
Urban area (*)	Takes a value of 1 if venture is located in a metropolitan area according to OECD FUA classification, 0 otherwise.	OECD FUA classification
Control variables		
GDP per capita (*)	GDP per capita in 2017 in constant 2010 US dollars. Value expressed in natural logarithm for the regression analysis.	World Bank
TMT size (*)	Number founding team members.	Crunchbase
Venture age (*)	Venture's age in years (as of 2020).	Crunchbase
Employees	Venture's number of employees, categorical variable ranging from 1 = 1–10 employees to 7 = > 1,000 employees. 0 = no data available.	Crunchbase
Funding rounds	Venture's number of funding rounds.	Crunchbase
Twitter account	Takes a value of 1 if the venture has a Twitter account according to Crunchbase, 0 otherwise.	Crunchbase
LinkedIn account	Takes a value of 1 if the venture has a LinkedIn account according to Crunchbase, 0 otherwise.	Crunchbase
Industries	Venture's number of different industry categories.	Crunchbase
Instrumental variables		
Industry dummies (*)	Set of dummy variables that capture whether the venture is active in financial services, data and analytics, hardware, IT, internet services, lending and investments, payments or software.	Crunchbase
Dependent variables		
ICO venture (*)	Takes a value of 1 if the venture conducted an initial coin offering (ICO), 0 otherwise.	Crunchbase
Funds raised (log.) (*)	Natural logarithm of the amount raised (in m$)	Crunchbase

Note: This table summarizes the variables used in Study I. The table also defines every variable and provides information on the data source. Variables marked by an asterisk (*) have a corresponding variable in Study II, as outlined in Table 4.

Table 2. Study I: descriptive statistics.

	Full sample (N = 1,468)				VC (N = 1,078)	ICO (N = 390)	
Variables	Mean	SD	Min.	Max.	Mean	Mean	Diff. (sig)
Dependent variable							
Funds raised (m USD)	–	–	–	–	–	38.78	–
Democratization variables							
# Female founders	0.16	0.42	0	4	0.17	0.16	0.01
Urban area (%)	75.75	42.87	0	100	77.46	71.03	6.43
Control variables							
GDP per capita (1,000 USD)	46.09	18.50	1.06	119.07	46.11	46.02	0.09
TMT size	2.13	1.13	1	8	2.13	2.12	0.02
Venture age (years)	3.86	2.80	0	46	3.63	4.48	−0.84***
Employees	1.52	0.98	0	7	1.46	1.67	−0.20***
Funding rounds	1.95	1.55	1	14	1.88	2.15	−0.26***
Twitter account (%)	83.86	36.81	0	100	80.80	92.31	−11.51*
LinkedIn account (%)	87.60	32.97	0	100	88.59	84.87	3.72
Industries	2.68	2.01	0	17	2.73	2.56	0.16

Note: This table displays descriptive statistics for our variables. The table also compares the mean values between the sample of VC-backed ventures and ICO ventures. The final column reports significance of a *t*-test (or *z*-test, in the case of proportions) on the difference between the means of the subsamples of VC-backed ventures and ICO ventures. ***, ** and * identify differences significant at less than 1%, 5%, or 10%, respectively.

received VC. On average, the ICO ventures raised 38.8 m USD in the respective ICOs. Funding information is available for 799 of the 1,078 VC-backed ventures in our sample. On average, these ventures raised 8.0 m USD in funding, which is significantly less than the ICO ventures. This finding illustrates the considerable funding opportunities offered by ICOs.

Regarding the democratization variables, Table 2 shows that the ventures in our sample have 0.16 female founders on average. In total, 14.9% of all venture founding teams have at least one female member. Conversely, this indicates that male-only teams constitute the vast majority of the sampled ventures (85.1%). The number of female founders is similar among ICO ventures (0.16) and VC-backed ventures (0.17). With 75.8%, most ventures in our sample are located in urban areas. However, this share is lower among ICO ventures (71.0%) than among VC-backed ventures (77.5%).

In contrast to the democratization variables, several significant differences emerge regarding our control variables. For example, significant differences exist concerning venture age, the number of employees, and the number of funding rounds. Interestingly, ICO ventures in our sample are older, have more employees, and received a larger number of funding rounds than VC-backed ventures. These findings indicate that ICO ventures, on average, seem to be more established than VC-backed ventures. This finding contradicts prior ICO research, which often argues that ICO ventures are in very preliminary stages when conducting an ICO (e.g. Fisch 2019; Howell, Niessner, and Yermack 2020), and potentially indicates that ICO ventures included in Crunchbase underlie a positive selection.

4.4. Econometric results

Our analysis implements a Cragg's double-hurdle model (Cragg 1971), which implements two equations. In the first equation, we assess whether our democratization variables drive the choice to pursue an ICO (vs. VC-backing). In the second equation, we analyze whether the same democratization variables correlate with ICO success (i.e. funds raised). The 'two hurdles' in our model are the choice of an ICO over VC-backing (modeled through the first equation), and the likelihood of success in the second equation (modeled by the Tobit regression, considering that zero values are censored). Given that our sample is choice-based (Manski and Lerman 1977), as we selected only firms that got financed through venture capital or through an ICO, we implement the strategy recommended by Arezzo and Guagnano (2018). Following this method, we use sampling weights, i.e. proportion of funding through ICO or VC, in the selection equation of our model, an approach which is feasible also in the Cragg's double hurdle model setting employed in our analysis.

The results are reported in Table 3. Model 1 shows the results of a probit regression with '*ICO venture*' as the dependent variable (first equation). The findings document a negative association between a venture location in an urban area and the choice of an ICO (coefficient = −0.166, *p*-value < 5%). This suggests that ventures in rural areas more often pursue funding in the form of an ICO. The results for ICO success (second equation) are displayed in Models 2.1–2.4. Model 2.4 is our full model and the results suggest that a higher number of female founders is associated with decreased funding success (coefficient = −0.204, *p*-value < 5%).

Additional relationships emerge for some of our control variables. For example, the results show that the likelihood of conducting an ICO vs. VC-backing (Model 1) is positively related to venture age (coefficient = 0.041, *p*-value < 1%) and a presence on Twitter (coefficient = 0.578, *p*-value < 1%), while it is negatively related to a presence on LinkedIn (coefficient = −0.397, *p*-value < 1%) and a higher number of different industry categories (coefficient = −0.058, *p*-value < 5%). Besides, the results displayed in Model 2.4 suggest that ICO success is related with larger GDP per capita (coefficient = 0.589, *p*-value < 1%) and a larger number of employees (coefficient = 0.501, *p*-value < 1%).

5. Study II: comparison of ICO ventures and REITs

5.1. Sample

Due to the absence of an official source, Study II started with an exploration of listed ICOs in the real estate sector ICObench.com serves as our main source of information, which is one of the most detailed websites on ICOs and has high accuracy (Fisch and Momtaz 2020; Huang, Meoli, and

Table 3. Study I: funds raised.

Model	(1)		(2.1)		(2.2)		(2.3)		(2.4)	
Dependent variable	ICO company		Funds raised (log.)		Funds raised (log.)		Funds raised (log.)		Funds raised (log.)	
Democratization var.										
# Female founders	0.018	(0.089)	–		−0.268	(0.146)*	–		−0.284	(0.144)**
Urban area	−0.166	(0.075)**	–		–		0.275	(0.201)	0.290	(0.200)
Control variables										
GDP per capita (log.)	−0.028	(0.041)	0.566	(0.139)***	0.561	(0.139)***	0.593	(0.140)***	0.589	(0.140)***
TMT Size	−0.021	(0.029)	−0.007	(0.070)	0.017	(0.072)	−0.023	(0.071)	0.002	(0.072)
Venture age	0.041	(0.013)***	0.012	(0.024)	0.012	(0.024)	0.010	(0.024)	0.010	(0.024)
Employees	0.071	(0.038)*	0.492	(0.108)***	0.495	(0.108)***	0.497	(0.109)***	0.501	(0.110)***
Funding rounds	0.034	(0.022)	0.022	(0.050)	0.029	(0.050)	0.017	(0.050)	0.024	(0.051)
Twitter account	0.578	(0.108)***	0.582	(0.430)	0.592	(0.429)	0.644	(0.424)	0.658	(0.423)
LinkedIn account	−0.397	(0.106)***	−0.195	(0.318)	−0.188	(0.317)	−0.202	(0.314)	−0.195	(0.313)
Industries	−0.058	(0.028)**	−0.029	(0.044)	−0.029	(0.044)	−0.031	(0.044)	−0.031	(0.044)
Industry dummies	Yes		No		No		No		No	
Constant	−1.115	(0.454)**	8.847	(1.518)***	8.857	(1.521)***	8.370	(1.582)***	8.354	(1.583)***
Sigma	–		1.605	(0.094)***	1.600	(0.094)***	1.600	(0.092)***	1.595	(0.092)***
Observations	1,468		390		390		390		390	
Log likelihood	–		−499.28		−499.00		−498.98		−498.67	

Note: This table reports the results of Cragg's double hurdle models, estimating two equations with Maximum Likelihood. The first equation is the selection equation, where the dependent variable is the ICO dummy (choice of ICO vs. VC-funding), estimated on the sample of 1,468 ventures (390 ICOs and 1,078 VC-backed ventures). This equation includes sub-industry dummies (unreported, jointly significant at less than 1%). The second equation is a Tobit model on the amount raised, estimated on the sample of 390 ICOs. In all second-equation columns, we report the estimation of sigma, namely the correlation between the error terms in the two equations. Models (2.2–2.3) separately test for female presence and urban area, while Model (2.4) jointly tests for the four variables. Due to the binary structure of our choice-based sample, we use sampling weights, i.e. proportion of funding through ICO or VC, in the selection equation of our model (Arezzo and Guagnano 2018). Robust standard errors in parentheses. ***, ** and * identify significance levels at less than 1, 5 and 10%, respectively.

Vismara 2020; Momtaz 2020c). In line with existing studies, we cross-checked information with other websites, such as coincheckup.com, coinspeaker.com, and coinist.io. We filtered the ICOs according to the industry and we only selected those with a presence of an underlying asset, namely real estate property. This process was essential to select only those ICO that are asset-backed equity offerings, discriminating and excluding, for instance, ICOs consisting of platform development or infrastructure offerings without any corresponding underlying asset. We also excluded ICOs that were not present on at least two websites and ICOs for which essential information was missing.

Similar to Study I, our data collection took place in July 2019 and our sample comprises ICOs between 1 January 2017 until 1 July 2019. From a total number of 3,948 ICOs in all industries, we identified 234 ICOs that belong to the real estate industry and, excluding ICOs with missing data and excluding criteria, 160 ICOs are ultimately included in our analysis.

With respect to publicly-traded REITs, our main source of information is Crunchbase. We considered all registered offerings starting from 1 January 2011 (i.e. after the global financial crisis of 2009) until 1 November 2019. Thus, our sample comprises REITs listed in a broader time period than ICOs. REITs missing essential data for the analysis were excluded. To maintain comparability between ICOs and REITs, we only considered deals belonging to the same range of variation in terms of size, namely with an issue amount greater than $125,000 and lower than $800 m. This procedure leads to the selection of 163 REITs.

5.2. Model, data, and variables

In Study II, we implement a similar setting as in Study I. We make use of two alternative two-equation modeling designs to assess whether ICOs contribute to a democratization of entrepreneurial finance in the real estate industry. The first equation is the same in both cases, as we choose a dependent variable named '*ICO venture*', which takes a value of 1 if the venture conducted an ICO and 0 otherwise (i.e. if funds were raised through REITs). In this equation, we always include sub-industry dummies to grant model identification.

The second equation in our analysis exclusively considers ICO ventures and assesses ICO success as the dependent variable. This model, though, is provided in both a simpler and more complete fashion. First, in a simpler setting, we define '*ICO success*' as a dummy variable equal to 1 when the venture's raised funds met the soft cap, and the ICO was therefore effective. In this case, the two-equation model is a Probit model with sample selection, estimated through Maximum Likelihood (Van de Ven and Van Praag 1981). Second, in a more complete set, we define ICO success by the amount of funding raised in the respective ICO ('*funds raised (log.)*'), which is a standard success measure in ICO research (e.g. Fisch 2019; Momtaz 2020b). We use the natural logarithm of the amount raised to account for the variable's skewness. In this case, the two-equation model is a Cragg's double hurdle model setting, estimated through Maximum Likelihood (Cragg 1971), under assumption of a joint distribution of the unobservables. The 'two hurdles' in our model are the choice of an ICO over a REIT (modeled through the first equation), and the likelihood of success in the second equation (modeled by the Tobit regression, considering that zero values are censored). Given that our sample is choice-based (Manski and Lerman 1977), as we selected only firms which got financed through an ICO or a REIT, we implement the strategy recommended by Arezzo and Guagnano (2018). Following this method, we use sampling weights, i.e. proportion of funding through ICO or REIT, in the selection equation of our model, an approach which is feasible also in the Cragg's double hurdle model setting employed in our analysis.

In Study II, we assess potential democratization effects with regard to gender, age, ethnicity, and geographical localization of ICOs' and REITs' proponents. As far as gender is concerned, we make use of information available on ventures' websites to define a dummy variable for '*female presence*', equal to 1 if the CEO or the co-CEO of a venture is female.[2] Identification and coding of gender were based on names and pictures provided on the website of each venture, with a double check on the main social media. To assess the role of age, we define '*TMT age*' as, the average age of the members of the top management team. Information for this variable was obtained from venture websites and social network profiles. *'Ethnical minority'* is our variable controlling for the role of ethnicity. This dummy variable equals 1 if at least one member of the top management team is non-caucasian. Again, this variable was coded based on the information and pictures available on the venture's website and social media profiles of the TMT members. This variable seizes the perception of the potential investor, rather than the actual individual's identity or their ethnicity. To follow a scientific assessment approach and to reconstruct the investors' viewpoint, the rating of this variable was conducted by at least two different individuals, who were requested to identify the ethnicity of the team members. If both raters agreed on their decision, the assessment resulted as positive, otherwise discarded. Last, to analyze the role of geographical location, we define an *'urban area'* dummy variable, equal to 1 if the venture is located in a metropolitan city, according to the definition of Functional Urban Areas by OECD classification (OECD 2020).

All our models are specified by including several control variables affecting the venture's decision to pursue funding in the form of an ICO vs. REITs (first equation) as well as ICO success (second equation). Most controls are in line with Study I, although a few differences exist due to data availability and due to the specificities of REITs. Venture specificities are controlled for by *'venture age'*, in years at the time of the offering announcement, and *'TMT size'*, as the number of members in the top management team. We take into account the specific regional context by including a few control variables measured in the year of the offering announcement, in the offering country: *'GDP per capita'* in 2010 US dollar; *'tertiary education level'*, as the ratio of total enrollment to total population; *'ease of doing business'*, a World Bank's composite index indicating the level of regulatory performance of a country.

While all the above-mentioned controls are included in both equations, we need a specific variable for methodological reasons in the first or the second equation, respectively. Our first equation includes a set of sub-industry dummy variables, identifying real-estate sectors invested by the ICO or by the REIT, following the Industry Classification Benchmark Structure.[3] The seven sub-industries are the following: industrial and office, retail, residential, diversified, specialty, mortgage, hotel and lodging. For REITs, this classification is recorded by the publicly available financial information of the venture. For ICOs, it is encoded from whitepapers and available information on the venture.

Our second equation also includes a measure for the *'target funding size'*, controlling for the role of issuing size for both the choice of financing method and for the project success. This variable is the minimum funding goal which, when not reached, leads to refunding money to interested contributors. Following extant literature (Cumming, Meoli, and Vismara 2019b), we treat this variable as endogenous. In practice, while the *'target funding size'* is primarily determined by real needs, proponents are likely to make adjustments for strategic purposes based on the desire to signal commitment, as well as on entrepreneurial expectations about their individual capability to attract investments. This variable is therefore estimated in an instrumental regression, implemented in the bivariate probit setting as in Newey (1986), and in the Cragg's double hurdle model according to Bettin, Lucchetti, and Zazzaro (2012). In the instrumental regression, we include all control variables and an instrumental variable, *'mimicking target'*, namely the average minimum funding goal set by offering in the same sub-industry in the previous offerings (the same year for the first year in the sample).

The variables, definitions, and data sources use din Study II are summarized in Table 4.

5.3. Descriptive statistics

Table 5 provides descriptive statistics on the firms in our sample used for Study II, enabling a comparison of ICO in the real-estate industry and REITs. The final sample comprises 160 observations on real estate ICOs and 163 REITs.

On average, the success frequency of ICOs is 39.3% in our sample, with an average of 3.72 m USD raised per ICO. As far as our main explanatory variables are concerned, there is no evidence of

Table 4. Study II: variables.

Variable	Definition	Data source
Democratization variables		
Female presence (*)	Takes a value of 1 if the venture's CEO is female, 0 otherwise.	Venture websites
Urban area (*)	Takes a value of 1 if venture is located in a metropolitan area according to OECD FUA classification, 0 otherwise.	OECD FUA classification
TMT age	Average age of all members of the venture's top management team (TMT).	Venture websites, LinkedIn
Ethnical minority	Takes a value of 1 if one member of the team belongs to an ethnical minority (i.e. Asian, Black, or Hispanic).	Venture websites, LinkedIn
Control variables		
Venture age (*)	Venture's age in years (as of the offering announcement)	Venture websites
TMT size (*)	Number of members in the top management team	Venture websites
GDP per capita	GDP per capita in 2017 in constant 2010 US dollars. Value expressed in natural logarithm for the regression analysis.	World Bank
Tertiary education	Tertiary enrollment ratio of total enrollment that corresponds to the highest level of education.	World Bank
Ease of doing business	Composite index indicating the level of regulatory performance for country economy in 2019. A high score means that the regulatory environment is conducive to the starting and operation of a local firm.	World Bank
Instrumental variables		
Industry dummies (*)	Set of dummy variables that identify sub-industries in the real estate sector invested by the investment trust.	Industry Classification Benchmark Structure
Mimicking target	Average minimum funding goal set by offering in the same sub-industry in the previous offerings (same year for first year in the sample).	Sample data
Dependent and endogenous variables		
ICO venture (*)	Takes a value of 1 if the venture conducted an initial coin offering (ICO), 0 otherwise.	ICObench
Funds raised (log.) (*)	Natural logarithm of the amount raised (in m$)	ICObench
Success	Takes a value of 1 if the venture's raised funds met the soft cap.	ICObench
Target funding size	The minimum funding goal, which, when not reached, leads to refund contributors. This variable is treated as endogeneous in all regression analyses and is only included in second-equation regressions.	ICObench

Note: This table summarizes the variables used in Study I. The table also defines every variable and provides information on the data source. Variables marked by an asterisk (*) have a corresponding variable in Study I, as outlined in Table 1.

Table 5. Study II: descriptive statistics.

	Full sample (N = 323)				REIT (N = 163)	ICO (N = 160)	
Variables	Mean	SD	Min.	Max.	Mean	Mean	Diff. (sig.)
Dependent variables							
Success (%)	40.76	49.17	0	100	–	39.30	–
Funds raised (m USD)	77.45	149.88	0	800.00	149.91	3.72	−146.19***
Explanatory variables							
Female presence (%)	17.03	12.41	0	100	19.68	15.42	4.26
Age (years)	42.20	8.44	26	62	45.56	38.81	−6.75**
Ethnical minority (%)	44.27	49.75	0	100	33.12	55.60	22.48***
Urban area (%)	72.76	44.59	0	100	66.39	79.46	13.07***
Endogenous variable							
Target size (m USD)	106.40	167.12	0	1,200.00	–	8.14	–
Control variables							
Venture age (years)	9.83	13.66	0	58	16.50	3.00	−13.50***
TMT size (No.)	4.07	2.29	1	15	5.24	2.90	−2.34***
GDP per capita (1,000 USD)	46.97	14.87	18.34	77.46	51.20	42.66	−8.54***
Tertiary education (index)	76.67	16.72	20.50	126.40	82.47	70.93	−11.54**
Ease of doing business	80.98	3.71	60.00	85.20	81.78	80.29	−1.49

Note: This table displays descriptive statistics for our variables. The table also compares the mean values between the sample of REITs and ICO ventures. The final column reports significance of a *t*-test (or *z*-test, in the case of proportions) on the difference between the means of the subsamples of REITs and ICO ventures. ***, ** and * identify differences significant at less than 1%, 5%, or 10%, respectively.

statistically significant differences between ICOs and REITs in terms of Female presence (15.42% vs. 19.68%), while ICOs are characterized by younger TMTs (45.56 vs. 38.81 years), a higher presence of Ethnical minorities (55.60% vs. 33.12%), and a higher likelihood of an urban location (79.46% vs. 66.39%).

Several other significant differences emerge between ICOs and REITs. For example, ventures using REITs are on the average older than those raising money through ICOs (16.5 vs. 3 years), have larger TMTs (5.24 vs. 2.9 members on average), and are located in wealthier areas (51.20 vs. 42.66 $K in GDP per capita), with more tertiary educated people (82.47 vs. 70.93). All of these differences will be accounted for by control variables in our empirical analyses.

5.4. Econometric results

Like Study I, our analysis for Study II implies the estimation of two equations. The first equation models whether our democratization variables drive the choice to pursue an ICO (vs. REITs). The second equation allows us to analyze whether the same democratization variables correlate with ICO success (either in terms of probability to reach the target or funds raised).

The results are reported in Table 6 (first equation and second equation modeling the probability of success) and 7 (second equation modeling the funds raised). Model 1 in Table 6 shows the results of a probit regression with '*ICO venture*' as the dependent variable (selection model). We find here weak evidence that teams characterized by Female presence are more likely to opt for a REIT vis-à-vis an ICO (coefficient = −0.536, *p*-value < 10%, equivalent to an 8% change in the probability). Teams characterized by the presence of Ethnical minorities, vice versa, are strongly correlated to the choice of an ICO (coefficient = 0.410, *p*-value < 5%, implying a 6% increase in probability), as well as teams that are not located in an urban area (coefficient = −0.185, *p*-value < 5%). Among control variables, we find evidence that ICOs are preferred by younger firms, with smaller TMT size, and located in areas characterized by lower levels of tertiary education.

In Models from 2.1 to 2.5 in Table 6, we report the second equation of our analysis (the estimation of the first equation is qualitatively the same in all cases) when adding to the ICO-success-probability regression one of the variable testing for democratization, while Model 2.6 jointly tests for the effect of gender, age, ethnical minority and belonging to an urban area. We find statistical significance in support that younger TMTs (in Model 2.6 coefficient = −0.020, *p*-value < 5%, implying a 2.6% change in the probability for a one-standard-deviation change in the age of TMT) and the presence of ethnic minorities (in Model 2.6 coefficient = 0.463, *p*-value < 5%, implying a 12% change in the probability) lead to an increase in the likelihood of success, while no statistical evidence is found concerning gender and urban location. Among controls, we find that projects targeting lower amounts, presented by younger companies, in countries with higher GDP per capita, and higher scores in the Ease of doing business variables are more likely to succeed.

Table 7 reports the results of the second equation of our analysis (the estimation of the first equation is qualitatively the same in all cases) when measuring the success of an ICO through raised funds, rather than through the probability of success. Again, in models from 2.1 to 2.5, we separately test for the variables assessing the role of gender, age, ethnic minorities, and urban area, while model 2.6 jointly test for the role of the four variables. We find weak evidence of a negative role for gender (in Model 2.6 coefficient −0.861, *p*-value < 10%, implying on average 5% lower funds raised by a female with respect to a male CEO), and a positive and significant effect for the presence of ethnic minorities (in Model 2.6 coefficient = 0.382, *p*-value < 1%, implying on average 2.6% higher funds raised by firms with at least one member belonging to ethnical minorities). Among control variables, we confirm the positive role of GDP per capita (significant at less than 10%), and we find that ventures targeting larger amounts, indeed, raise more funds.

All in all, our results suggest that ICOs do not improve access to finance for women, which are discouraged to pursue ICOs in contrast to REITs. By contrast, teams from remote (non-urban) areas seem to prefer ICOs. Younger teams are more likely to succeed, while we have statistical

Table 6. Study II. Probability of success.

Model	(1)		(2.1)		(2.2)		(2.3)		(2.4)		(2.5)		(2.6)	
Dependent Variable	ICO company (dummy)		Success (dummy)		Success (dummy)		Success (dummy)		Success (dummy)		Success (dummy)		Success (dummy)	
Democratization var.														
Female presence	−0.536	(0.290)*	–		−0.385	(0.297)	–		–		–		−0.217	(0.204)
TMT age	−0.026	(0.018)	–		–		−0.028	(0.012)**	–		–		−0.020	(0.009)**
Ethnical minority	0.410	(0.190)**	–		–		–		0.426	(0.200)**	–		0.463	(0.209)**
Urban area	−0.185	(0.190)**	–		–		–		–		−0.149	(0.276)	−0.235	(0.273)
Control variables														
Target size	–		−0.156	(0.048)***	−0.159	(0.049)***	−0.150	(0.054)***	−0.154	(0.048)***	−0.153	(0.054)***	−0.143	(0.053)***
Firm age	−0.088	(0.026)***	−0.056	(0.026)**	−0.057	(0.029)*	−0.055	(0.028)*	−0.052	(0.028)*	−0.057	(0.029)*	−0.052	(0.025)**
TMT size	−0.423	(0.079)***	−0.015	(0.090)	−0.024	(0.103)	−0.015	(0.090)	−0.010	(0.091)	−0.016	(0.091)	−0.035	(0.144)
GDP per capita	−0.224	(0.320)	0.309	(0.191)	0.382	(0.296)	0.310	(0.192)	0.370	(0.199)*	0.371	(0.216)*	0.304	(0.168)*
Tertiary education	−0.034	(0.020)***	−0.009	(0.006)	−0.011	(0.007)	−0.009	(0.006)	−0.009	(0.006)	−0.008	(0.006)	−0.011	(0.011)
Ease of doing business	0.033	(0.040)	0.051	(0.028)*	0.062	(0.032)*	0.051	(0.028)*	0.047	(0.028)*	0.060	(0.031)*	0.112	(0.067)*
Industry dummies	Yes		–		–		–		–		–		–	
Constant	9.941	(3.268)***	−0.354	(2.183)	−0.352	(2.090)	−0.207	(2.256)	0.294	(2.259)	−0.255	(2.200)	1.094	(0.778)
Rho	–		−0.415	(0.634)	−0.432	(0.638)	−0.406	(0.632)	−0.429	(0.646)	−0.384	(0.636)	−0.311	(0.209)
Observations	323		160		160		160		160		160		160	
Log-likelihood	–		−101.06		−101.63		−102.52		−100.61		−102.25		−99.80	

Note: This table reports the results of Probit models with sample selection, estimating two equations with Maximum Likelihood (Van de Ven and Van Praag 1981). The first equation is the selection equation, where the dependent variable is the ICO dummy (choice of ICO vs. REIT), estimated on the sample of 323 financing (160 ICOs and 163 REITs). This equation includes sub-industry dummies (unreported, jointly significant at less than 1%). The second equation is a Probit model on the probability of success, estimated on the sample of 160 ICOS. Target size is included in the second equation and treated as endogenous. The instrumental variable (implemented as in Newey 1986) in the instrumental regression (unreported) is the Mimicking Target (significant at less than 1%). For each second state equation we report the estimation of rho, namely the correlation between the error terms in the two equations. Model (1) reports the estimation of the first equation estimated for model (2.1). All other regressions for the first equation are qualitative the same and unreported. Model (2.1) is the baseline regression for the second equation. Models (2.2–2.5) separately test for Female presence, Age, Ethnical minority and Urban area, while Model (2.6) jointly tests for the four variables. Due to the binary structure of our choice-based sample, we use sampling weights, i.e. proportion of funding through ICO or VC, in the selection equation of our model (Arezzo and Guagnano 2018). Robust standard errors in parentheses. ***, ** and * identify significance levels at less than 1, 5 and 10%, respectively.

Table 7. Study II. Funds raised (log.).

Model	(2.1)		(2.2)		(2.3)		(2.4)		(2.5)		(2.6)	
Dependent Variable	Funds raised (log)		Funds raised (log)		Funds raised (log)		Funds raised (log)		Funds raised (log)		Funds raised (log)	
Democratization variables												
Female presence	–		−0.918	(0.401)**	–		–		–		−0.861	(0.396)*
TMT age	–		–		0.019	(0.018)	–		–		−0.017	(0.018)
Ethnical minority	–		–		–		0.421	(0.206)**	–		0.382	(0.155)***
Urban area	–		–		–		–		0.060	(0.368)	−0.072	(0.380)
Control variables												
Target size	0.877	(0.084)***	0.880	(0.288)***	0.841	(0.093)***	0.860	(0.090)***	0.875	(0.083)***	0.832	(0.100)***
Firm age	−0.037	(0.038)	−0.039	(0.041)	−0.044	(0.040)	−0.032	(0.041)	−0.038	(0.039)	−0.041	(0.047)
TMT size	−0.148	(0.113)	−0.142	(0.127)	−0.146	(0.118)	−0.122	(0.114)	−0.147	(0.114)	−0.118	(0.130)
GDP per capita	0.522	(0.272)*	0.508	(0.265)*	0.575	(0.276)**	0.506	(0.264)*	0.535	(0.273)*	0.562	(0.291)*
Tertiary education	0.260	(0.483)	0.175	(0.419)	0.481	(0.446)	0.310	(0.426)	0.245	(0.425)	0.124	(0.071)
Ease of doing business	0.023	(0.055)	0.023	(0.061)	0.016	(0.054)	0.008	(0.053)	0.020	(0.053)	0.029	(0.049)
Industry dummies	–		–		–		–		–		–	
Constant	1.685	(3.626)	1.664	(3.606)	1.286	(3.429)	1.674	(3.552)	1.656	(3.737)	1.262	(3.526)
Sigma	2.233	(1.508)	2.353	(1.505)	2.015	(1.595)	2.691	(1.407)	2.088	(1.512)	2.274	(1.585)
Observations	160		160		160		160		160		160	
Log-likelihood	−334.18		−334.12		−334.56		−331.71		−334.45		−330.89	

Note: This table reports the results of Cragg's double hurdle models, estimated with Maximum Likelihood. The first equation is the selection equation, where the dependent variable is the ICO dummy (choice of ICO vs. REIT), estimated on the sample of 323 financing (160 ICOs and 163 REITs). This stage includes sub-industry dummies (unreported, jointly significant at less than 1%). Results are qualitatively the same as those reported in Table 7, Model (1), and are not reported. The second equation is a Tobit model on the amount raised, estimated on the sample of 160 ICOS. In the second equation, Target size is treated as endogenous. The instrumental variable (implemented as in Bettin, Lucchetti, and Zazzaro 2012) in the instrumental regression (unreported) is the Mimicking Target (significant at less than 1%). For all second state equation we report the estimation of sigma, namely the correlation between the error terms in the two equations. Models (2.2–2.5) separately test for Female presence, Age, Ethnical minority and Urban area, while Model (2.6) jointly tests for the four variables. ***, ** and * identify significance levels at less than 1, 5 and 10%, respectively.

evidence that teams with the presence of ethnical minorities are more likely to succeed as well as to raise more money than purely Caucasian teams.

6. Conclusions

Blockchain technology has a strong potential to 'democratize' entrepreneurship. ICOs are novel mechanisms of entrepreneurial finance that leverage blockchain technology. As such, ICOs are a promising candidate to alleviate existing financial constraints. Despite high expectations, very few studies have investigated whether digital finance provides such a neutral and meritocratic space for categories that are underrepresented in traditional entrepreneurial finance markets. Our study contributes to this debate by assessing the extent to which ICOs provide a neutral framework for individuals to raise capital and finance their entrepreneurial ventures, or whether inequalities found in the 'offline world' are echoed online.

Clear associations between gender, ethnic, or geographic disadvantages and funding are difficult to isolate given that exogenous variables intrude into the process of finance and performance in general. This is why, in this paper, we conduct two empirical studies to provide a nuanced picture of how underrepresented categories perform when raising funds through ICOs. This way, we are unable to show that some characteristics are more or less likely to obtain funding through an ICO. We acknowledge that our analysis reveals a choice or a realized outcome, not the range of outcomes that were a priori possible. The analysis does not show that in the absence of ICOs, underrepresented groups would have been less likely to receive more traditional forms of funding.

The combination of the results from the two studies provides the opportunity to summarize some preliminary evidence on the topic: we find evidence of ameliorated financing conditions for young teams, ethnic minorities, and remotely located entrepreneurs. Entrepreneurial boards with minority representation have a higher likelihood to opt for ICOs over traditional finance, are more likely to succeed in their campaign, and are expected to raise more funding than ethnically homogenous teams. This is an interesting result with implications for team diversity and the democratization of access to financial resources. We interpret this evidence as higher sensitivity to ethnicity from small investors, relative to professional investors, as highlighted by extant literature on equity crowdfunding (Cumming, Meoli, and Vismara 2019b). While professional investors might follow a market logic, small investors might also consider a community logic, as proposed by Vismara (2019). This would explain why ethnic entrepreneurs are more successful both in terms of success probability and expected amount raised.

For women, financial constraints generally found in traditional entrepreneurial markets do not seem to be mitigated by ICOs (so far). This result paves the way for considerations by policymakers, and further investigation on the social rationale behind this financing gap. To some extent, this gap might be alleviated by policy interventions. A recent study by Link and van Hasselt (2020, Forthcoming) about SBIR-funded research projects found that minority-owned firms are associated with 0.51 more patent applications than non-minority-owned firms, although women-owned firms are associated with slightly fewer patent applications, than men-owned firms. Future studies should further address how to calibrate policy intervention in the context of blockchain finance, encompassing how financial inclusion is linked to financial literacy.

Notes

1. The quotation reported is from the White House Press Release, accessed at https://www.whitehouse.gov/the-press-office/2012/04/05/remarks-president-jobs-act-bill-signing.
2. During an ICO, potentially, the CEO of a firm could change. We carried out a Google search for all companies in our sample, and when available we went through the post-ICO documentation reporting information on the CEO identity. Through this search, we did not find any evidence of CEO change during the ICOs in our sample.
3. Available at http://www.icbenchmark.com/Site/ICB_Structure.

Disclosure statement

No potential conflict of interest was reported by the author(s).

ORCID

Silvio Vismara http://orcid.org/0000-0001-5411-0326

References

Amatucci, F., and J. Sohl. 2004. "Women Entrepreneurs Securing Business Angel Financing: Tales from the Field." *Venture Capital* 6 (2–3): 181–196.

Arezzo, M. F., and G. Guagnano. 2018. "Response-based Sampling for Binary Choice Models with Sample Selection." *Econometrics* 6 (1): 12.

Arrow, K. J. 1998. "What has Economics to Say About Racial Discrimination?" *Journal of Economic Perspectives* 12 (2): 91–100.

Audretsch, D. B., E. E. Lehmann, and K. Wirsching. 2017. "Female Immigrant Entrepreneurship in Germany." In *Gender and Entrepreneurial Activity*, edited by A. N. Link (pp. 46–68). Cheltenham, UK: Edward Elgar Publishing.

Baum, A. 2020. "PropTech 2020: The Future of Real Estate." Accessed 28 August 2020. https://www.sbs.ox.ac.uk/sites/default/files/2020-02/proptech2020.pdf.

Baum, J., and B. Silverman. 2004. "Picking Winners or Building Them? Alliance, Intellectual, and Human Capital as Selection Criteria in Venture Financing and Performance of Biotechnology Startups." *Journal of Business Venturing* 19 (3): 411–436.

Becker, G. 1957. *The Economics of Discrimination*. Chicago: University of Chicago Press.

Bednar, S., D. Gicheva, and A. N. Link. 2019. "Innovative Activity and Gender Dynamics." *Small Business Economics*. Advance online publication. doi:10.1007/s11187-019-00282-2.

Bernstein, S., A. Korteweg, and K. Laws. 2017. "Attracting Early-stage Investors: Evidence from a Randomized Field Experiment." *The Journal of Finance* 72 (2): 509–538.

Bettin, G., R. Lucchetti, and A. Zazzaro. 2012. "Endogeneity and Sample Selection in a Model for Remittances." *Journal of Development Economics* 99 (2): 370–384.

Block, J., M. G. Colombo, D. J. Cumming, and S. Vismara. 2018. "New Players in Entrepreneurial Finance and Why They are There." *Small Business Economics* 50 (2): 239–250.

Block, J., C. Fisch, M. Obschonka, and P. Sandner. 2019. "A Personality Perspective on Business Angel Syndication." *Journal of Banking & Finance* 100: 306–327.

Block, J., A. Groh, L. Hornuf, T. Vanacker, and S. Vismara. 2020. "The Entrepreneurial Finance Markets of the Future: A Comparison of Crowdfunding and Initial Coin Offerings." *Small Business Economics*. Advance online publication. doi:10.1007/s11187-020-00330-2.

Brush, C. G., N. M. Carter, E. J. Gatwood, P. G. Greene, and M. Hart. 2004. *Gatekeepers of Venture Growth: A Diana Project Report on the Role and Participation of Women in the Venture Capital Industry*. Kansas City, MO: The Kauffman Foundation.

Coval, J., and T. Moskowitz. 2001. "The Geography of Investment: Informed Trading and Asset Prices." *Journal of Political Economy* 109: 811–841.

Cragg, J. G. 1971. "Some Statistical Models for Limited Dependent Variables with Application to the Demand for Durable Goods." *Econometrica* 39: 829–844.

Cumming, D., M. Meoli, and S. Vismara. 2019a. "Does Equity Crowdfunding Democratize Entrepreneurial Finance?" *Small Business Economics*. Advance online publication. doi:10.1007/s11187-019-00188-z.

Cumming, D., M. Meoli, and S. Vismara. 2019b. "Investors' Choices between Cash and Voting Rights: Evidence from Dual-class Equity Crowdfunding." *Research Policy* 48 (8): 103740.

Daniels, J. 2009. "Rethinking Cyberfeminism(s): Race, Gender, and Embodiment." *Women's Studies Quarterly* 37 (1–2): 101–124.

Dy, A. M., S. Marlow, and L. Martin. 2017. "A Web of Opportunity or the Same Old Story? Women Digital Entrepreneurs and Intersectionality Theory." *Human Relations* 70 (3): 286–311.

Fairlie, R. W., and A. Robb. 2007. "Why are Black-owned Businesses Less Successful Than White-owned Businesses? The Role of Families, Inheritances, and Business Human Capital." *Journal of Labor Economics* 25 (2): 289–323.

Fisch, C. 2019. "Initial Coin Offerings (ICOs) to Finance New Ventures." *Journal of Business Venturing* 34 (1): 1–22.

Fisch, C., and J. H. Block. 2020. "How does Entrepreneurial Failure Change an Entrepreneur's Digital Identity? Evidence from Twitter Data." *Journal of Business Venturing*. Advance online publication. doi:10.1016/j.jbusvent.2020.106015.

Fisch, C., C. Masiak, S. Vismara, and J. Block. 2019. "Motives and Profiles of ICO Investors." *Journal of Business Research*. Advance online publication. doi:10.1016/j.jbusres.2019.07.036.

Fisch, C., and P. P. Momtaz. 2020. "Institutional Investors and Post-ICO Performance: An Empirical Analysis of Investor Returns in Initial Coin Offerings (ICOs)." *Journal of Corporate Finance* 64 (10): 101679.

French, K. R., and J. M. Poterba. 1991. "Investor Diversification and International Equity Markets." *American Economic Review* 81: 222–226.

Gicheva, D., and A. N. Link. 2013. "Leveraging Entrepreneurship Through Private Investments: Does Gender Matter?" *Small Business Economics* 40 (2): 199–210.

Gicheva, D., and A. N. Link. 2015. "The Gender Gap in Federal and Private Support for Entrepreneurship." *Small Business Economics* 45 (4): 729–733.

Giudici, G., M. Guerini, and C. Rossi-Lamastra. 2020. "Elective Affinities: Exploring the Matching between Entrepreneurs and Investors in Equity Crowdfunding." *Baltic Journal of Managament*. Advance online publication. doi:10.1108/BJM-08-2019-0287.

Gompers, P., and J. Lerner. 2001. "The Venture Capital Revolution." *Journal of Economic Perspectives* 15 (2): 145–168.

Greene, P., C. Brush, M. Hart, and P. Saparito. 2001. "Patterns of Venture Capital Funding: is Gender a Factor?" *Venture Capital* 3: 63–83.

Herzenstein, M., R. Andrews, U. Dholakia, and E. Lyandres. 2008. "The Democratization of Personal Consumer Loans? Determinants of Success in Online Peer-to-peer Lending Communities." *Boston University School of Management Research Paper* 14 (6): 1–36.

Howell, S., M. Niessner, and D. Yermack. 2020. "Initial Coin Offerings: Financing Growth with Cryptocurrency Token Sales." *Review of Financial Studies* 33 (9): 3925–3974.

Hsu, D. 2007. "Experienced Entrepreneurial Founders, Organizational Capital, and Venture Capital Funding." *Research Policy* 36 (5): 722–741.

Huang, W., M. Meoli, and S. Vismara. 2020. "The Geography of Initial Coin Offerings." *Small Business Economics* 55: 77–102.

Link, A. 2017. *Gender and Entrepreneurial Activity*. Cheltenham: Edward Elgar.

Link, A. N., van Hasselt, M., Vismara, S. (2020, Forthcoming). Going Public with Public Money. *Small Business Economics*. doi:10.1007/s11187-020-00355-7

Lyandres, E., B. Palazzo, and D. Rabetti. 2019. "Are tokens securities? An anatomy of initial coin offerings." Working Paper.

Manski, C. F., and S. R. Lerman. 1977. "The Estimation of Choice Probabilities from Choice Based Samples." *Econometrica: Journal of the Econometric Society* 45, 1977–1988.

Momtaz, P. P. 2020a. "Entrepreneurial Finance and Moral Hazard: Evidence from Token Offerings." *Journal of Business Venturing*. Advance online publication. doi:10.1016/j.jbusvent.2020.106001.

Momtaz, P. P. 2020b. "Initial Coin Offerings, Asymmetric Information, and Loyal CEOs." *Small Business Economics*. Advance online publication. doi:10.1007/s11187-020-00335-x.

Momtaz, P. P. 2020c. "CEO Emotions and Firm Valuation in Initial Coin Offerings: An Artificial Emotional Intelligence Approach." *Strategic Management Journal*. Advance online publication. doi:10.1002/smj.3235.

Morgan-Thomas, A. 2016. "Rethinking Technology in the SME Context: Affordances, Practices and ICTs." *International Small Business Journal* 34 (8): 1122–1136.

Morse, A. 2015. "Peer-to-peer Crowd Funding: Information and the Potential for Disruption in Consumer Lending." NBER Working Paper.

Nambisan, S., K. Lyytinen, A. Majchrzak, and M. Song. 2017. "Digital Innovation Management: Reinventing Innovation Management Research in a Digital World." *MIS Quarterly* 41 (1): 223–238.

Newey, W. K. 1986. "Linear Instrumental Variable Estimation of Limited Dependent Variable Models with Endogenous Explanatory Variables." *Journal of Econometrics* 32 (1): 127–141.

OECD. 2020. "List of OECD Member Countries." Accessed 28 August 2020. https://www.oecd.org/about/document/list-oecd-member-countries.htm.

Orser, B., S. Coleman, and Y. Li. 2020. "Progress or Pinkwashing: Who Benefits from Women-focused Capital Funds?" *Small Business Economics* 55: 363–387.

Pope, D. G., and J. R. Sydnor. 2011. "What's in a Picture? Evidence of Discrimination from Prosper.com." *Journal of Human Resources* 46 (1): 53–92.

Prokop, J., and D. Wang. 2018. "Is there a Gender gap in Equity Crowdfunding?" Proceedings of the INFINITI Conference on International finance 2018.

Puri, M., and R. Zarutskie. 2012. "On the Life Cycle Dynamics of Venture-capital- and Non-venture-capital-financed Firms." *The Journal of Finance* 67 (6): 2247–2293.

Roubini, N. 2018. "Blockchain isn't about Democracy and Decentralization – It's about Greed." Accessed 28 August 2020. https://www.theguardian.com/technology/2018/oct/15/blockchain-democracy-decentralisation-bitcoin-price-cryptocurrencies.

SEC (U.S. Securities and Exchange Commission). 2019. *Real Estate Investment Trusts (REITS): What are REITs?* Accessed 28 August 2020. https://www.investor.gov/introduction-investing/basics/investment-products/real-estate-investment-trusts-reits.

Smith, J., M. Vora, H. E. Benedetti, K. Yoshida, and Z. Vogel. 2019. "Tokenized Securities and Commercial Real Estate." Working Paper.

Sorenson, O., and T. Stuart. 2001. "Syndication Networks and the Spatial Distribution of Venture Capital Investments." *American Journal of Sociology* 106: 1546–1588.

Ter Wal, A., O. Alexy, J. Block, and P. G. Sandner. 2016. "The Best of Both Worlds: The Benefits of Open-specialized and Closed-diverse Syndication Networks for New Ventures' Success." *Administrative Science Quarterly* 61 (3): 393–432.

Ughetto, E., C. Rossi, D. B. Audretsch, and E. E. Lehmann. 2020. "Female Entrepreneurship in the Digital Era." *Small Business Economics*. Advance online publication. doi:10.1007/s11187-019-00298-8.

Van de Ven, W., and B. Van Praag. 1981. "The Demand for Deductibles in Private Health Insurance: A Probit Model with Sample Selection." *Journal of Econometrics* 17: 229–252.

Verheul, I., and R. Thurik. 2001. "Start-up Capital: Does Gender Matter?" *Small Business Economics* 16 (4): 329–346.

Vismara, S. 2019. "Sustainability in Equity Crowdfunding." *Technological Forecasting and Social Change* 141: 98–106.

Vismara, S., D. Benaroio, and F. Carne. 2017. "Gender in Entrepreneurial Finance: Matching Investors and Entrepreneurs in Equity Crowdfunding." In *Gender and Entrepreneurial Activity*, edited by A. N. Link (pp. 271–288). Cheltenham, UK: Edward Elgar Publishing.

Yermack, D. 2017. "Corporate Governance and Blockchains." *Review of Finance* 21 (1): 7–31.

Innovation in women-led firms: an empirical analysis

David B. Audretsch, Maksim Belitski and Candida Brush

ABSTRACT

The availability of resources is paramount for innovation in women-led firms. We define a women-led firm where a chief executive officer (CEO) is a woman. We examine how nature – a pervasive and arbitrary type of institutional environment as well as access to resources is associated with different propensity to innovate between women and men-led firms.

Using micro-level cross-country data of 12,412 firms and a reduced sample of 5,052 firms during 2008–2015 and across 75 economies, we find that the differences in risk perception between women and men-led firms ae not associated with innovation propensity. Instead, the availability of resources proxied by a country's fiscal freedom and availability of internal resources lead to an increase in innovation in women-led firms. The relationship is non-linear and increases with the availability of finance. This work has important policy implications for the role of institutions to spur innovation in women-led firms.

1. Introduction

It has been long argued that innovation is gender-biased (Still and Timms 2000; Thursby and Thursby 2005; Ding, Murray, and Stuart 2006; De Tienne and Chandler 2007; Gicheva and Link 2015). The general perception is that women are less innovative than men (Nählinder 2010). However, this is not the case when we look at the data. The world bank enterprise survey for 75 developing countries reports for 2007–2014, there was 19.86 percent of women-led firms that created new to market products, whereas only 14.60 percent of firms are women-led (World Bank 2015). There are significant differences in women-led firms between countries such as Argentina, Bangladesh, Georgia, Mexico, India, Turkey, Senegal, Tajikistan, Tanzania, and Uzbekistan, with less than 8 percent of total firms which are women-led. Afghanistan, Armenia, Bolivia, Cameroon, Egypt, Yemen have less than 4 percent of total firms with a woman as a CEO. Other developing countries such as Estonia, Latvia, Romania, Serbia, Mongolia, Ukraine have at least a quarter of women-led firms (World Bank 2015).

Recent research for the United States has also demonstrated that the Phase II Small Business Innovation Research (SBIR) research-funded projects had a greater probability of being commercialized in women- than in men-owned and led firms (Bednar, Gicheva, and Link 2019)

Despite this non-obvious empirical fact, there is a paucity of empirical research on the gender differences in a firm's innovation (Turner 2009; Carrasco 2014; Dohse, Goel, and Nelson 2019; Wellalage, Fernandez, and Thrikawala 2020) and the impact of institutional change on firm innovation (Link and Scott 2019). Research on innovation and growth in women-led firms has become more prominent in recent years (Belitski and Desai 2019; Balachandra et al. 2019) and has found significant differences between men and women CEOs in firm productivity and job creation.

Similar research in the entrepreneurship and management literature has recently shifted its focus on nature's role in firm innovation (Greene et al. 2001; Brush 2006, 2009; Weber and Zulehner 2010). Researchers have also found a significant funding gap between men and women ambitious entrepreneurs because of possible bias against women (Jennings and Brush 2013).

Literature gaps in the gender differences in innovation include an explanation of why women are less visible as inventors, innovators or entrepreneurs than men, and the conditions that make women take innovation risk and increase survival and growth rates (Link and Strong 2016). The literature on entrepreneurial finance has demonstrated that investors might evaluate the pitches by men founders more favorably than those by women (De Bruin, Brush, and Welter 2006), resulting in a lack of financial resources for women-owned firms (Gicheva and Link 2013, 2015; World Bank 2019).

Differences in how the investors perceive women-led firms as a riskier investment compared to men-led firms (Greene et al. 2001) influences the country's business culture and institutional environment. Differences in risk perceptions among the investors change the access to finance for women-led firms compared to men-led firms (Estrin, Korosteleva, and Mickiewicz 2013; Belitski and Desai 2019; Bednar, Gicheva, and Link 2019), which in turns affects the likelihood of innovation and the perception of women in business.

While prior empirical research has found that family support, access to external financing, and networks are the main criteria affecting women CEO decision to innovate (Jabeen et al. 2019), very little attention has been paid to how this relationship changes in countries with different level of institutional quality, for example in countries with the high and low level of market uncertainty related to corruption (Olsen and Cox 2001; De Bruin, Brush, and Welter 2006).

The evidence on the connection between women-led innovation, institutional environment, and corruption in the literature on innovation remains mixed (Alatas et al. 2009; Wellalage, Locke, and Samujh 2018, 2020).

In order to address this gap and respond to a recent call in the economics of innovation and new technology literature (Gicheva and Link 2013, 2015; Link 2019b) the purpose of this study is to investigate how nature – pervasive and arbitrary types of corruption, a country's fiscal freedom and availability of internal resources – is associated with innovation propensity in women-led firms.

This paper draws on three main theoretical arguments that explain gender differences in innovation (i) institutional theory, (ii) risk-aversion theory, and (iii) resource dependency theory.

This study makes two main contributions to the innovation literature. First, we contribute to the cross-over of knowledge in the relationship between innovation and institutional factors (corruption type, access to finance, and internal resources), and how this relationship varies between women- and men-led firms (De Bruin, Brush, and Welter 2006; Brush 2006, 2009; Carrasco 2014; Gicheva and Link 2013, 2015). Second, we contribute to the innovation literature by demonstrating how gender aspects may change firms' propensity to innovate and whether the differences in innovation are gender-biased or resource-dependent? (Brush 2006, 2009; Balachandra et al. 2019). In doing so, we empirically test whether the state of nature, related to the perception of risk, uncertainty, and differences in moral of women CEO (Swamy et al. 2001; Sung 2003; Esarey and Chirillo 2013) can explain the differences in innovation rates (Verheul, van Stel, and Thurik 2006).

Unlike prior research, which typically has resorted to cross-sectional data (Carrasco 2014) and single-country studies (Nählinder 2010; Bednar and Gicheva 2014; Link 2019a; Link and Scott 2019), we advance innovation research by using firm-level data and two samples for 12,412 firms and 5,052 firms across 75 developing countries during 2008–2015.

The remainder of the paper is as follows. In the next section, we discuss the links between institutional context and innovation. We present our data and method in the third section, followed by results in the fourth section. Our fifth section offers discussion and conclusions.

2. Theory and hypotheses

Innovation decisions are taken based on a set of internal and external (institutional) factors, which affect the level of risk it may impose on the execution of the decision and the likelihood of a successful outcome.

Traditionally, the economic literature has explained innovation by linking it to the economic stock of knowledge (Griliches 1990; Cohen and Levinthal 1989). These theories have been enriched by others that suggest that institutions matter for innovation (Shleifer and Vishny 1993; Estrin, Korosteleva, and Mickiewicz 2013) along with the innovator's decision-making process (Teece 1996; Link and Scott 2005).

We define institutions following Williamson's (2000) four levels of social analysis –norms, customs, traditions, values, religion, etc. operate and constitutes informal institutions; formal rules (such as constitutions, laws, property rights, etc.); institutions of governance; and resource allocation. While formal institutions present similar opportunities and status to women- and men-led firms, informal institutions demonstrate a different context for women (Carrasco 2014) and may affect their decision-making as a CEO to take risks and innovate.

Pervasive and arbitrary corruption as an informal institution is usually associated with different perceptions of risk and uncertainty of doing business (Cuervo-Cazurra 2006, 2008). Women-led firms may respond differently from men-led firms to each type of corruption due to the differences in preferences and social culture, uncertainty, and risk perceptions between women and men (Croson and Gneezy 2009). This argument builds on Swamy et al. (2001) and who found using micro-data that women are less involved in bribery and may respond differently to the two types of corrupt environments and on Dollar, Fisman, and Gatti (2001) and Sung (2003) on women as the fairer sex. Gender differences were also found to affect preferences, behaviors, and cultural norms and change the relationship between corruption and firm innovation (Alatas et al. 2009; Brush, De Bruin, and Welter 2009; Nelson 2015).

There have been several attempts to explain these differences in innovation activity between women-led and men-led firms both theoretically and empirically (Brush et al. 2006; Alsos, Isaksen, and Ljunggren 2006; Verheul, van Stel, and Thurik 2006; Elam and Terjesen 2010).

First, when a CEO makes a decision, he/she evaluates the level of risk, uncertainty, and the likelihood of a successful outcome such as product or process innovation. Thus, the domination of informal institutions in a country may lead to greater uncertainty and risk and deter decisions leading to innovation. For example, in countries where it is expected that bureaucrats change the frequency and amount of bribes (Fredriksson 2014) (arbitrary corruption) may increase transaction costs of innovation, which may discourage CEOs from innovating.

Women are generally perceived in the literature as more risk-averse than men (Charness and Gneezy 2012; Palvia, Vähämaa, and Vähämaa 2015) and are more likely to defer innovation activity if the environment is perceived as more uncertain and risky (Estrin and Mickiewicz 2011; Belitski, Chowdhury, and Desai 2016; Hsieh et al. 2018). Corruption may increase their transaction costs, reduce the profit and sustainability of a business. Considering a set of gender-specific determinants of innovation behavior (e.g. attitude to risk, tolerance to uncertainty, social-focus, morale, opportunism, etc.), innovation policies have long been conducive to women being promoted into CEO positions on the basis that they have inherently superior moral qualities, however these policies can be misguided if both men and women equally perceive and are exposed to corruption (Wellalage, Fernandez, and Thrikawala 2020)

Research on understanding the origins and the consequences of pervasive and arbitrary corruption (Cuervo-Cazurra 2006) as the state of 'nature' is important in explaining the extent of risk-aversion and the propensity of innovation women- and men-led firms. These two types of corruption can be effectively used as a proxy for institutional quality and the environment that affects gender differences in preferences, behaviors, and cultural norms (Alatas et al. 2009; Wellalage, Fernandez, and Thrikawala 2020). On the one hand, pervasive institutionalized corruption could facilitate transactions by reducing inefficiency under conditions of severe formal voids (Webb, Khoury, and Hitt 2020) and uncertainty. Paying a bribe could help to overcome the 'red tape' and may become an attractive option to a firm if the bribe size is less than the amount of taxes and that a firm may expect the authorities to comply with the agreement. The nature of pervasive corruption helps to bypass regulatory burdens, and reducing uncertainty as a bribe is associated with less risk of doing business. Under the assumption that women CEO is more risk-averse (Charness and Gneezy 2012; Palvia, Vähämaa, and Vähämaa 2015) leads us to the following hypotheses:

> H1: Women-led firms are more innovative in countries with higher pervasive corruption when uncertainty and risks are low.

Arbitrary corruption hurts business, and it increases uncertainty and transaction costs for business if bribes are not institutionalized (Cuervo-Cazurra 2006). Arbitrary corruption relates to informal practices and norms when the expectations are not well-defined, and execution of the agreement is either unexpected (in other words, unpredictable) (Méon and Sekkat 2005), or it cannot be guaranteed by authorities (Cuervo-Cazurra 2006).

The nature of arbitrary corruption makes the risk of non-compliance with the agreements high (Cuervo-Cazurra 2008; Estrin, Korosteleva, and Mickiewicz 2013). Arbitrary corruption also means the manager may have to set aside resources for a 'just in case' scenario each time there will be a transaction. It is less predictable, as the manager knows there will be no secure reduction in costs if the bribe is paid. This type of nature is associated with a higher cost of innovation, and the impediments to develop and commercialize new products remain highly unknown. This setting will particularly deter women CEOs decision-making on innovation (Alatas et al. 2009).

While both scenarios are undesirable and women are more risk-averse (Croson and Gneezy 2009) and more altruistic (Eckel and Grossman 1998) than men, a straightforward interpretation is women-led firms will either postpone the innovation decision or abandon innovation. This implies that women-led firms will be more careful when it comes to innovation in the arbitrary environment (Charness and Gneezy 2012). We hypothesize:

> H2: Women-led firms are less innovative in countries with a higher arbitrary corruption when uncertainty and risks are high.

The theory of resource dependency providers provides another reason why woman can incur more (less) risks (Alsos, Isaksen, and Ljunggren 2006; Ngoasong and Kimbu 2019). This is associated with their access to resources (Brush 2006; Brush et al. 2006; De Bruin, Brush, and Welter 2006; Gicheva and Link 2015; Wellalage, Fernandez, and Thrikawala 2020). In the institutionally strong and economically developed countries such as the United States, women seek angel financing at rates substantially lower than men but have an equal probability of receiving investment (Becker-Blease and Sohl 2007). This may not be the case in developing economies. Estrin and Mickiewicz (2011) argued that women-led firms are disadvantaged in countries with weak institutions and corruption. Other studies also found that in many institutional contexts, women are restricted in their access to the economic resources needed for innovation, particularly in the early stage of business growth (Brush 2006; World Bank 2019). That can be the reason why women respond differently to investment risks (Olsen and Cox 2001), including limited venture investments in women-led firms (Balachandra et al. 2019). Countries with a high tax burden impose additional costs on innovation and are likely to hit women-led firms harder, who already experience resource limitations (Jennings and Brush 2013).

The institutional environment (Williamson 2000) may not affect innovation in women-led firms directly (Carrasco 2014). Gender differences may affect investor perception of the intensity and success of innovation in women-led firms. Women-led firms in developing countries, and in those where patriarchal society dominates, are more likely to experience gender-based discrimination, limiting their access to finance (Balachandra et al. 2019) working in a "man's world" (Gupta et al. 2009).

A large literature has found mixed effects of fiscal freedom on business activity (Baliamoune-Lutz 2015), with an increase in tax burden likely to drain financial resources for innovation (Braunerhjelm, Eklund, and Thulin 2019), hamper risk-taking behavior, R&D, and market entry. Women-led firms may be particularly sensitive to tax changes as it increases the cost of doing business (Becker-Blease and Sohl 2007). An increase in resource availability and fiscal freedom creates the motivation to engage in entrepreneurial action and innovation activities (McMullen, Bagby, and Palich 2008), with women-led firms most affected. We hypothesize:

H3: Women-led firms are more innovative in countries with higher fiscal freedom.

Access to resources for innovation is different across different stages of the firm life cycle (Belitski and Desai 2019; Mickiewicz et al. 2017), with more mature firms accumulating substantial internal resources for innovation, while younger firms and start-ups will rely on external equity investment, debt finance and will be squeezed in resource availability (Olsen and Cox 2001; Brush 2006; Brush et al. 2006; De Bruin, Brush, and Welter 2006). In addition, equity investment is substantially limited for women-led firms at the start-up stage that hinders the propensity to engage in innovation (Jennings and Brush 2013; World Bank 2019). We hypothesize:

H4: Women-led firms are more innovative in the later stages of the firm lifecycle.

3. Data and method

3.1. Sample

We combine firm and country-level data for our sample. Our source for firm-level data is the World Bank Enterprise Surveys (World Bank 2015) and world bank development indicators (World Bank 2018). We use one to two waves of the data for 75 countries during 2008–2015. The World Bank enterprise survey (2015) covers a wide range of topics, including leadership and ownership, performance, human capital, industry and business environment, institutional characteristics (e.g. corruption, financial and administrative obstacles of doing business). Self-reported data from firms is useful because 'experience-based' information (Gonzalez, Lopez-Cordova, and Valladares 2007) is more likely to be accurate than objective data, especially if managers in many developing economies underreport accounting data. The surveys include retrospective information, which spans three years for a focal firm input.

We cleaned the data for outliers and used the maximum number of observations available for non-missing values for our model (1) and replaced all non-applicable with missing values, achieving two distinctive samples. Our full sample of 12,412 firms is used to test the women-led likelihood of innovation in a pervasive institutional environment, while the reduced sample consists of 5,052 firms is used to test this relationship in an arbitrary institutional environment. The number of observations varies between two samples due to data availability for firms' characteristics related to an arbitrary type of corruption, which is less reported as they contain more sensitive corruption data. Interestingly, we do not find significant differences in means and standard deviations for dependent and explanatory variables in two samples (Table 1).

A composition of industries and firm size across both samples also demonstrates they are largely representative (see Table 2). Industries, including food, metals, and machinery, chemicals and pharmaceuticals, non-metallic and plastic materials, make up to more than half of each sample. The Enterprise Surveys classifies small firms (<20 fulltime employees), medium firms (20–99 fulltime employees), and large firms (>100 fulltime employees). Both models have a smaller proportion of small firms than medium firms.

The list of countries included in this study, and additional information about our variables are in Table A1 (Appendix).

Table 1. Descriptive statistics.

Variables	Description	Full sample (12,412 obs.)				Reduced sample (4,714 obs.)				
		Mean	St.dev	Min	Max	Mean	St.dev	Min	Max	
Innovation	Firm introduced new to market product or service during the last 3 years1 = yes, 0 = no	0.13	0.33	0.00	1.00	0.09	0.29	0.00	1.00	
Foreign Technology	Technology licensed from a foreign-owned company1 = yes, 0 = no	0.83	0.38	0.00	1.00	0.79	0.40	0.00	1.00	
Firm age	Age of firm, years	19.72	13.85	0.00	74.00	20.54	14.98	0.00	72.00	
Women-led firm	Chief Information Officer (Top manager) is a female 1 = yes, 0 = no	0.11	0.31	0.00	1.00	0.11	0.31	0.00	1.00	
Female high-skill	Proportion of women employed full-time in non-production activities (high-skilled) in total number of employees	8.33	10.99	0.00	100.00	9.25	11.60	0.00	100.00	
Female low-skill	Proportion of women in production activities (low -skilled) in total number of employees	17.59	24.07	0.00	100.00	17.33	23.25	0.00	100.00	
Firm size	Number of Full Time Employees (FTEs), in logs	3.85	1.38	0.69	9.74	3.99	1.40	0.69	9.74	
Digital readiness- Email	Email is used to communicate value chain	0.79	0.40	0.00	1.00	0.84	0.37	0.00	1.00	
Digital readiness- Web	Wed-site is used to communicate value chain	0.55	0.50	0.00	1.00	0.60	0.49	0.00	1.00	
Senior management time	% of C-level management time spent in dealing with government regulations?	11.50	18.32	0.00	100.00	13.66	19.03	0.00	100.00	
Frequency of inspections	Frequency of inspections a year /requirement for meeting by tax officials	3.42	4.53	1.00	30.00	4.26	5.57	1.00	30.00	
Court system perception	Court system is unfair and corrupted −1 corrupted - 4 not corrupted	−2.39	1.02	−4.00	−1.00	−2.23	1.00	−4.00	−1.00	
Pervasive corruption	Cronbach alpha (>0.70) of pervasive corruption in the host country, from −3 (low) to 3 (high), composite of share sales paid in informal payments % (1); need to offer a gift when expected by public officials, (2) share of contract value in informal gifts to government officials to secure contract, (3)	−0.05	0.79	−0.41	9.06					
Arbitrary corruption	Cronbach alpha (>0.70) of arbitrary corruption in the host country, from −3 (low) to 3 (high) unofficial payment when applied for a water connection (1), applied for a telephone connection and an informal gift requested (2), applied for an import license and an informal gift requested (3), applied for an operating license and an informal gift requested (4).					−0.003	0.94	−3.70	0.45	
FFI	Fiscal freedom Index ij = 100 – α (Factor ij) ^{2} where Fiscal Freedom ij represents the fiscal freedom in country i for factor j; Factor ij represents the value (based on a scale of 0–100) in country i for factor j; and α is a coefficient set equal to 0.03 (Heritage Foundation 2020).	79.82	5.76	60.20	96.60		79.53	5.30	60.20	96.60

(*Continued*)

Table 1. Continued.

Variables	Description	Full sample (12,412 obs.)				Reduced sample (4,714 obs.)				
		Mean	St.dev	Min	Max	Mean	St.dev	Min	Max	
Seats	Proportion of seats held by women in national parliaments (%), World Bank (2018)	15.86	9.34	0.00	43.30		16.84	8.93	0.00	43.30
Discrimination	Binary variable = 1 if country ratified the C111 – Discrimination (Employment and Occupation) Convention, 1958 (No. 111), zero otherwise (ILO 2018)	0.93	0.26	0.00	1.00		0.89	0.31	0.00	1.00
Maternity	Binary variable = 1 if country ratified C003 – Maternity Protection Convention, 1919 (No. 3), zero otherwise (ILO 2018)	0.12	0.32	0.00	1.00		0.14	0.34	0.00	1.00
FLPR	Female labor participation rate, World Bank (2018)	41.78	16.34	6.88	86.70		44.36051	16.11	6.84	86.69
Low income	Countries classified by the World Bank (2018) as low income and low-middle income (<3,895 Gross National Income per capita).	0.64	0.48	0.00	1.00		0.57	0.49	0.00	1.00
Economic development	GDP per capita in constant 2010 prices (logarithm)	3.47	0.42	2.50	4.56		3.51	0.42	2.50	4.56

Source: World Bank (2015, 2018), ILO (2018).

Table 2. Averages of main variables split by industry and firm across two models.

	Full sample = 12,412 obs.				Reduced sample = 5,052 obs.			
Industry	obs.	% in total	Women-led firm	pervasive corruption	obs.	% in total	Women-led firm	arbitrary corruption
Textiles	873	7.03	0.10	0.01	256	5.07	0.14	0.10
Leather	62	0.50	0.03	−0.09	54	1.07	0.00	−0.50
Garments	1105	8.90	0.23	−0.03	373	7.38	0.23	−0.03
Food	2345	18.89	0.12	−0.06	935	18.51	0.13	0.09
Metals and machinery	2433	19.60	0.06	−0.06	943	18.67	0.06	−0.05
Electronics	372	3.00	0.10	0.06	138	2.73	0.11	0.00
Chemicals and pharmaceuticals	1022	8.23	0.12	−0.08	450	8.91	0.14	0.04
Wood and furniture	448	3.61	0.09	0.04	196	3.88	0.18	−0.05
Non-metallic and plastic materials	1668	13.44	0.07	0.00	717	14.19	0.06	0.02
Auto and auto components	236	1.90	0.03	0.06	88	1.74	0.02	−0.47
Other manufacturing	975	7.86	0.10	−0.08	397	7.86	0.09	−0.02
Retail and wholesale trade	179	1.44	0.09	0.03	155	3.07	0.11	−0.12
Hotels and restaurants	174	1.40	0.12	−0.04	110	2.18	0.18	0.23
Other services	325	2.62	0.04	0.15	126	2.49	0.05	−0.36
Other: Construction, Transportation	195	1.57	0.04	0.29	114	2.26	0.06	−0.66
Firm size split								
Small (<20)	3760	30.29	0.11	−0.01	1,534	30.36	0.13	−0.01
Medium Small (20–99)	4997	40.26	0.09	0.00	1,906	37.73	0.10	−0.09
Medium large and large (100 and over)	3655	29.45	0.10	−0.08	1,612	31.91	0.10	0.08

Source: World Bank (2015, 2018), ILO (2018).

3.2. Dependent variable

Our firm-level dependent variable is product innovation, calculated as a binary variable equal to one if a firm introduced new to market product or service and zero otherwise (Hsieh et al. 2018; Audretsch and Belitski 2019, 2020).

The Measure of innovation based on products (our dependent variable) is characterized by a lower bound of zero as no negative values are possible. Firms report zero in cases where no innovation project was undertaken, or this was not completed over the three-year period to which the questionnaire referred. Innovation plans may not have been completed within the three-year period because of one of the following reasons: the project was abandoned or seriously suspended; the project was seriously delayed with respect to initial planning; the project required more than three years to be completed. Firms reporting positive innovation values have demonstrated commercialization of new products, while firms reporting missing values were not included.

3.3. Key explanatory variables

We use two corruption measures, drawn from the World Bank Enterprise Survey (World Bank 2015). Pervasive corruption measures the likelihood that a firm will encounter the demand for bribes when dealing with the government. Arbitrary corruption measures uncertainty regarding the demand for bribes (Cuervo-Cazurra 2008) to know in advance the expected bribe amount when applying for a water and telephone connection, import and operating licenses, or getting the service delivered after paying a bribe. Our corruption measures were created as aggregates using Cronbach alpha (Cronbach 1951).

We use a binary variable 'Women-led firm' if a CEO is a female (1 = yes; o = no), sourced from the question 'Chief executive officer is Male/Female' from the Enterprise Surveys. We also know if the owner is a female or male.

The Fiscal Freedom Index refers to the absence of burdensome tax rates and government expenditures as a portion of GDP (McMullen, Bagby, and Palich 2008). Tax rates reflect the price of engaging in innovation activity. Increases in this price are expected to correspond to fewer individuals taking risks of new product development to market (Brush 2006). Calculation of the Fiscal Freedom Index (FFI) includes three components:

The top marginal tax rate on individual income; The top marginal tax rate on corporate income, and the total tax burden as a percentage of GDP, with all three equally weighted (Heritage Foundation 2020). Our final explanatory variable is firm age in years and is included with a quadratic term in the equation to capture differences in the level of innovation and resource availability across different stages of the firm lifecycle (Belitski and Desai 2019). We created four interactions by multiplying a binary variable 'women-led firm' with both types of corruption, FFI, and firm age.

3.4. Control variables

We control for the country and firm-level characteristics. The inclusion of country characteristics enables us to further control the impact of the institutional environment (Williamson 2000) on innovation in women-led firms. We include gender-specific institutions reflecting the state of female labor market access, level of maternity protection, and equal rights (Cuervo-Cazurra 2008). More specifically, we include the share of seats held by women in national parliaments as a proxy for women's political empowerment from the World Bank. We used binary variable discrimination to identify whether or not a country ratified the C111 – Discrimination (Employment and Occupation) Convention, 1958 (No. 111), which concerns discrimination in respect of employment and occupation (entry into force 15 Jun 1960) (ILO 2018). We used binary variable maternity to identify whether or not a country ratified the C003 – Maternity Protection Convention, 1919 (No. 3), which concerns the employment of women before and after childbirth (Entry into force:13 Jun 1921) (ILO 2018).

We include female labor force participation rate, female (% of female population ages 15+) from the World Bank (2018). To measure the level of economic development, we included the logarithm of gross domestic product (GDP) per capita in constant 2010 prices as well as a binary variable of the low-income country according to the World Bank classification (2018). We interacted a binary variable for a low-income country and GDP per capita to understand how the extent of economic development may change innovation for firms in low-income countries.

We also control for firm-level characteristics that may affect the likelihood of innovation. We use the number of full-time employees as a proxy for firm size, taken in logarithms. We also included if a firm licenses foreign technology from a foreign firm (yes = 1; 0 = no) to measure the extent of advanced technology use and knowledge collaboration with external partners (Belitski and Desai 2016). Besides, we measure the use of digital technologies by including a binary variable whether or not firms employ emails for communication with partners and clients (1 = yes, 0 = no), which may be an indicator of internet connectedness and e-commerce for developing countries. We include a binary variable Web if a firm has a corporate website to connect with customers and suppliers, operating within a vertical supply and demand chain (Li et al. 2016). Manager perceptions about fairness in the court system may change the decision to innovate and enforce contracts (Audretsch, Belitski, and Desai 2019), affecting subsequent decision-making. Court system perception illustrates the extent to which a manager considers the legislative system fair and uncorrupted (–4) or unfair (–1) (Chowdhury, Audretsch, and Belitski 2019).

In order to control for female labor force participation in a firm (Bednar and Gicheva 2014) we include female high-skill engagement, which is measured as the proportion of female employees engaged in high-skilled activity in a firm. We measured female production engagement as the proportion of female employees engaged in non-skilled production activity in a firm (Weber and Zulehner 2010; Belitski and Desai 2019). Finally, we use industry and year fixed effects to control for industry-specific and year unobserved heterogeneity.

3.5. Estimation strategy

Our estimation strategy is congruent with the firm and country-level data availability and design (Siepel and Dejardin 2020). We estimate two logistic (logit) models for product innovation using pervasive and arbitrary institutional environments and FFI in each model (Wooldridge 2009). Our dependent variable is binary y_i (firm's propensity to introduce new to market products/ services):

$$Prob(y_i = 1) = \beta_0 + \beta_{1i}x_{1i} + \lambda_1 S_{ir} + \beta_{2i}x_{2i} + \delta_i + \omega_r + \varphi_t + u_i \quad (1)$$

Equation (1) is the logistic cumulative distribution function. Vector S_{ir} is explanatory variables (corruption type, Fiscal Freedom Index, women-led firm) of while x_{1i} is a vector of the firm's characteristics and x_{2i} is a vector of the country characteristics and u_i is an error term. (Wooldridge 2009). Vectors δ_i, ω_r, φ_t are industry, region and time fixed effects. A bootstrapping of errors was also applied and OLS which led to similar results in terms of the sign and significance of all confidents, but of a different size.

We started by exploring the multicollinearity of the variables by examining the variance inflation factors for all variables, finding each less than 10. In addition, we analysed the correlation coefficients ensuring that no coefficients were greater than 0.70. We analysed all the variables' histograms and found the errors were identically and independently distributed with constant variance.

4. Results

Results related to the main hypothesis are reported in Table 3.

Our results are robust across all five specifications in the full (specification 1–6) and reduced samples (specification 7–12), including and excluding country-level characteristics and gender-specific national institutions. Our findings do not support H1 and H2, which predict that innovation propensity in women-led firms depends on the level of pervasive or arbitrary corruption; interestingly that both interactions of a women-led firm and pervasive environment (specifications 1–6) as well as a women-led firm and arbitrary (specifications 7–12) environment are not statistically significant and are not associated with the decision-making on innovation (Wellalage, Fernandez, and Thrikawala 2020).

Corruption is endogenous by nature, meaning that bureaucrats can modify their bribe-seeking behavior, increasing the risk of doing business, also known as an arbitrary type of corruption (Cuervo-Cazurra 2008). Officials may arbitrarily decide to raise the bribe fees or non-comply for a transaction, then corruption raises innovation costs, and thus both the pervasive and arbitrary nature of corruption is perceived by women and men-led firms as risky, deferring innovation decision-making.

Figure 1A and B illustrate the predictive margins of innovation propensity in women-led firms vs. men-led firms across two types of a corrupt environment using the full and reduced samples. Our results are consistent with Wellalage, Fernandez, and Thrikawala (2020), who reject the proposition that women behave differently concerning bribing on the grounds of higher ethical/moral standards, which supports the differential association and opportunity (DAO) view, which argues that women and men in positions of influence are equally associated with firm-level bribing (Alatas et al. 2009).

We find that women- and men-led firms react similarly to differences in bribing behavior and differences associated with the pervasive and arbitrary corruption type in the country does not change their propensity to innovate. By paying bribes or avoiding bribes in the same way, women-led firms may aim to avoid discrimination (Wellalage, Locke, and Samujh 2018) with the incentives to innovate and bribe independently on the environment may be even higher for women-led firms. We also found that it is the extent of resources available for innovation rather than institutional nature, which changes the propensity of innovation in women-led firms.

Our results do not directly support Nelson (2015), Palvia, Vähämaa, and Vähämaa (2015), and Croson and Gneezy (2009) as we found that innovation in women-led firms does not vary across countries where the pervasive or arbitrary type of corruption prevails and hence the decision about innovation is not gender-specific or different between women- and men-led firms in a level of market risk.

Our results also add to the DAO theory by demonstrating other factors that explain why and when women-led firms will exhibit higher innovation efforts.

Interestingly, the prior research on the role of finance for women-led firms emphasizes that women-led firms diverge from men-led firms as they need "distinctively different financial investment advice" (Nelson 2015, 566). Our findings support H3, which means that women-led firms will increase the likelihood of innovation from 1.03–1.04 times with every one-unit increase in country's fiscal freedom index (specification 3–6, Table 3) and from 1.03–1.06 times (specification 9–12, Table 3). This finding supports Brush (2006), Estrin and Mickiewicz (2011) and, more recently by Balachandra et al. (2019), who found that resource dependency and discrimination of women-led firms might be a major reason for lower innovation intensity. As discussed earlier, women are more likely to be constrained with access to resources, which explains the propensity to innovate in the environments with different types of corruption.

We found that women-led firms in countries with a lower FFI will be less innovative as the tax burden is high and fewer resources are left to invest in R&D and innovation (McMullen, Bagby, and Palich 2008; Chowdhury, Audretsch, and Belitski 2019). Figures 1C and 1B illustrate that using the full and reduced samples that high levels of financial freedom (after 80) result in an exponential increase in the probability of innovating. While both women and men-led firms increase innovation propensity, the rise is higher for women-led firms (see Figures 1C, D), which leads us to infer a non-linear relationship between the availability of finance and innovation for women-led firms. The interaction coefficients' confidence intervals remain robust between specifications 4, 5 and 9, 10 (Table 3). A woman CEO is more likely to innovate at a later stage of the firm lifecycle (30 years since establishment and more), supporting H4. Figures 1E and 1F illustrate different innovation levels for women-led firms at the early stages of the firm life cycle and firm maturity. While innovation in men-led firms decreases over time, the propensity to innovate in women-led firms increases at the later stages. This may point out that women-led firms are more innovative in the later stages when firms may leverage potential external shocks with greater resource availability and tested business models.

The results for our control variables are similar when using pervasive or arbitrary corruption and consistent across the two models. Our findings indicate a neutral relationship between firm age and innovation, while a lower firm size is negative related to innovation propensity. The use of digital technologies such as email and websites boost the innovation propensity (Li et al. 2016), and bureaucratic burden proxied by the frequency of inspections as well as institutional trust is negatively associated with innovation propensity. Firms that use foreign technology are less likely to innovate new to market products as they use ready-made solutions by providers of such technology. We found that the share of female employment specialized in a high and low level of skill jobs was positively associated with innovation propensity. This finding supports Weber and Zulehner (2010), who studied the relationship between female hires in startup firms in Austria with firm performance. They found that firms that start with more female employees have higher survival rates. A decrease in trust in court institutions is negatively associated with innovation, as firm managers will be less likely to take risks of innovation and uncertainty. Economic development is positively associated with innovation propensity, increasing it between 1.6 (specification 10, Table 3) and 2.4 times for every one percent increase in GDP per capita (Specification 5, Table 3). We also found that an increase in low-income countries' economic development may not be enough to start innovating.

Table 3. Logistic estimation results for innovation in women-led firms: Dependent variable = product (service) innovation [0,1] results reported ion odd ratios.

Sample	Full sample = 12,412 firms						Reduced sample = 5,052 firms					
Specifications	(1)	(2)	(3)	(4)	(5)	(6)	(7)	(8)	(9)	(10)	(11)	(12)
Foreign Technology	0.74***	0.70***	0.71***	0.85**	0.81**	0.81**	0.64***	0.63***	0.63***	0.75**	0.77*	0.78*
	(0.05)	(0.05)	(0.05)	(0.06)	(0.07)	(0.06)	(0.07)	(0.07)	(0.07)	(0.09)	(0.10)	(0.10)
Firm Age	1.04*	1.03*	1.03*	1.01*	1.05*	1.01*	1.01	1.02	1.001	1.05	1.02	0.98
	(0.01)	(0.01)	(0.01)	(0.01)	(0.01)	(0.01)	(0.01)	(0.01)	(0.01)	(0.01)	(0.01)	(0.01)
Firm Age (squared)	1.01***	1.02**	1.02**	0.99***	1.00***	0.99***	0.99	0.99	0.99	0.99	0.99	0.99
	(0.00)	(0.00)	(0.00)	(0.00)	(0.00)	(0.00)	(0.00)	(0.00)	(0.00)	(0.00)	(0.00)	(0.01)
Women-led firm	1.01	1.02	0.07**	0.03**	0.05*	0.03*	1.11	1.06	0.06	0.01	0.03	0.001*
	(0.09)	(0.09)	(0.09)	(0.04)	(0.08)	(0.05)	(0.17)	(0.17)	(0.16)	(0.04)	(0.11)	(0.00)
Female high-skill	1.01***	1.01***	1.01***	1.01***	0.998	0.99	0.99	0.99	0.99	0.99*	0.98**	0.98**
	(0.00)	(0.00)	(0.00)	(0.00)	(0.00)	(0.00)	(0.00)	(0.00)	(0.00)	(0.01)	(0.01)	(0.01)
Female low-skill	1.01***	1.02***	1.02***	1.02***	1.01***	1.01**	1.01***	1.04***	1.01***	1.01***	1.01***	1.02***
	(0.00)	(0.00)	(0.00)	(0.00)	(0.00)	(0.00)	(0.00)	(0.00)	(0.00)	(0.00)	(0.00)	(0.00)
Firm size	0.71***	0.73***	0.73***	0.72***	0.75***	0.75***	0.81***	0.80***	0.87***	0.79***	0.81***	0.80***
	(0.02)	(0.02)	(0.02)	(0.02)	(0.02)	(0.02)	(0.03)	(0.04)	(0.04)	(0.04)	(0.04)	(0.04)
Digital readiness-Email	2.06***	2.26***	2.24***	2.24***	1.49***	1.48***	1.71***	1.84***	1.84***	1.76***	1.19	1.20
	(0.18)	(0.20)	(0.20)	(0.22)	(0.16)	(0.16)	(0.32)	(0.35)	(0.35)	(0.34)	(0.26)	(0.26)
Digital readiness-Web	1.94***	1.96***	1.96***	1.86***	1.43***	1.43***	1.93***	1.93***	1.93***	1.76***	1.35**	1.39**
	(0.13)	(0.13)	(0.13)	(0.14)	(0.12)	(0.12)	(0.24)	(0.25)	(0.25)	(0.24)	(0.20)	(0.20)
Frequency of inspections	0.92***	0.93***	0.92***	0.93***	0.93***	0.93***	0.88***	0.89***	0.89***	0.90***	0.91***	0.90**
	(0.01)	(0.01)	(0.01)	(0.01)	(0.01)	(0.01)	(0.02)	(0.02)	(0.02)	(0.02)	(0.02)	(0.02)
Court system perception	1.09***	1.08***	1.08***	0.91***	0.86***	0.86***	0.84***	0.86***	0.86***	0.78***	0.80***	0.80**
	(0.03)	(0.03)	(0.03)	(0.03)	(0.03)	(0.03)	(0.04)	(0.04)	(0.04)	(0.04)	(0.05)	(0.05)
Pervasive institutional environment	0.88***	0.88***	0.88***	0.92*	1.05	1.06						
	(0.03)	(0.04)	(0.04)	(0.04)	(0.05)	(0.04)						
Arbitrary institutional environment							1.06	1.03	1.05	1.00	0.93	0.93
							(0.06)	(0.06)	(0.07)	(0.07)	(0.07)	(0.07)
Fiscal freedom Index	1.12***	1.12***	1.12***	1.08***	1.16***	1.16***	1.11***	1.11***	1.11***	1.08***	1.15***	1.16***
	(0.01)	(0.01)	(0.01)	(0.01)	(0.01)	(0.00)	(0.01)	(0.01)	(0.01)	(0.01)	(0.02)	(0.01)
Women-led firm x Pervasive environment ***(H1)***			0.99	0.99	0.95	0.96						
			(0.11)	(0.11)	(0.12)	(0.11)						
Women-led firm x Arbitrary environment ***(H2)***									0.91	0.85	0.98	0.96
									(0.15)	(0.15)	(0.19)	(0.18)
Women-led firm x Fiscal freedom Index ***(H3)***			1.03**	1.04***	1.03**	1.03**			1.03*	1.05*	1.04*	1.06*
			(0.02)	(0.02)	(0.02)	(0.02)			(0.03)	(0.03)	(0.04)	(0.05)

(*Continued*)

Table 3. Continued.

Sample	Full sample = 12,412 firms						Reduced sample = 5,052 firms					
Specifications	(1)	(2)	(3)	(4)	(5)	(6)	(7)	(8)	(9)	(10)	(11)	(12)
Women-led firm x						1.01**						1.13***
Firm Age (H4)						(0.05)						(0.05)
Women-led firm x						0.99						0.99**
Firm Age (squared) (H4)						(0.00)						(0.00)
Country characteristics												
Seats				1.04***	0.99	0.99				1.09**	0.96***	0.96***
				(0.00)	(0.00)	(0.00)				(0.01)	(0.01)	(0.01)
Discrimination				1.05	0.30***	0.30***				1.60**	0.39***	0.40***
				(0.11)	(0.04)	(0.03)				(0.31)	(0.09)	(0.09)
Maternity				0.84*	0.35***	0.34***				1.19	0.52***	0.52***
				(0.08)	(0.04)	(0.04)				(0.22)	(0.11)	(0.11)
FLPR				0.99***	1.00	1.00				0.98***	0.99*	0.99*
				(0.00)	(0.00)	(0.00)				(0.00)	(0.01)	(0.01)
Economic development					2.30***	2.31***					1.68*	1.75*
					(0.39)	(0.39)					(0.54)	(0.54)
Economic development x low income					0.44**	0.44**					0.45***	0.45***
					(0.02)	(0.01)					(0.04)	(0.04)
Industry fixed effects	No	Yes	Yes	Yes	Yes	Yes	No	Yes	Yes	Yes	Yes	Yes
Year fixed effects	No	No	No	Yes	Yes	Yes	No	No	No	Yes	Yes	Yes
chi-squared	1691.88	1997.37	2001.97	3068.57	4589.57	4593.77	415.02	509.91	511.63	779.07	1157.10	1166.10
loglikelihood	−4604.01	−4451.26	−4448.96	−3915.66	−3155.16	−3153.0	−1433.00	−1385.56	−1384.70	−1250.98	−1061.96	−1057.01
pseudo R2	.15	.18	.18	.28	.42	.43	.12	.15	.15	.23	.35	.37

Note: Number of countries: 75. Number of firms in the full sample = 12,412, while number of firms in reduced sample = 5,052. Level of statistical significance is * 0.10%; ** 0.05%. and *** 0.01%. Standard errors are in parenthesis and are robust for heteroskedasticity. Industry and year fixed – effects are included and suppressed to save space. Reference industry: Other manufacturing. Source: Authors calculation based on World Bank (2015, 2018), ILO (2018).

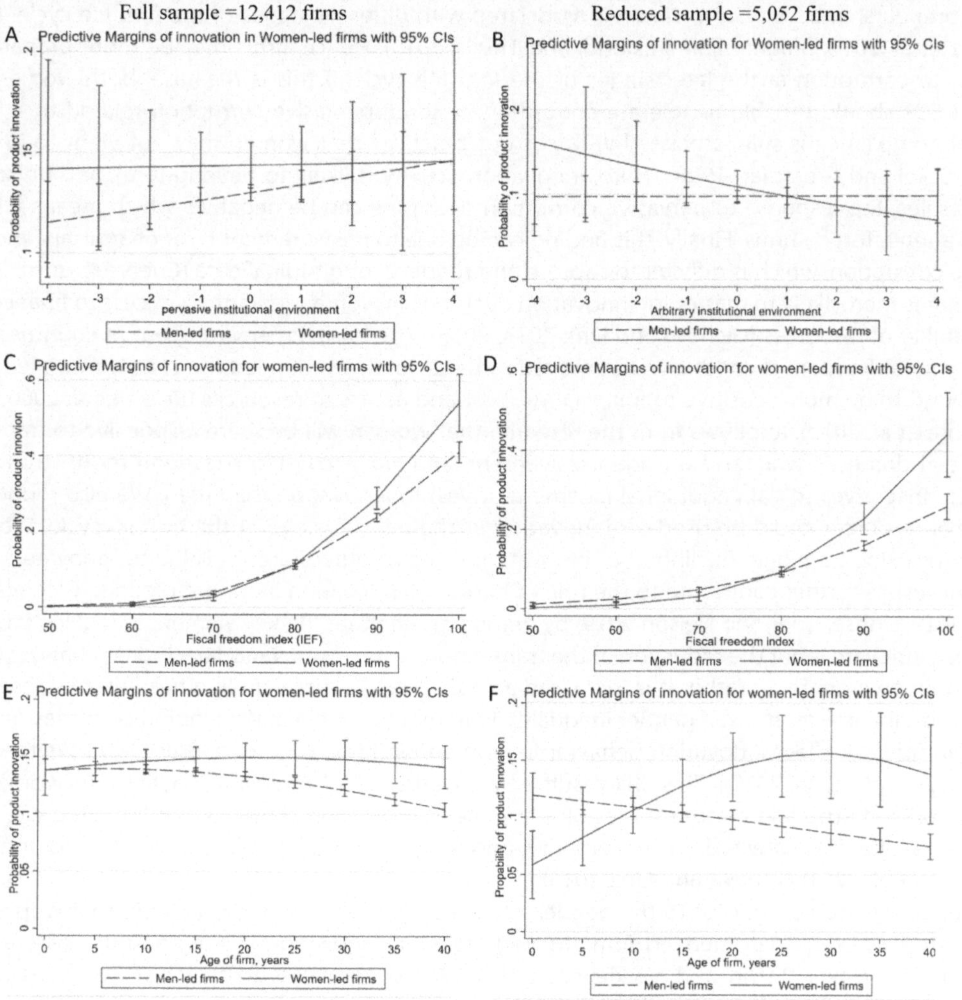

Figure 1. Predictive Margins of the effect of pervasive and arbitrary institutional environment as well as Fiscal Freedom on innovation propensity in women and men-led firms. Source: Authors calculations based on World Bank (2015, 2018), ILO (2018).

5. Discussion and conclusion

Our findings provide new insight into nature's role in shaping innovation in women-led firms (Brush 2006; Elam and Terjesen 2010; Ding, Murray, and Stuart 2006; Dohse, Goel, and Nelson 2019; Link 2019b).

First, we present a model and explain why and at which circumstances of nature, women-led firms are likely to exhibit more innovative activity. Our results confirm that neither a pervasive nor an arbitrary institutional environment, which is associated with different levels of risk-taking, explains innovation in women-led firms, contrasting prior research on the higher degree of risk-aversion and higher moral exhibited by women (Swamy et al. 2001; Charness and Gneezy 2012; Palvia, Vähämaa, and Vähämaa 2015). Our findings suggest that differences in informal institutions related to uncertainty and risk and their effect on innovation decision-making are not gender-biased. This is surprising as both women and men-led firms respond similarly to market risks and uncertainty related to corruption (Wellalage, Locke, and Samujh 2018, 2020). Our finding contrasts with Estrin and Mickiewicz (2011), who found that women-led firms are less likely than men-led firms to undertake entrepreneurial activity in countries where institutions are weaker. Unlike entrepreneurship activity, innovation is associated with different stages of the firm life cycle (Mickiewicz et al. 2017; Braunerhjelm, Eklund, and Thulin 2019). Hence, firms may be more prepared to adjust to corruption at the later stages of the firm life cycle. If this is the case, both women and men CEOs should be able to tolerate corruption. Second, pervasive corruption related to a lower risk of compliance is still associated with corrupt practices that women may not want to engage with (Eckel and Grossman 1998). Third, innovation activity is likely to be long-term, and unlike the firm's sales, the response to pervasive corruption over time can be negative, which means a lower innovation effort by firms. Finally, this finding can be due to measurement error of arbitrary and pervasive corruption, which is difficult to capture and requires longitudinal data (Cuervo-Cazurra 2008).

What is more likely to matter for innovation decisions in women-led firms is access to finance and availability of resources (Gicheva and Link 2013, 2015). The business environment in countries with higher fiscal freedom is conducive to innovation behavior in women-led firms, as women-led firms are found to be more sensitive to financial support and access to resources (Brush et al. 2006; Balachandra et al. 2019). It follows from the research that women will be more responsive to trade-offs between domestic work and outside involvement, and will accordingly respond more strongly to greater incentives to gain additional income to invest in innovation than men. We also found that internal resources could be used for innovation at the mature stage of the firm lifecycle. Women-led firms exhibit a higher likelihood of innovation if the resources are available to innovate.

Our results further contribute to the role of nature in innovation literature (Bednar, Gicheva, and Link 2019; Dohse, Goel, and Nelson 2019) by demonstrating that the key element in making women-led firm innovate is not the reduction of the transaction costs of innovation (including changes in the uncertain environment), rather it is increased access to resources, including firm internal resources and firm's income after tax. If gender inequality in access to capital in developing countries persists, the former may affect innovation behavior in women-led firms (De Bruin, Brush, and Welter 2006; Jennings and Brush 2013). This will result in a divergence of innovation activity in women-led firms in the startup and mature stages of a firm lifecycle. At later stages of the firm lifecycle, these firms may be less affected by uncertainty and may accumulate more resources to innovate (Greene et al. 2001; Gicheva and Link 2015).

Our study also contributes to the gender and innovation literature by showing that women-led firms are less likely than men-led firms to undertake an innovation in the countries where fiscal freedom is weaker (Estrin and Mickiewicz 2011). Moreover, access to financial resources means that, in relative terms, women-led firms have to rely to a greater extent on informal social networks for resource acquisition at startup stages, and those networks tend to be male-dominated in developing countries (Aidis, Estrin, and Mickiewicz 2008; World Bank 2019).

Our findings for gender institutions call for further research on the role of gender institutions. Countries that adopted gender equality institutions, such as maternity leave and non-discrimination in the labor market on average, exhibit women-led firms innovating less than men-led firms. This is puzzling as one would expect more women-led firms in countries where women are more protected. This finding supports earlier findings by Estrin and Mickiewicz (2011) for transition economies who found that a maternity leave provision does not affect high aspiration female entrepreneurship. However, it is the provision of childcare which increases female entrepreneurship. Our study further supports Estrin and Mickiewicz (2011) by finding that both maternity protection and labor market non-discrimination, in addition to other improvements in gender-related institutional quality, are negatively associated with innovation propensity in women-led firms. One explanation for this finding is that institutionalized equality between men and women creates a 'safety net,' increasing the opportunity costs of doing business or taking additional risks in business, such as innovating in women-led firms. More research is required to unpack the effects, which are likely non-linear (Audretsch, Belitski, and Desai 2019). We also advanced management literature on the role that nature can play in driving innovation (Carrasco 2014; Bednar, Gicheva, and Link 2019) when women-led firms operate in the institutional environment with different levels of uncertainty and attitude towards corruption (pervasive vs. arbitrary).

5.1. Limitations

Our study has several limitations. First, we could not consider psychological or neurological factors that could determine women's and men's CEO intrinsic qualities when making decisions related to risk and uncertainty. While our H1-H2 are not supported, the reason for this could be the measurement of the risk environment associated with two types of informal practices. Using other proxies for the pervasive and arbitrary corruption can be useful for further research. Without controlling for female CEOs' individual characteristics, we cannot confirm that corruption and innovation are gender-free or that women are not prone to engage in corrupt behavior at all. In addition to nature, CEO age and experience in the industry could be important in risk-taking behavior. If we analyze women entrepreneurs at different age groups, one can find different risk-taking patterns.

Second, our data is cross-sectional, which does not enforce the causal interpretation of our findings. Future research needs to analyze longitudinal cross-country data to measure innovation behavior changes in women-led firms as the institutional environment changes.

5.2. Policy implications

Policymakers have put stronger demands on the quality of institutions supporting the share of women-owned and women-led businesses. For women CEOs, this means special attention and greater access to acquiring sufficient financial resources to their businesses to reach desired levels of business growth (Alsos, Isaksen, and Ljunggren 2006). Unfortunately, in many developing countries, the policymakers' efforts have been compromised by bribery that impairs gender-based asymmetries in product and process innovation in developing economies (Wellalage, Fernandez, and Thrikawala 2020). Their results in our call for further research on returns from corrupt behavior for women-led firms compared to men-led firms and how access to financial resources and heterogeneity in nature (e.g. pervasive vs. arbitrary type of corruption) changes the propensity to innovate.

This study has found that it is not risk-aversion or differences in morals between women and men which lead to differences in innovation behavior as, has been found in earlier studies (Esarey and Chirillo 2013), rather than the access to financial resources (Becker-Blease and Sohl 2007) increases the propensity of women-led firms to innovate exponentially. While policymakers' efforts are focused on securing gender equality, the focus here should be on providing more debt and equity capital to women CEOs rather than changing their risk-taking behavior, creativity, or change society's perception of a woman.

Capital supply should allow women-led firms to accelerate growth and innovation quickly with every unit increase in access to finance. As our study has found, the relationship is non-linear. As the availability of resources increases, women-led firms exhibit a significantly higher propensity to innovate than men-led firms.

Pandemic and other world crises in developing countries may shrink credit markets and increase government spending, higher taxes, and less take-home income. This may endanger women-led businesses, who struggle to accumulate scarce resources and access finance but are more willing to take innovation decisions as access to capital grows.

Policymakers should bear in mind that innovation in women-led firms is unlikely to be enhanced with a high tax burden and fiscal freedom quality (McMullen, Bagby, and Palich 2008). Further research needs to explore the consequences in government institutional support to women CEOs and entrepreneurs and how effective it is to spur innovation. Policies designed to reduce the gap for women in innovation activities usually fight against gender segregation in society. At the same time, they need to refocus to fight against gender segregation in the financial markets and competition for funding. Gender segregation is most pervasive at the startup and pre-market stages, when women-led firms are limited in internal resources for financing and instead rely on equity markets. Programs aiming to increase the variety of equity and debt financing, crowdfunding, and grants for women are the most efficient tool and may help to reconcile internal resources with external finances to reduce the gap in innovation activity in women-led firms.

Disclosure statement

No potential conflict of interest was reported by the author(s).

References

Aidis, R., S. Estrin, and T. Mickiewicz. 2008. "Institutions and Entrepreneurship Development in Russia: A Comparative Perspective." *Journal of Business Venturing* 23 (6): 656–672.

Alatas, V., L. Cameron, A. Chaudhuri, N. Erkal, and L. Gangadharan. 2009. "Gender, Culture, and Corruption: Insights from an Experimental Analysis." *Southern Economic Journal* 75 (3): 663–680.

Alsos, G. A., E. J. Isaksen, and E. Ljunggren. 2006. "New Venture Financing and Subsequent Business Growth in men–and Women–led Businesses." *Entrepreneurship Theory & Practice* 30 (5): 667–686.

Audretsch, D. B., and M. Belitski. 2019. "The Limits to Collaboration Across Four of the Most Innovative UK Industries." *British Journal of Management*. doi:10.1111/1467-8551.12353.

Audretsch, D. B., and M. Belitski. 2020. "The Role of R&D and Knowledge Spillovers in Innovation and Productivity." *European Economic Review* 123: 103391.

Audretsch, D. B., M. Belitski, and S. Desai. 2019. "National Business Regulations and City Entrepreneurship in Europe: A Multilevel Nested Analysis." *Entrepreneurship Theory & Practice* 43 (6): 1148–1165.

Balachandra, L., T. Briggs, K. Eddleston, and C. Brush. 2019. "Don't Pitch Like a Girl!: how Gender Stereotypes Influence Investor Decisions." *Entrepreneurship Theory & Practice* 43 (1): 116–137.

Baliamoune-Lutz, M. 2015. "Taxes and Entrepreneurship in OECD Countries." *Contemporary Economic Policy* 33 (2): 369–380.

Becker-Blease, J. R., and J. E. Sohl. 2007. "Do Women-Owned Businesses Have Equal Access to Angel Capital?" *Journal of Business Venturing* 22 (4): 503–521.

Bednar, S., and D. Gicheva. 2014. "Are Female Supervisors More Female-Friendly?" *American Economic Review* 104: 370–375.

Bednar, S., D. Gicheva, and A. N. Link. 2019. "Innovative Activity and Gender Dynamics." *Small Business Economics*. doi:10.1007/s11187-019-00282-2.

Belitski, M., F. Chowdhury, and S. Desai. 2016. "Taxes, Corruption, and Entry." *Small Business Economics* 47 (1): 201–216.

Belitski, M., and S. Desai. 2016. "What Drives ICT Clustering in European Cities?" *The Journal of Technology Transfer* 41 (3): 430–450.

Belitski, M., and S. Desai. 2019. "Female Ownership, Firm age and Firm Growth: A Study of South Asian Firms." *Asia Pacific Journal of Management*. doi:10.1007/s10490-019-09689-7.

Braunerhjelm, P., J. E. Eklund, and P. Thulin. 2019. "Taxes, the tax Administrative Burden and the Entrepreneurial Life Cycle." *Small Business Economics*. doi:10.1007/s11187-019-00195-0.

Brush, C. G. 2006. "Women Entrepreneurs: A Research Overview." In *Oxford Handbook of Entrepreneurship*, edited by M. Casson, B. Yeung, A. Basu, and N. Wadeson, 611–628. Oxford, UK: Oxford University Press.

Brush, C. G., N. M. Carter, E. J. Gatewood, P. G. Greene, and M. M. Hart. 2006. *Growth-oriented Women Entrepreneurs and Their Businesses: A Global Research Perspective*. Cheltenham: Edward Elgar Publishing.

Brush, C. G., A. De Bruin, and F. Welter. 2009. "A Gender-Aware Framework for Women's Entrepreneurship." *International Journal of Gender and Entrepreneurship* 1 (1): 8–24.

Carrasco, I. 2014. "Gender gap in Innovation: An Institutionalist Explanation." *Management Decision* 52 (2): 410–424.

Charness, G., and U. Gneezy. 2012. "Strong Evidence for Gender Differences in Risk Taking." *Journal of Economic Behavior & Organization* 83 (1): 50–58.

Chowdhury, F., D. B. Audretsch, and M. Belitski. 2019. "Institutions and Entrepreneurship Quality." *Entrepreneurship Theory & Practice* 43 (1): 51–81.

Cohen, W. M., and D. A. Levinthal. 1989. "Innovation and Learning: The two Faces of R&D." *The Economic Journal* 99 (397): 569–596.

Cronbach, L. J. 1951. "Coefficient Alpha and the Internal Structure of Tests." *Psychometrika* 16 (3): 297–334.

Croson, R., and U. Gneezy. 2009. "Gender Differences in Preferences." *Journal of Economic Literature* 47 (2): 448–474.

Cuervo-Cazurra, C. 2006. ""Who Cares About Corruption?" *Journal of International Business Studies* 37: 807–822.

Cuervo-Cazurra, C. 2008. "Better the Devil you Don't Know: Types of Corruption and FDI in Transition Economies." *Journal of International Management* 14: 12–27.

De Bruin, A., C. G. Brush, and F. Welter. 2006. "Introduction to the Special Issue: Towards Building Cumulative Knowledge on Women's Entrepreneurship." *Entrepreneurship Theory and Practice* 30 (5): 585–593.

De Tienne, D. R., and G. N. Chandler. 2007. "The Role of Gender in Opportunity Identification." *Entrepreneurship Theory & Practice* 31 (3): 365–386.

Ding, W. W., F. Murray, and T. E. Stuart. 2006. "Gender Differences in Patenting in the Academic Life Sciences." *Science* 313 (5787): 665–667.

Dohse, D., R. K. Goel, and M. A. Nelson. 2019. "Female Owners Versus Female Managers: Who is Better at Introducing Innovations?" *Journal of Technology Transfer* 44: 520–539.

Dollar, D., R. Fisman, and R. Gatti. 2001. "Are Women Really the 'Fairer' sex? Corruption and Women in Government." *Journal of Economic Behavior and Organization* 46 (4): 423–429.

Eckel, C., and P. Grossman. 1998. "Are Women Less Selfish Than men? Evidence from Dictator Experiments." *The Economic Journal* 108: 726–735.

Elam, A., and S. Terjesen. 2010. "Gendered Institutions and Cross-National Patterns of Business Creation for men and Women." *European Journal of Development Research* 22: 331–348.

Esarey, J., and G. Chirillo. 2013. "Fairer sex or Purity Myth? Corruption, Gender, and Institutional Context." *Politics & Gender* 9 (4): 361–389.

Estrin, S., J. Korosteleva, and T. Mickiewicz. 2013. ""Which Institutions Encourage Entrepreneurial Growth Aspirations?" *Journal of Business Venturing* 28 (4): 564–580.

Estrin, S., and T. Mickiewicz. 2011. "Institutions and Female Entrepreneurship." *Small Business Economics* 37 (4): 397.

Fredriksson, A. 2014. "Bureaucracy Intermediaries, Corruption and red Tape." *Journal of Development Economics* 108: 256–273.

Gicheva, D., and A. N. Link. 2013. ""Leveraging Entrepreneurship Through Private Investments: Does Gender Matter?" *Small Business Economics* 40: 199–210.

Gicheva, D., and A. N. Link. 2015. "The Gender gap in Federal and Private Support for Entrepreneurship." *Small Business Economics* 45: 729–733.

Gonzalez, A., J. Lopez-Cordova, and E. Valladares. 2007. "The Incidence of Graft on Developing-Country Firms." *World Bank Policy Research Working Paper* 4394.

Greene, P. G., C. G. Brush, C. G, M. M. Hart, and P. Saparito. 2001. ""Patterns of Venture Capital Funding: Is Gender a Factor?" *Venture Capital: An International Journal of Entrepreneurial Finance* 3 (1): 63–83.

Griliches, Z. 1990. "Patent Statistics as Economic Indicators: A Survey." *Journal of Economic Literature* 28 (4): 92–116.

Gupta, V. K., D. Turban, S. A. Wasti, and A. Sikdar. 2009. "The Role of Gender Stereotypes in Perceptions of Entrepreneurs and Intentions to Become an Entrepreneur." *Entrepreneurship Theory & Practice* 33 (2): 397–417.

Heritage Foundation. 2020. "Index of Economic Freedom." Fiscal freedom. Accessed February 13 2020. https://www.heritage.org/index/fiscal-freedom.

Hsieh, W. L., P. Ganotakis, M. Kafouros, and C. Wang. 2018. "Foreign and Domestic Collaboration, Product Innovation Novelty, and Firm Growth." *Journal of Product Innovation Management* 35 (4): 652–672.

ILO. 2018. International Labour Organization. Ratifications of C111 - Discrimination (Employment and Occupation) Convention, 1958 (No. 111) and Ratifications of C003 - Maternity Protection Convention, 1919 (No. 3). Accessed April 15 2019. https://www.ilo.org/dyn/normlex/en/f?p=1000:11300:0::NO:11300:P11300_INSTRUMENT_ID.

Jabeen, F., M. N. Faisal, H. Al Matroushi, and S. Farouk. 2019. "Determinants of Innovation Decisions among Emirati Female-Owned Small and Medium Enterprises." *International Journal of Gender and Entrepreneurship 11(4): 408-434.*

Jennings, J., and C. G. Brush. 2013. "Research on Women Entrepreneurs: Challenges to (and from) the Broader Entrepreneurship Literature." *Academy of Management Annals* 7 (1): 661–713.

Li, W., K. Liu, M. Belitski, A. Ghobadian, and N. O'Regan. 2016. "e-Leadership Through Strategic Alignment: An Empirical Study of Small-and Medium-Sized Enterprises in the Digital age." *Journal of Information Technology* 31 (2): 185–206.

Link, A. N. 2019a. "Technology Transfer at the U.S. National Institute of Standards and Technology (NIST)." *Science and Public Policy* 46(6): 906–912.

Link, A. N. 2019b. "Innovative Behavior of Minorities, Women, and Immigrants." *Economics of Innovation and New Technology* 28 (7): 758.

Link, A. N., and J. T. Scott. 2005. "Opening the Ivory Tower's Door: An Analysis of the Determinants of the Formation of US University Spin-off Companies." *Research Policy* 34 (7): 1106–1112.

Link, A. N., and J. T. Scott. 2019. "Creativity-Enhancing Technological Change in the Production of Scientific Knowledge." *Economics of Innovation and New Technology*. doi:10.1080/10438599.2019.1636449.

Link, A. N., and D. R. Strong. 2016. "Gender and Entrepreneurship: An Annotated Bibliography." *Foundations and Trends in Entrepreneurship* 12: 3–156.

McMullen, J. S., D. R. Bagby, and L. E. Palich. 2008. "Economic Freedom and the Motivation to Engage in Entrepreneurial Action." *Entrepreneurship Theory and Practice* 32 (5): 875–895.

Méon, P.-G., and K. Sekkat. 2005. ""Does Corruption Grease or Sand the Wheels of Growth?" *Public Choice* 122 (1): 69–97.

Mickiewicz, T., F. W. Nyakudya, N. Theodorakopoulos, and M. Hart. 2017. "Resource Endowment and Opportunity Cost Effects Along the Stages of Entrepreneurship." *Small Business Economics* 48 (4): 953–976.

Nählinder, J. 2010. "Where are all the Female Innovators?: Nurses as Innovators in a Public Sector Innovation Project." *Journal of Technology Management & Innovation* 5 (1): 13–29.

Nelson, J. A. 2015. "Are Women Really More Risk-Averse Than men? A re-Analysis of the Literature Using Expanded Methods." *Journal of Economic Surveys* 29 (3): 566–585.

Ngoasong, M. Z., and A. N. Kimbu. 2019. "Why Hurry? The Slow Process of High Growth in Women-Owned Businesses in a Resource-Scarce Context." *Journal of Small Business Management* 57 (1): 40–58.

Olsen, R. A., and C. M. Cox. 2001. "The Influence of Gender on the Perception and Response to Investment Risk: The Case of Professional Investors." *The Journal of Psychology and Financial Markets* 2 (1): 29–36.

Palvia, A., E. Vähämaa, and S. Vähämaa. 2015. "Are Female CEOs and Chairwomen More Conservative and Risk Averse? Evidence from the Banking Industry During the Financial Crisis." *Journal of Business Ethics* 131 (3): 577–594.

Shleifer, A., and R. W. Vishny. 1993. "Corruption." *Quarterly Journal of Economics* 108: 599–617.

Siepel, J., and M. Dejardin. 2020. "How do we Measure Firm Performance? A Review of Issues Facing Entrepreneurship Researchers." In *Handbook of Quantitative Research Methods in Entrepreneurship*, edited by G. Saridakis and M. Cowling, 1–19. Cheltenham: Edward Elgar Publishing.

Still, L. V., and W. Timms. 2000. "Women's Business: The Flexible Alternative Workstyle for Women." *Women in Management Review* 15 (5/6): 272–283.

Sung, H.-E. 2003. "Fairer sex or Fairer System? Gender and Corruption Revisited." *Social Forces* 82 (2): 703–723.

Swamy, A., S. Knack, Y. Lee, and O. Azfar. 2001. "Gender and Corruption." *Journal of Development Economics* 64 (1): 25–55.

Teece, D. J. 1996. "Firm Organisation, Industrial Structure and Technological Innovation." *Journal of Economic Behaviour and Organisation* 31: 193–224.

Thursby, J. G., and M. C. Thursby. 2005. "Gender Patterns of Research and Licensing Activity of Science and Engineering Faculty." *The Journal of Technology Transfer* 30 (4): 343–353.

Turner, L. 2009. "Gender Diversity and Innovative Performance." *International Journal of Innovation and Sustainable Development* 4 (2–3): 123–134.

Verheul, I., A. van Stel, and R. Thurik. 2006. "Explaining Female and Male Entrepreneurship Across 29 Countries." *Entrepreneurship and Regional Development* 18 (2): 151–183.

Webb, J. W., T. A. Khoury, and M. A. Hitt. 2020. "The Influence of Formal and Informal Institutional Voids on Entrepreneurship." *Entrepreneurship Theory and Practice* 44 (3): 504–526.

Weber, A., and C. Zulehner. 2010. "Female Hires and the Success of Start-up Firms." *American Economic Review* 100 (2): 358–361.

Wellalage, N. H., V. Fernandez, and S. Thrikawala. 2020. "Corruption and Innovation in Private Firms: Does Gender Matter?" *International Review of Financial Analysis* 70. doi:10.1016/j.irfa.2020.101500.

Wellalage, N. H., S. Locke, and H. Samujh. 2018. "Corruption, Gender and Credit Constraints: Evidence from South Asian SMEs." *Journal of Business Ethics* 159(1): 267-280.

Williamson, O. 2000. "The new Institutional Economics: Taking Stock, Looking Ahead." *Journal of Economics Literature* 38 (3): 595–613.

Wooldridge, J. M. 2009. *Introductory Economics: A Modern Approach*. Mason: Cengage-Learning.

World Bank. 2015. *World Bank Enterprise Survey*. Accessed April 15 2019. http://www.enterprisesurveys.org/.

World Bank. 2018. *World Bank Indicators*. Accessed February 5 2019. https://data.worldbank.org/indicator.

World Bank. 2019. "Female Entrepreneurship Resource Point - Introduction and Module 1: Why Gender Matters." Accessed March 14 2019. http://www.worldbank.org/en/topic/gender/publication/female-entrepreneurship-resource-point-introduction-and-module-1-why-gender-matters.

Appendix

Table A1. Averages for female management and corruption type, by country.

Country in this study	Obs.	Women-led firm	Pervasive Corruption	Obs.	Women-led firm	Arbitrary Corruption
Afghanistan	57	0.04	0.41	36	0.06	0.16
Albania	41	0.12	0.23	41	0.00	−0.54
Angola	41	0.15	0.48	14	0.07	−1.49
Argentina	402	0.06	−0.13	207	0.03	0.15
Armenia	107	0.04	−0.19	32	0.03	0.14
Azerbaijan	73	0.05	0.04	50	0.10	−0.09
Bangladesh	628	0.06	0.51	61	0.13	−1.28
Belarus	55	0.18	−0.24	18	0.11	0.42
Bhutan	46	0.11	−0.27	71	0.12	0.44
Bolivia	36	0.03	0.04	30	0.03	0.15
Bosnia	103	0.10	−0.28	35	0.09	0.38
Bulgaria	76	0.20	−0.35	34	0.07	0.40
Burkina Faso	46	0.20	−0.19	28	0.11	0.20
Burundi	27	0.15	−0.07	14	0.14	0.21
Cameroon	87	0.05	0.62	32	0.06	−0.82
Chile	446	0.09	−0.31	258	0.09	0.28
Colombia	274	0.17	−0.25	200	0.14	0.28
Costa Rica	67	0.12	−0.31	35	0.11	0.02
Croatia	33	0.18	−0.24	16	0.25	0.32
Czech Rep.	86	0.13	−0.33	23	0.22	0.38
Djibouti	11	0.07	−0.28	47	0.13	0.42
Dominica	31	0.13	−0.14	47	0.12	0.15
Ecuador	36	0.08	−0.33	30	0.10	0.37
Egypt	975	0.05	−0.18	65	0.03	−0.12
El Salvador	55	0.15	−0.33	50	0.15	0.37
Estonia	26	0.27	−0.33	28	0.25	−0.12
Ethiopia	93	0.14	−0.21	18	0.06	−0.34
Georgia	25	0.08	−0.31	25	0.20	0.38
Ghana	127	0.11	0.11	55	0.12	−0.02
Guatemala	150	0.15	−0.11	102	0.14	0.20
Honduras	66	0.11	−0.24	51	0.10	0.34
Hungary	77	0.09	−0.35	54	0.07	0.02
India	3,046	0.07	0.00	1,131	0.06	−0.16
Indonesia	191	0.14	0.10	78	0.18	−0.19
Israel	117	0.07	−0.34	20	0.15	0.40
Jamaica	32	0.06	−0.08	10	0.10	0.36
Kazakhstan	83	0.20	0.09	41	0.24	0.03
Kyrgyz Rep	114	0.22	0.41	38	0.16	−0.13
Lao PDR	53	0.25	0.15	49	0.24	−0.38
Latvia	57	0.32	−0.32	17	0.24	0.33
Lebanon	65	0.03	0.28	14	0.07	−0.07
Lithuania	52	0.12	−0.28	22	0.14	0.27
Madagascar	33	0.18	−0.02	8	0.13	0.00
Malawi	73	0.16	−0.06	30	0.27	0.29
Mali	30	0.17	0.09	4	0.25	0.38
Mauritania	10	0.10	0.10	7	0.00	−0.54
Mauritius	6	0.12	−0.12	4	0.00	0.38
Mexico	404	0.08	−0.13	233	0.09	0.12
Moldova	92	0.24	−0.10	46	0.17	0.10
Mongolia	147	0.31	−0.01	82	0.32	−0.32
Montenegro	13	0.15	−0.19	8	0.25	0.39
Myanmar	160	0.21	0.62	121	0.20	−0.52
Nepal	233	0.08	0.18	49	0.07	0.25
Nicaragua	44	0.25	−0.12	29	0.28	0.15
Pakistan	166	0.03	0.27	16	0.00	−0.77
Panama	18	0.17	−0.41	7	0.00	0.39
Paraguay	36	0.11	0.12	23	0.04	−0.02
Peru	365	0.11	−0.19	228	0.10	0.14
Poland	72	0.14	−0.35	14	0.14	0.34

(Continued)

Table A1. Continued.

Country in this study	Obs.	Women-led firm	Pervasive Corruption	Obs.	Women-led firm	Arbitrary Corruption
Romania	133	0.20	−0.23	42	0.10	0.37
Russia	219	0.18	0.02	119	0.14	−0.14
Senegal	48	0.08	−0.24	8	0.13	0.41
Serbia	95	0.19	−0.26	29	0.17	0.27
Slovak Rep.	49	0.10	−0.24	8	0.13	0.39
Slovenia	22	0.18	−0.38	6	0.17	0.40
Sri Lanka	126	0.14	−0.19	19	0.21	0.00
Tajikistan	82	0.07	0.39	40	0.10	−0.32
Tanzania	104	0.06	−0.22	42	0.10	0.19
Turkey	578	0.08	−0.24	232	0.10	0.24
Ukraine	310	0.20	0.21	117	0.19	−0.22
Uruguay	110	0.14	−0.30	58	0.16	0.29
Uzbekistan	83	0.07	−0.08	17	0.06	0.03
Venezuela	51	0.16	0.11	36	0.22	−0.06
Yemen	172	0.01	1.10	57	0.00	−1.22
Zambia	130	0.13	−0.13	80	0.13	0.20

Averages are calculated for the following variables related to testing our hypothesis. Source: World Bank (2015, 2018).

The use of intellectual property protection mechanisms by publicly supported firms

Albert N. Link and Martijn van Hasselt

ABSTRACT

Technology-based firms use intellectual property protection mechanisms (IPPMs) to appropriate the returns to their research investments. The empirical literature has generally focused on the use of IPPMs by private sector firms to appropriate the returns to their *privately financed* R&D-based technologies. To date, studies have not considered the use of IPPMs by private sector firms whose research is *publicly financed*. We identify empirically a number of significant covariates with the use of a portfolio of formal IPPMs consisting of patents, copyrights, and trademarks. However, our multivariate empirical analyses show that caution is needed in generalizing about such covariates when discussing any one particular formal IPPM.

Nature is all that a man brings with himself into the world; nurture is every influence from without that affects him after his birth.[1]
— Francis Galton

1. Introduction

Firms, especially technology-based firms, use intellectual property protection mechanisms (IPPMs) to appropriate the returns to their research investments. The academic and policy literatures are rich in studies that examine the effectiveness of this use of IPPMs; however, less researched in these literatures are the economic factors associated with a firm's choice of which IPPMs to adopt.

The attendant empirical literature has generally focused on the use of IPPMs by private sector firms to appropriate the returns to their in-house research investments. These are the returns to the firms' *privately financed* R&D-based technologies. As discussed in Amoroso and Link (2019), this literature has considered firm and sectoral characteristics associated with the choice among IPPMs (e.g. Veugelers and Schneider 2017); the complementarity among formal (e.g. patents) and informal (e.g. trade secrets) IPPMs (e.g. Gallié and Legros 2012); and the situations in which informal IPPMs may be more appropriate to use than formal IPPMs (e.g. Hall et al. 2014). To date, to the best of our knowledge, no studies have considered the use of IPPMs by private sector firms whose research is *publicly financed*. This is an important void to begin to fill as more and more economic growth policies, especially those that are targeted to small firms, are focused on public sector financial support of innovative activity.

In this paper, we build on the existing literature by exploring the use of IPPMs by firms to appropriate the returns to their *publicly financed* R&D-based technologies. In other words, the research question that we address in this paper is, Which, if any, IPPMs are used by private sector firms to protect the technologies developed with the support of public sector money, and what are the characteristics of owners and principal investigators (PIs) relevant to the IPPMs that are used?[2] A secondary research question that we consider is, What is the appropriate framework for identifying empirically the relevant characteristics associated with the use of IPPMs?

The former is an important question to consider for at least two reasons. At an academic level, the answer to this question contributes to the existing literature on the appropriability-related use of IPPMs; at a policy level, the answer provides information to public-sector funding agencies on possible advice or guidance to offer to funded firms, especially nascent and small firms, to protect their publicly funded technologies.[3] And, protection of publicly funded technologies is a step forward to ensuring that the public's investment dollars are effective in meeting the public's intended funding objective.[4] The latter is also an important question to consider because it relates to the accuracy of answers to the former question.

In Section II, we discuss the data that we use to explore the relationship between the use of IPPMs and the characteristics of involved individuals. We divide the characteristics of interest into those that reflect nature (i.e. demographic) characteristics of the funded firm's owner and the principal investigator (PI) involved in the research, versus the nurture (i.e. experiential) characteristics of the funded firm and its founders.[5,6,7] In Section III, we present our empirical model of the use of alternative IPPMs, followed by our empirical findings in Section IV. We offer concluding remarks in Section V.

2. Description of the data

The data that we study in this paper relate to Phase II research projects funded by the U.S. Small Business Innovation Research (SBIR) program.[8] The SBIR program was initiated through the Small Business Innovation Development Act of 1982 (Public Law 97–219). This legislation was not only a response to the success of the prototype SBIR program that began at the National Science Foundation in 1977, but also it was a response to the pervasive productivity slowdown in the United States that began in the early-to-mid 1970s and continued into the early 1980s.

In response to the productivity slowdown, U.S. President Jimmy Carter initiated in 1979 a Domestic Policy Review, and among his eight corrective policy initiatives was one to foster the development of small, innovative firms (Carter 1979, 65).

As legislative background, the mission of the SBIR program created through the Act of 1982 is:[9]

> ... to support scientific excellence and technological innovation through the investment of Federal research funds in critical American priorities to build a strong national economy. The program's goals are four-fold:

- Stimulate technological innovation.
- Meet Federal research and development needs.
- Foster and encourage participation in innovation and entrepreneurship by women and socially or economically disadvantaged persons.
- Increase private-sector commercialization of innovations derived from Federal research and development funding.

Eleven agencies currently participate in the SBIR program. These programs fund Phase I and Phase II projects. The objective of a Phase I project is to establish proof of concept of the research as well as the technical merit and commercial potential of the proposed R&D effort. These six-month projects are legislatively funded at no more than $150,000. The objective of a Phase II project is to continue the R&D efforts from Phase I. Only Phase I awardees can apply for a competitive Phase II award. It is anticipated that by the end of the two-year Phase II projects, which are legislatively funded at no more than $1 million, the awardees will have commercialized the newly developed technologies.[10,11]

As part of the SBIR program reauthorization in 2000, the U.S. Congress authorized the National Research Council (NRC) of the National Academies[12] to conduct a survey of Phase II projects that were previously funded by the Department of Defense (DOD), the National Institutes of Health (NIH), the National Aeronautics and Space Administration (NASA), the Department of Energy (DOE), and the National Science Foundation (NSF). Based on the success of that survey and the NRC reports that followed, Congress reauthorized a second assessment survey. Phase II projects funded by the DOD and NASA were surveyed in 2011,[13] and Phase II projects funded by the NIH and DOE were surveyed in 2014. We have unique access to the data from the second survey of the DOD, NASA, NIH, and DOE funded projects; and these project data frame the empirical analyses in this paper.

Our sampling population of Phase II projects is described in Table 1, by funding agency. To arrive at the final sample of projects, we deleted projects that were not completed at the time of the NRC survey and projects that were discontinued prior to realizing any sales up to the time of the survey. The projects that were discontinued without sales have been referred to in the literature as *failed projects* (Link and Wright 2015; Andersen, Bray, and Link 2017). We also note in Table 1 the number of projects that were deleted due to nonresponses to key survey questions (i.e. we deleted projects with missing data).

The academic literature on IPPMs defines patents, copyrights, and trademarks as formal IPPMs.[14] The formal IPPM variables of emphasis in the analyses that follow are based on the NRC Phase II survey question:[15]

> Please give the number of patents, copyrights, trademarks received … for the technology developed as a result of this funded Phase II project.

Figures 1 and 2 overview the responses to this survey question for those Phase II projects that were completed and did not fail ($n = 1{,}647$; see Table 1). Figure 1 shows the percentage of Phase II projects using each of the three IPPMs considered in the NRC survey question. Patents are the most frequently used IPPM by the Phase II project firms, and copyrights are the least frequently used.[16] Figure 2 shows the percentage of Phase II projects that use no IPPMs or only one IPPM. More than 60 percent of the 1,647 Phase II projects in our sampling population use no IPPMs, while just over 20 percent use only patents.[17] About 2 percent of the sampling population uses only copyrights or only trademarks.

Table 2 defines the IPPM, nature (i.e. demographic), and nurture (i.e. experiential) variables used in this paper.

Descriptive statistics for all the variables listed in Table 2 are in Table 3, by funding agency as well as for the full sample.

3. The empirical model

Our first empirical model explores covariates with the use of any IPPM from a completed and successful Phase II project. It takes the general functional form:

Table 1. Data Reduction Process.

	DOD	NIH	NASA	DOE	All Agencies
Random sample of Ph II projects from NRC surveys	1155	572	298	244	2269
Sample after removal of incomplete and failed projects	803	456	213	175	1647
Number of projects with missing data	554	266	160	89	1069
Final Sample	249 (43.08%)	190 (32.87%)	53 (9.17%)	86 (14.88%)	578

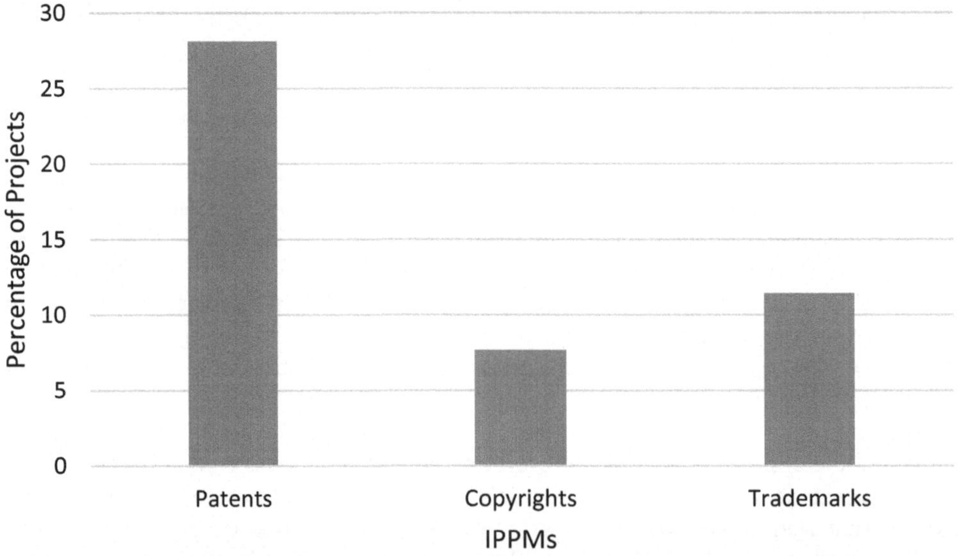

Figure 1. Percentage of Phase II SBIR Projects Using Alternative IPPMs ($n = 1647$). Note: A firm can use more than 1 IPPM to protect its Phase II intellectual property.

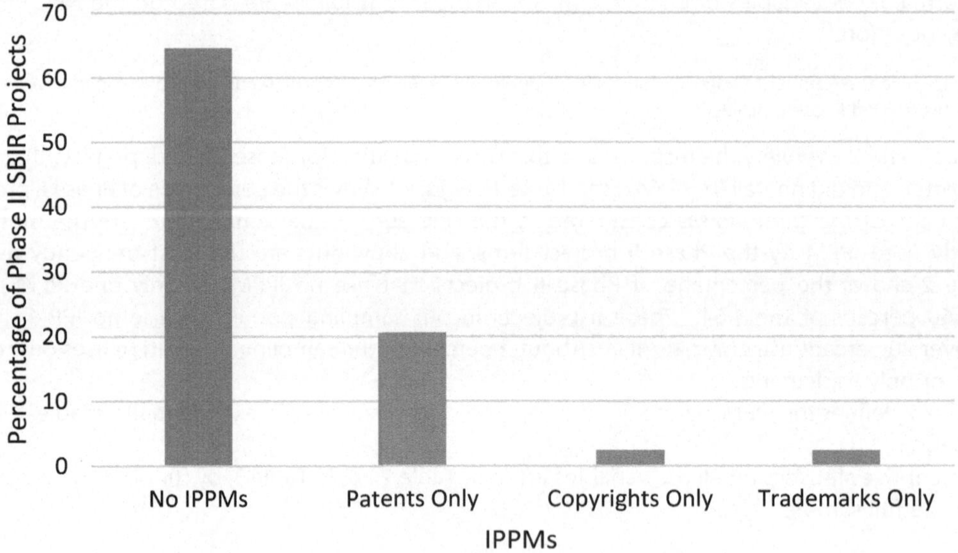

Figure 2. Percentage of Phase II SBIR Projects Using No or Only One IPPM ($n = 1647$)

(1) Pr(*AnyFormalIPPMDmy* = 1) = f (**Nature**, **Nurture**, **Funding Agency Controls**),

where Pr(·) denotes probability, the specific variables in the vectors **Nature** and **Nurture** vector are defined in Table 2, and the funding agency controls are a set of indicator variables to account for differences in the propensity to use IPPMs by funding agency.

We do not offer hypotheses about the directional effect of the nature variables on the probability that the firm will use a formal IPPM to protect its Phase II technology; these variables in this context are relatively new to the literature (Link and Morrison 2019).[18] We do note, however, that homophilic firms (e.g. woman owned and woman PI) have been shown empirically to commercialize more often

Table 2. Definition of Variables.

Variable	Definition
IPPM	
AnyFormalIPPMDmy	Equals 1 if the firm received any patents, copyrights, or trademarks for the technology developed during the Phase II project, 0 otherwise
PatentsDmy	Equals 1 if the firm received any patents for the technology developed during the Phase II project, 0 otherwise
CopyrightsDmy	Equals 1 if the firm received any copyrights for the technology developed during the Phase II project, 0 otherwise
TrademarksDmy	Equals 1 if the firm received any trademarks for the technology developed during the Phase II project, 0 otherwise
Nature	
WomanOwned	Equals 1 if the firm is owned by a woman, 0 otherwise
WomanPI	Equals 1 if the PI is a woman, 0 otherwise
HomophWoman	Equals 1 if the firm is owned by a woman and the PI is a woman, 0 otherwise
PIAge	The midpoint of the PI's age bracket (measured in 5-year intervals)
Nurture	
ProjectYears	Year of the NRC Phase II survey minus the year the Phase II funding was awarded
NumFounders	Number of founders of the firm
EmpAtAward	Number of employees at the time of the current Phase II award
AddlDevelFunding	Equals 1 if the firm received additional development funding for the technology developed during the Phase II project, 0 otherwise
NumPrevPhII	Number of prior Phase II awards received related to the technology supported by the current Phase II award

Note:
PIAge could also be considered a nurture variable to the extent it reflects accumulated experience that comes with age.

than other owner/PI combinations (Bednar, Gicheva, and Link 2019). To the extent that firms that are successful in commercialization are also firms that seek to protect the IP of their commercialized technology, *HomophWoman* should have a positive sign.

Regarding the nurture variables, we hypothesize that *ProjectYears* will be positively related to the likelihood of using a formal IPPM. One might logically expect that the more time a firm has from the time it began its Phase II project until it was surveyed about its use of IPPMs, the greater the likelihood that an IPPM could be used if for no other reason but to ensure that the firm was able to navigate around any related institutional barriers (e.g. the time to apply and time to receive a patent).[19]

We offer no hypothesis about the human capital endowment with the funded firm as measured by the variable *NumFounders*. On the one hand, the more founders of a firm, the greater the collective experience base of the firm and the more likely the firm would have the human capital resources to construct meaningful IPPMs. On the other hand, with more such experience, the firm might be in the position to know if and when IPPMs are important. Thus, the relationship of this variable to the likelihood of using a formal IPPM could be positive or negative.

The extent to which the variable *EmpAtAward* proxies firm size, its relationship to the likelihood of using formal IPPMs is also ambiguous. One the one hand, firm size might reflect relevant internal resources requisite for successfully adopting a relevant IPPM; but on the other hand, firms with more internal resources might not require IP protection to the same extent as a smaller firm.

We hypothesize that the variable *AddlDevelPhII* is positively related to the likelihood of using formal IPPMs. The presence of additional development funding often implies the presence of additional investors in the Phase II project itself, or at least in the subsequent development of the Phase II technology. It is not unreasonable to expect such investors to encourage the use of IPPMs to protect their investments.

We hypothesize that the variable *NumPrevPhII* is positively related to the likelihood of using formal IPPMs. To the extent that a greater focused knowledge base implies that the firm is wedded to or dependent on the particular technology developed thought the Phase II award, the more important it might be for the firm to adopt an IP protection strategy to protect such a strategic and thus critical technology.

Table 3. Descriptive Statistics ($n = 578$).

Variable	DOD	DOE	NASA	NIH	Full Sample
IMMP					
AnyFormalIPPMDmy	0.23	0.38	0.30	0.63	0.39
	(0.42)	(0.49)	(0.46)	(0.49)	(0.49)
PatentsDmy	0.16	0.33	0.19	0.46	0.29
	(0.36)	(0.47)	(0.39)	(0.50)	(0.45)
CopyrightsDmy	0.07	0.03	0.15	0.24	0.13
	(0.25)	(0.18)	(0.36)	(0.43)	(0.33)
TrademarksDmy	0.10	0.09	0.11	0.33	0.17
	(0.30)	(0.29)	(0.32)	(0.47)	(0.38)
Nature					
WomanOwned	0.13	0.09	0.15	0.15	0.13
	(0.34)	(0.29)	(0.36)	(0.36)	(0.34)
WomanPI	0.05	0.08	0.08	0.15	0.09
	(0.22)	(0.28)	(0.27)	(0.36)	(0.29)
HomophWoman	0.02	0.03	0.08	0.10	0.05
	(0.14)	(0.18)	(0.27)	(0.30)	(0.23)
PIAge	45.78	48.28	45.11	48.66	47.03
	(9.73)	(9.71)	(9.05)	(10.08)	(9.87)
	[22, 67]	[32, 67]	[27, 62]	[27, 67]	[22, 67]
Nurture					
ProjectYears	6.03	6.49	7.03	7.52	6.68
	(1.97)	(2.45)	(2.95)	(2.79)	(2.51)
	[4, 13]	[4, 13]	[4, 13]	[4, 13]	[4, 13]
NumFounders	2.40	2.29	2.17	2.37	2.35
	(2.76)	1.84	(1.66)	(1.46)	(2.18)
	[1, 30]	[1, 12]	[1, 12]	[1, 10]	[1, 30]
EmpAtAward	41.48	26.51	31.91	16.92	30.30
	(63.10)	30.22	(59.12)	(32.98)	(51.30)
	[1, 480]	[1, 150]	[1, 400]	[1, 300]	[1, 480]
AddlDevelFunding	0.73	0.92	0.77	0.91	0.82
	(0.44)	(0.27)	(0.42)	(0.29)	(0.38)
NumPrevPhII	1.49	1.24	1.57	1.44	1.44
	(1.81)	(1.64)	(2.11)	(1.75)	(1.79)
	[0, 10]	[0, 10]	[0, 10]	[0, 11]	[0, 11]

Note:
The table contains sample means and, in parentheses, standard deviations. Numbers in square brackets, where reported, indicate the minimum and maximum values.

The choice model in equation (1) focuses on the use of *any* IPPM versus *none*. In our second empirical specification, we consider firms' choices for the three specific types of IPPM, namely patents, copyrights, and trademarks. Specifically, we use a multivariate Probit model (e.g. Wooldridge 2010) to model the distribution of the trivariate binary vector (*PatentsDmy, CopyrightsDmy, TrademarksDmy*). The control variables in this model are the same as in equation (1). The advantage of the multivariate Probit model in this context is twofold. First, we can learn about the relation between various nature and nurture characteristics and the propensity to use different IPPMs. Second, the model allows for the possibility that these choices are correlated, even after controlling for observed characteristics.

4. Empirical findings

The Probit results from the estimation of three specification of equation (1) are presented in Table 4. The differences among the three specifications are related to the inclusion/exclusion of the variable *HomophWoman*.[20]

The Probit results in Table 4 confirm the directional effects hypothesized above, including those for which directional ambiguity is reflected in a statistically insignificant Probit coefficient.

We referenced a number of studies in the Introduction to this paper that explored covariates with the use of formal, as well as informal, IPPMs. However, greater insight into covariates with the use of

Table 4. Estimates from the Probit Model for the Use of Any IPPM ($n = 578$).

Variable	(1)	(2)	(3)
WomanOwned	0.3316*	–	0.2403
	(0.1783)		(0.2058)
WomanPI	−0.0820	–	−0.2727
	(0.2147)		(0.3100)
HomophWoman	–	0.3666	0.4030
		(0.2409)	(0.4348)
PIAge	0.0048	0.0047	0.0045
	(0.0058)	(0.0058)	(0.0058)
ProjectYears	0.0561**	0.0547**	0.0550**
	(0.0226)	(0.0225)	(0.0226)
NumFounders	0.0099	0.0140	0.0110
	(0.0290)	(0.0282)	(0.0288)
EmpAtAward	−0.0016	−0.0017	−0.0016
	(0.0014)	(0.0013)	(0.0013)
AddlDevelFunding	0.4242***	0.4234***	0.4267***
	(0.1633)	(0.1634)	(0.1634)
NumPrevPhII	0.0831**	0.0786**	0.0816**
	(0.0327)	(0.0327)	(0.0329)
Agency funded controls	yes	yes	yes
Wald chi-square statistic	93.24	93.26	94.32
(*p*-value)	(<0.00)	(<0.00)	(<0.00)
Log-likelihood	−335.53	−336.24	−335.11

Notes:
Robust standard errors in parentheses.
*** significant at the .01-level, ** significant at the .05-level, * significant at the .10-level.

a particular IPPM might provide new evidence to inform the extant literature. Thus, we use a multivariate Probit specification to model the three dependent variables *PatentsDmy, CopyrightsDmy,* and *TrademarksDmy* jointly. The independent variables in each of these three models are the same as discussed with reference to Table 4. As mentioned in Section III, the advantage of the multivariate model is that it allows for the possibility that the unobservables affecting the choices for the types of IPPMs are correlated across the three equations.

The multivariate probit model was estimated using the **mvprobit** package in Stata 15.1 (Cappellari and Jenkins 2003). Estimation is performed by simulated maximum likelihood, which requires the user to specify a seed number for the random number generator, as well as the number of random draws used to simulate the likelihood function. We set the number of random draws equal to 100, which substantially exceeds the empirical rule-of-thumb of the square root of the sample size.[21] We also experimented with different seed numbers and found our estimates to be robust.[22]

The multivariate Probit results are in Table 5. The first observation from these results is that the significant covariates differ across IPPMs.[23] For example, the only significant covariate with the variable *PatentsDmy* is *AddlDevelFund*, and this relationship is positive as we hypothesized. That same independent variable is significant and positive in the *TrademarksDmy* equation but not in the *CopyrightsDmy* equation.

In the *CopyrightsDmy* equation, both nurture and nature independent variables are significant, as they are in the *TrademarksDmy* equation. Woman-owned firms are associated with a greater likelihood of using copyrights to protect their Phase II project's technology, but projects with a woman PI have a lesser likelihood (in the specification in column (3)) of using trademarks for the same purpose. If the owner-PI relationship is female homophilic (i.e. woman owned and woman PI), there is a positive association with the use of both copyrights and trademarks as IPPMs.

Firm size, as measured in terms of the variable *EmpAtAward*, is negatively associated with the use of both copyrights and trademarks as IPPMs. The coefficients for this variable are also negative in the *PatentsDmy* equation, but not significant.

Table 5. Estimates from the Multivariate Probit Model for Patents, Copyrights, and Trademarks ($n = 578$).

Variable	(1)	(2)	(3)
PatentsDmy			
WomanOwned	0.0559	–	0.1310
	(0.1935)		(0.2216)
WomanPI	−0.2913	–	−0.1593
	(0.2292)		(0.3088)
HomophWoman	–	−0.3209	−0.2920
		(0.2605)	(0.4524)
PIAge	0.0004	0.0007	0.0006
	(0.0061)	(0.0061)	(0.0061)
ProjectYears	0.0336	0.0345	0.0346
	(0.0236)	(0.0236)	(0.0237)
NumFounders	0.0411	0.0420	0.0401
	(0.0260)	(0.0260)	(0.0260)
EmpAtAward	−0.0014	−0.0014	−0.0014
	(0.0013)	(0.0013)	(0.0013)
AddlDevelFunding	0.7017***	0.6976***	0.7005***
	(0.1973)	(0.1971)	(0.1974)
NumPrevPhII	0.0300	0.0303	0.0317
	(0.0318)	(0.0319)	(0.0320)
CopyrightsDmy			
WomanOwned	0.4781**	–	0.4757*
	(0.2129)		(0.2453)
WomanPI	0.1288	–	0.0680
	(0.2541)		(0.3828)
HomophWoman	–	0.5923**	0.0893
		(0.2506)	(0.5055)
PIAge	0.0061	0.0053	0.0060
	(0.0074)	(0.0074)	(0.0074)
ProjectYears	0.0086	0.0051	0.0083
	(0.0283)	(0.0282)	(0.0283)
NumFounders	−0.1333**	−0.1293**	−0.1349**
	(0.0617)	(0.0607)	(0.0620)
EmpAtAward	−0.0034*	−0.0036*	−0.0034*
	(0.0020)	(0.0021)	(0.0020)
AddlDevelFunding	−0.1247	−0.1300	−0.1257
	(0.1983)	(0.1982)	(0.1983)
NumPrevPhII	0.1158***	0.1083***	0.1157***
	(0.0355)	(0.0354)	(0.0355)
TrademarksDmy			
WomanOwned	0.3364	–	0.1407
	(0.2083)		(0.2447)
WomanPI	−0.3985	–	−1.0415**
	(0.2582)		(0.4796)
HomophWoman	–	0.1464	1.0103*
		(0.2542)	(0.5847)
PIAge	0.0018	0.0023	0.0016
	(0.0068)	(0.0067)	(0.0068)
ProjectYears	0.0461*	0.0432*	0.0440*
	(0.0257)	(0.0256)	(0.0258)
NumFounders	−0.0253	−0.0157	−0.0205
	(0.0433)	(0.0413)	(0.0426)
EmpAtAward	−0.0026*	−0.0027*	−0.0027*
	(0.0015)	(0.0016)	(0.0015)
AddlDevelFunding	0.5374**	0.5462**	0.5570**
	(0.2190)	(0.2201)	(0.2199)
NumPrevPhII	0.0624*	0.0552*	0.0573*
	(0.0325)	(0.0325)	(0.0325)
Wald chi-square statistic	144.87	139.47	147.99
(*p*-value)	(<0.00)	(<0.00)	(<0.00)
Log-likelihood	−672.68	−676.31	−670.16

Notes:
Standard errors in parentheses. The sample size is $n = 578$. The coefficients are estimated using simulated maximum likelihood. The number of random draws to simulate the likelihood function is $M = 100$.
*** significant at the .01-level, ** significant at the .05-level, * significant at the .10-level

Other relationships showing a greater or lesser likelihood for the use of either copyrights or trademarks as IPPMs are observable in Table 5. As a final note, we did not report the correlations between the errors in the three equations of the multivariate Probit model.[24] These correlations were all positive and statistically significant. The error correlation between copyrights and trademarks was particularly high, ranging between 0.78 and 0.80 across the three model specifications. Thus, after controlling for nature, nurture and agency effects, firms that use copyrights as an IPPM are more likely to also use trademarks, and vice versa.

5. Concluding remarks

In the Introduction we raised the two questions that would be addressed in this paper. First, Which, if any, IPPMs are used by private sector firms to protect the technologies developed through their use of public sector money, and what are the characteristics of owners and principal investigators (PIs) relevant to the IPPMs that are used? And second, What is the appropriate framework for identifying empirically the relevant characteristics associated with the use of IPPMs?

Focusing on technologies developed through publicly financed R&D, we identified empirically a number of significant covariates with the use of a portfolio of formal IPPMs consisting of patents, copyrights, and trademarks. However, our multivariate empirical analyses show that caution is needed in generalizing about such covariates when discussing any one particular formal IPPM. We did not identify a covariate that was simultaneously statistically related to the use of patents, the use of copyrights, as well as the use of trademarks.

Notes

1. *English Men of Science: Their Nature and Nurture* (1895, 9).
2. An ideal experiment would be to study matched pairs of private sector firms, one-half that fund their technologies with their own R&D and one-half that fund their technologies with publicly funded R&D.
3. See Santamaría, Barge-Gil, and Modrego (2010) and Antonelli (2020) on factors that influence a firm's likelihood of receiving public-sector funds, and see Busom (2000) on the benefits of such funds.
4. We elaborate on this final point below in our discussion of the mission of the SBIR program; the data that we examine related to SBIR funded projects.
5. Conley (1984) argues that the origin of the nature versus nurture controversy traces to William Shakespeare's *The Tempest* (1610): 'A devil, a born devil, on whose nature nurture can never stick … '.
6. See Audretsch and Link (2018) and Link (2020) for a discussion of John Locke's view of experiences (i.e. nurture) over nature, and the role of experiences in crafting public sector and private sector entrepreneurial behavior.
7. We are not the first researchers to address nature versus nurture aspects of the innovation process. See, for example, Aghion et al. (2017); Bell et al. (2019); and Nicolaou et al. (2008).
8. We have written about the institutional and policy history of the SBIR program many times, so duplication of text and quoted materials from the enabling legislation is inevitable. See Link and Scott (2012); the collection of papers in Link (2013); Hayter, Link, and Scott (2018); and most recently Audretsch, Link, and van Hasselt (2019).
9. See, https://www.sbir.gov/about/about-sbir (accessed September 13, 2020).
10. To the extent that the small firm that receives SBIR Phase II funding is able to protect the intellectual property of its newly developed technology, the greater the commercialization success of the technology and thus the greater the extent to which the purpose of the Phase II funding is achieved.
11. There are agency-specific exceptions to the upper limits of a Phase I and Phase II award.
12. See, https://www.nationalacademies.org/ (accessed September 13, 2020).
13. Phase II projects funded by NSF were also surveyed, but the data at our access on those projects is limited.
14. See, Amoroso and Link 2019, and the papers summarized and referenced therein.
15. Our study is limited to these three IPPMs. Amoroso and Link (2019) study a broader set of IPPMs, but none of the firms in their sample are protecting publicly funded technologies. Patents have been studied extensively in the economics and policy literatures. To the best of our knowledge, the only economics study of copyrights is by Rooksby and Hayter (2017), and we know of no studies related to trademarks individually as an IPPM.
16. We thank Silvio Vismara for pointing out that little is known about the timing of the adoption of different IPPMs. Are such mechanisms adopted contemporaneously or over time as a technology matures?
17. Potekhina and Blind (2020) provide empirical evidence that technology as well as human motivation (e.g. reward recognition) influence the decision to patent.

18. See also Swanson (2016).
19. Perhaps more subtle reason for a positive relationship relates to SBIR-funded firms being in a state of liminality in which they are attempting to define their identity as a technology-based organization and adopt attendant strategies. See, for example, Beech (2011) and the references therein.
20. Variance inflation factor (VIF) tests show no multicollinearity in any of these specifications. These results are available from the authors on request.
21. The rule of thumb suggests using at least sqrt(578) or 24 random draws. Using a higher number increases estimation accuracy but also computing time. We experimented with 25, 50, 75 and 100 random draws. The estimates were robust in the sense that the coefficient signs remained the same and, at the 1% and 5% significance levels, no coefficients switched from being statistically significant to insignificant, or vice versa. The results reported here correspond to 100 random draws.
22. Robustness refers to the sign and significance of the estimated coefficients (see footnote 17). Estimates from the robustness checks are available from the authors on request.
23. We are using the term *significant* in the following description of the multivariate Probit results to refer to estimated coefficients that are significant at the .10-level or better in at least one of the specifications considered.
24. These statistics are available from the authors on request.

Disclosure statement

No potential conflict of interest was reported by the author(s).

References

Aghion, Philippe, Ufuk Akcigit, Ari Hyytinen, and Otto Toivanen. 2017. "The Social Origins of Inventors." NBER Working Paper 24110.

Amoroso, Sara, and Albert N. Link. 2019. "Intellectual Property Protection Mechanisms and the Characteristics of Founding Teams." *European Commission Joint Research Centre Working Paper 01-2019*.

Andersen, Martin S., Jeremy W. Bray, and Albert N. Link. 2017. "On the Failure of Scientific Research: An Analysis of SBIR Projects Funded by the U.S. National Institutes of Health." *Scientometrics* 112: 431–442.

Antonelli, Cristiano. 2020. "Knowledge Exhaustibility Public Support to Business R&D and the Additionality Constraint." *Journal of Technology Transfer* 45: 649–663.

Audretsch, David B., and Albert N. Link. 2018. *Sources of Knowledge and Entrepreneurial Behavior*. Toronto: University of Toronto Press.

Audretsch, David B., Albert N. Link, and Martijn van Hasselt. 2019. "Knowledge Begets Knowledge: University Knowledge Spillovers and the Output of Scientific Papers from U.S. Small Business Innovation Research (SBIR) Projects." *Scientometrics* 121: 1367–1383.

Bednar, Steven, Dora Gicheva, and Albert N. Link. 2019. "Innovative Activity and Gender Dynamics." *Small Business Economics*. doi:10.1007/s11187-019-00282-2.

Beech, Nic. 2011. "Liminality and the Practices of Identity Reconstruction." *Human Relations* 64: 285–302.

Bell, Alexander M., Raj Chetty, Xavier Jaravel, Neviana Petkova, and John Van Reenen. 2019. "Who Becomes an Inventor in America? The Importance of Exposure to Innovation." NBER Working Paper 24062.

Busom, Isabel. 2000. "An Empirical Evaluation of The Effects of R&D Subsidies." *Economics of Innovation and New Technology* 9: 111–148.

Cappellari, Lorenzo, and Stephen P. Jenkins. 2003. "Multivariate Probit Regression Using Simulated Maximum Likelihood." *The Stata Journal* 3: 278–294.

Carter, President Jimmy. 1979. *Industrial Innovation: Joint Hearings before the U.S. Senate Committee on Commerce, Science, and Transportation and the Select Committee on Small Business; and to the U.S. House of Representatives Committee on Science and Technology and the Committee on Small Business*. Washington, DC: Government Printing Office.

Conley, James J. 1984. "Not Galton, but Shakespeare: A Note on the Origin of the Term 'Nature and Nurture'." *Journal of the History of the Behavioral Sciences* 20: 184–185.

Gallié, Emilie-Pauline, and Diego Legros. 2012. "French Firms' Strategies for Protecting their Intellectual Property." *Research Policy* 41: 780–794.

Hall, Bronwyn H., Christian Helmers, Mark Rogers, and Vania Sena. 2014. "The Choice between Formal and Informal Intellectual Property: A Review." *Journal of Economic Literature* 52: 375–423.

Hayter, Christopher S., Albert N. Link, and John T. Scott. 2018. "Public-Sector Entrepreneurship." *Oxford Review of Economic Policy* 34: 676–694.

Link, Albert N. 2013. *Public Support of Innovation in Entrepreneurial Firms*. Northampton, MA: Edward Elgar Publishers.

Link, Albert N. 2020. *Invention, Innovation, and U.S. Federal Laboratories*. Northampton, MA: Edward Elgar Publisher.

Link, Albert N., and Laura T. R. Morrison. 2019. *Innovative Activity in Minority-Owned and Women-Owned Business*. New York: Springer.

Link, Albert N., and John T. Scott. 2012. *Employment Growth from Public Support of Innovation in Small Firms*. Kalamazoo, MI: W.E. Upjohn Institute for Employment Research.

Link, Albert N., and Mike Wright. 2015. "On the Failure of R&D Projects." *IEEE Transactions on Engineering Management* 62: 442–448.

Nicolaou, Nicos, Scott Shane, Lynn Cherkas, Janice Hunkin, and Tim D. Spector. 2008. "Is the Tendency to Engage in Entrepreneurship Genetic?" *Management Science* 54: 167–179.

Potekhina, Anna, and Knut Blind. 2020. "What Motivates the Engineers to Patent? A Study of the Chinese R&D Laboratories of a European MNC." *Journal of Technology Transfer* 45: 461–480.

Rooksby, Jacob H., and Christopher S. Hayter. 2017. "Copyrights in Higher Education: Motivating a Research Agenda." *Journal of Technology Transfer* 44: 250–263.

Santamaría, Lluís, Andrés Barge-Gil, and Aurelia Modrego. 2010. "Public Selection and Financing of R&D Cooperative Projects: Credit Versus Subsidy Funding." *Research Policy* 39: 549–563.

Swanson, Kara W. 2016. "Intellectual Property and Gender: Reflections on Accomplishments and Methodology." *Journal of Gender, Social Policy & the Law* 24: 175–198.

Veugelers, Reinhilde, and Cédric Schneider. 2017. "Which IP Strategies Do Young Highly Innovative Firms Choose?" *Small Business Economics* 50: 113–129.

Wooldridge, J. M. 2010. *Econometric Analysis of Cross Section and Panel Data*. Cambridge, MA: MIT Press.

Index